THE DYING LION

Feudalism and Modernization in Ethiopia

THE DYING LION
Feudalism and Modernization in Ethiopia

Patrick Gilkes

JULIAN FRIEDMANN
PUBLISHERS LTD

Published in 1975 by

JULIAN FRIEDMANN PUBLISHERS LTD.

6–30 International Press Centre,
76 Shoe Lane, London E.C.4. England.

© *Patrick Gilkes 1975*

ISBN 0 904014 07 X

Published for Africa (excluding South Africa and Rhodesia)
and the Middle East (excluding Israel)
by Davison Publishing Limited,
20 Northgate Street, Devizes, Wiltshire, England.
Made and printed in Great Britain by
The Garden City Press Limited
Letchworth, Hertfordshire SG6 1JS

Table of Contents

Tables

Genealogical Tables

Maps

Author's Note

Chapters 1 and 2 are largely historical and are intended for the more specialist reader.

Transcription

There is no generally accepted form of Ethiopian transcription and most of the various systems belong to the realm of linguistics. I have therefore used forms that are to be found in official government documents, in the *Ethiopian Herald* and in the telephone directory. While these are not necessarily consistent in the transcription of palatized or explosive consonants, nor do they use such linguistic devices as diacritical marks, they are easy to use. I fully realize that this is scarcely satisfactory from the linguistic point of view, but my concern has not been with the minutiae of linguistics. In this sense conventional usage has been my main guide.

Calendar

The Ethiopian calendar differs from the Gregorian in having the year begin on 11 September, and in being seven or eight years behind. From 11 September to 31 December it runs seven years in arrears; from 1 January to 10 September there is eight years difference. All dates have been put into the Gregorian form or have Gregorian equivalents.

Money

Since 1945 the Ethiopian dollar has remained stable against the US dollar, the rate being 1 Ethiopian dollar = US$0·40. Against the pound sterling it has fluctuated—until 1945 when the present dollar was introduced the rate of the Maria Theresa thaler fluctuated with the price of silver, but was approximately 10 to £1·00. After 1945 the rate was 7·00 Ethiopian dollars to the pound; in 1967 the British devaluation changed the rate to £1·00—E$6.00 and since then the rate has steadily dropped—in 1974 it was £1·00—E$4·80.

ix

Acknowledgements

The genesis of this book lies in the six years that I spent teaching in Ethiopia, at secondary school and at the University, and in the two years of research I did in Ethiopia, in Rome and in London. Some of the material incorporated here was originally intended for a doctorate. I was however unable to finish this after I was expelled from Ethiopia in 1972 for involvement in political affairs. Most of my research papers were taken, and are still held, by the security authorities.

I am thus more than usually indebted to those who have continued to keep me informed of events in Ethiopia. Indeed my debt to all those many Ethiopians, both officials and others, who have helped me especially in discussions of political matters is inestimable. Since there are many whose names I cannot give, I have not acknowledged individual contributions except in a few general cases. However I hope that they will accept this intimation of my gratitude which is very real. This book is essentially dependent upon their information though the use to which I have put it is of course my responsibility.

I am also deeply indebted to Dr. Richard Rathbone, my former supervisor, for his support and valuable criticisms. Various other scholars, both inside and outside Ethiopia, have been extremely helpful with suggestions concerning research and analysis. To mention names would again be invidious, but to all of them I am most grateful. I would also like to express my appreciation to those who helped me with the preparation of the manuscript and did editorial work. It must have been a thankless task for them although most necessary for me.

PATRICK GILKES

London, August 1974

Preface

In January 1974 the Ethiopian government was facing an extremely serious famine situation and rapidly rising prices. At the end of February, this escalated into a political crisis as strikes by taxi drivers, students and teachers were backed up by mutinies among the 2nd and 4th Army Divisions, the Navy and the Airforce. On the 27th February, the Armed Forces, with support from other sections of the community, mainly workers and students in Addis Ababa, were responsible for the removal of the then Prime Minister, Aklilu Habtewold, and his Council of Ministers. At the time, the appointment by Haile Selassie of *Lij* Endalkatchew Makonnen as the new Prime Minister proved to be acceptable because it was attached to the promise of a wide-ranging series of reforms. The most important of these were the promised investigation into corruption, the reform of the land tenure system and the setting up of a Commission to produce a new constitution.

However, progress in carrying out these reforms was not found to be so satisfactory. During the following three months certain conservative elements among the Emperor's closest advisors and the great aristocracy were making efforts to reassert themselves; the new administration did not actually seem to do much, and there were suspicions of *Lij* Endalkatchew's own aristocratic background (as the leading member of one of the most important Shoan noble families); some Deputies in Parliament even suggested that the ex-Ministers should be released on bail pending their investigation by the anti-corruption Commission that had been set up.

But, the most serious potential threat to the Armed Forces was the efforts to divide them. These were not entirely unsuccessful. The first public appearance of the Armed Forces Co-ordinating Committee was under the chairmanship of Colonel Alem Zewde; by June he had been removed by his colleagues on the committee because of his efforts to draw together a Gojjami group to support his own position, and because of his ties with *Lij* Endalkatchew. Colonel

Alem had also been responsible for moving the paratroops into the airbase in April and, according to official reports, stopping an attempted coup by the Air Force. Other signs of strain were also to be seen among the committee members and it was not until the end of June that they produced a concensus over their next moves and acted on it.

The need for an agreed concensus was implicit in the make-up of the Committee that emerged from the February mutinies. The Committee was entitled the Co-ordinating Committee of the Armed Forces, Police and Territorial Army. It was composed of elected representatives from all the units in these services, and the democratic nature of it was taken seriously; the representatives remained responsible to their units and could be, and were, dismissed for failing to put the unit's point of view adequately. The number on the committee fluctuated between 80 and 120, and the ranks ranged from private to major although the majority of representatives were in fact officers. Within the larger Committee there were a number of sub-committees, the most important of which was the central planning group organized around a smaller caucus of key figures. The views of the whole Committee, not surprisingly, covered a wide spectrum of opinion from the near conservative to the strongly radical and in this sense represented the attitudes of their units—the most radical being the Air Force and, after the deposition of Haile Selassie on 12 September, the Bodyguard. There was little sign of any single ideological approach to Ethiopia's problems. Actions were carried out in the name of the rather vague motto "Ethiopia first", and the Committee claimed to be anti-imperialist and anti-communist. They were swift to deny rumours that foreign companies were going to be nationalized or that foreign policy would be changed, and this held true even after the Committee's assumption of power as the Provisional Military Government.

One thing however that the Committee could easily agree on was to remove any potential threats to their own position. At the end of June a new wave of arrests was started, which included leading aristocracy such as *Leul-Ras* Asrate Kassa, *Dejazmatch* Kassa Woldemariam and *Ras* Mesfin Sileshi; members of the Crown Council and the Emperor's closest advisers; a series of security and police personnel including Colonel Solomon Kadir, the Chief of Security; a number of *enderassies* and other provincial officers; senior officials in the Ministry of Defence, including the Minister of Defence in *Lij* Endalkatchew's Government, General Abiy Abebe;

many others suspected of corruption and finally after his dismissal as Prime Minister, *Lij* Endalkatchew. Since then the arrests have continued, concentrating especially on those accused of corruption in the Administration and the Judiciary.

The Armed Forces Co-ordinating Committee also presented the Emperor with a series of demands that he had to accept—the release of political prisoners and the return of exiles, the speeding-up of constitutional reform and a permanent status for the Armed Forces vis-a-vis the Council of Ministers. At this point the Armed Forces were still not prepared to take over themselves and preferred to act behind the scenes and through a civilian Administration. In place of *Lij* Endalkatchew they put *Lij* Michael Imru, son of *Ras* Imru who, although a member of the leading aristocracy, had a liberal reputation and had been out of the country for many years and was thus untainted by the scandals that were emerging.

It was clear at this point that the Armed Forces were serious in their claim that they were going to destroy feudalism; inevitably they began to get closer and closer to the prime symbol of that system, Emperor Haile Selassie. With the Emperor isolated and most of his suporters arrested, the next step was the nationalization of his palaces and the seizure of the imperial records. With the aid of these, publicity was given to a series of revelations and attacks that emphasized that the Emperor's own hands were no cleaner than those of his Ministers.

Figures published in the Amharic press showed, for example, that the profits from the St. George Brewery, a company brought by the Ministry of Finance in 1952, had been taken exclusively by the Emperor. The total signed for and received from the brewery by Haile Selassie apparently came to over Eth.$11 million, some of which was distributed to close associates like Wolde-Giyorgis, Wolde-Yohannis, *Abba* Hana Jema and *Blatta* Admassu Reta.[1] Other evidence showed that the Emperor personally intervened to make the Ministry of Finance cut taxes on individual landowners—in one case the amount due was dropped from Eth.$90,000 to a mere Eth.$3,000. Details were also released of the assets (over Eth.$40 million) and income (Eth.$6·7 million) of the Haile Selassie Foundation. Part of this income came from the Government (Eth.$0·6 million) and from its hospitals (over Eth.$3 million), one of which was the St. Paul's Hospital for the Poor.[2] Even more damaging were the allegations that Haile Selassie had sent huge sums abroad to be deposited in Swiss banks and invested in property in France and other countries. The sums mentioned—up to Eth.$10,000 million—are obviously exaggerated, but the fact they were publicized helped gain support for his removal, for few Ethiopians believe that there is no truth in the stories. The accusations were rounded-off by claims that the Emperor was also fully aware of the famine disaster long before it became public and refused to do anything about it.

Finally on the second day of the Ethiopian New Year, 12 September, the Armed Forces deposed Haile Selassie, and at the same time abolished the constitution and dismissed Parliament. They did not, however abolish the monarchy and the throne was offered to Haile Selassie's only surviving son, Prince Asfa Wossen, still recovering in Geneva from the stroke he had in 1973. After some deliberation he agreed to accept it under the conditions imposed—a purely ceremonial monarchy without the title of Emperor, King without any power. The Co-ordinating Committee themselves took power as the Provisional Military Government headed by General Aman Michael Andom, a popular figure with the Armed Forces and with the people; General Aman was also made Prime Minister and the Council of Ministers remained unchanged except for the move of *Lij* Michael Imru to the Ministry of Information.

This situation was not reached without considerable debate in the Committee. There was serious consideration given to the future course of the revolution and especially to the type of Government that the Armed Forces actually wanted. In fact the arrangements of September represented a compromise, the more radical units wanting the monarchy to go and a republic to be set up. It was partly because of the possibility of a republic that such prominence was given to General Aman in August and September for he was considered as an excellent figurehead (he was not himself a member of the Committee) and as a potential Presidential candidate. The continuation of the monarchy was agreed upon to satisfy the conservative elements in the country including the Church and the smaller landowners, and to inhibit any objections to the deposition of Haile Selassie.

A closely related topic that also caused argument within the Committee was the question of a return to civilian rule. As the Co-ordinating Committee and as the Provisional Military Government the military issued several statements that they were going to return to barracks and had no intention of setting up a military tyranny to replace the one overthrown. Some opposition was however quick to surface from both workers and students who feared for a continuation of army rule; the lack of a timetable for the drawing up of a new constitution and for elections was the main point at issue.

By and large, however, most people were prepared to accept the somewhat general aims of the Armed Forces published on 12 September, and to give them time to carry them out:

The aims of the (military administration) committee:

1. This committee will see to it that the equality, rights and progress of all Ethiopians, i.e. of the farmer, the worker and people generally, are properly safeguarded.

2. In the spirit of the motto "Ethipoia first" the committee will do away with the longstanding tribal and religious differences and the gap in the standard of living among Ethiopians.

3. The committee will re-organize, in a modern way, some customary beliefs which are obstacles to the modern progress and unity of the Ethiopians, including systems of provincial administration.

4. Law on land tenancy, which will particularly satisfy the common farmer whose livelihood depends on agriculture and which will increase the country's agricultural produce, will be urgently acclaimed and implemented. Until such time, all tenants will have a guarantee that they will be able to live on and benefit from the land on which they are settled and which they cultivate.

5. The set-up of the courts and the process of prosecution, under which the whole people of our country have suffered, will be reorganized in a modern manner, so that all Ethiopians have the right of speedy justice.

6. A big campaign will be launched against diseases in various parts of the country for the benefit and health of the whole community.

7. Since education is the basis for the country's improvement and progress, every Ethiopian will get a free basic education, related to his progress, and a foundation for a modern and permanent education system, related to progress and development, will be laid. In addition, a big campaign will be launched to reduce the existing number of illiterates.

8. Obstacles to good and moral living standards for society will be swept away, so that the whole society of our country can live by establishing a family based on equality and love.

9. It (the committee) will see to it, by safeguarding the equal rights of Ethiopians, that the people's basic rights and national obligations are guaranteed by law without any pressure.

10. It believes that all Ethiopians, free from personal inclination
or pressure from other cultures, should believe in love for their
country and nationalism, and must wholeheartedly participate in
the progress of modern civilization.

11. It is required that all Ethiopians believe in the theory that
trust among Ethiopians, together with co-operation and equality,
is the foundation of our country's development and unity.

12. Since, in accordance with the belief of modern civilization,
all kinds of work and handicraft are necessary for development
and prosperity, all occupations, such as potteries and tanneries and
cloth-weaving, will be recognized as honourable jobs and will be
expanded, like any other work or skill.

13. Since the economy is the basis for a country's development
and progress, products manufactured in our country by industry
and the activities of the factories will be increased.

14. Our cultural heritages and the arts, renowned abroad, will be
organized in an honourable and dependable manner, so that all
Ethiopians know about them and take pride in them, and also make
them known to the rest of the world.

15. Believing that all Ethiopians should take part in the
country's development and unity, spearheaded by the military
committee, a policy statement aimed at laying a foundation for the
change and improvement of our country, in justice, administration,
agriculture, trade, education, [word indistinct] and social life, will
be issued at a future date.[3]

Within a fortnight it was thought necessary to provide a supplement to explain item four, which was intended as a compromise until
a final solution was worked out:

We have discovered that some tenants, not having studied and
understood the provisional decision and having been instigated by
some mischief-makers, have interpreted the words "have a
guarantee to live and benefit" as meaning that they owned the land
and had the right to benefit from it forever, and accordingly
have been trying to deny some landlords the right to their
land.

We warn everybody that they must realize that such action would
disturb the security of the country and these people must bear the
responsibility for disturbing security. Therefore, the meaning of this
provisional decision is that until such time as a solution to the land

tenancy issue is found, the landlord and the tenant must work in accordance with the agreement they had hitherto entered into—that is the landlord must not evict the tenant indiscriminately, and the tenant must not consider the land on which he has settled as his own and must continue giving profits to the landlord in accordance with their agreement, and must not evict the owner of the land or take possession of the land. We, therefore, warn against such action[4]

This illustrates the problems that the Provisional Military Government is facing. It is not only students that are impatient for action. Indeed a substantial amount of land has already been taken over by tenants in the south and west, especially since the arrest of such landowners as *Ras* Mesfin Sileshi. It underlines Ethiopia's need for a solution to the whole problem of land tenure, now that expectations have been raised. This is the case for all sections of the community.

A start has been made with the removal of the symbols of the feudal state, with the arrest of the leading members of the old regime. A Commission of Enquiry is investigating corruption, and, by implication, its brief is steadily being extended as arrests have continued since the deposition of Haile Selassie. A fifty-man civilian Commission has been set up to draft a new constitution and to organize the necessary administration for the election of a genuinely democratic People's Assembly. Considerable energy has been put into organizing more effective relief for the drought-stricken provinces—Wollo was declared a disaster area and it was decided that the entire province should be put under the administration of the Drought Relief and Rehabilitation Committee.

The long-term aim of the Military is the complete overthrow of feudalism and the restructuring of Ethiopian society. The easy part of this revolution was the removal of the old regime. The stages that have to follow this will be the difficult ones. At the very least, whatever direction the revolution takes in the next months and years, Ethiopia has at last accepted the necessity for real change, and has begun to modernize the structure of the State. However the crisis of 1974 is regarded, it is clear that it demonstrated the corruption of the regime of Haile Selassie, and its inability to deal with the famine disaster of 1973/4 and inflation. It showed that Government policies, especially since the restoration of 1941, had not begun to solve the deep-rooted problems that threaten the future of the country. In more than forty years as Emperor any reforming or modernizing zeal shown by Haile Selassie appears to have had little effect on Ethiopian society.

In fact, the contrast that has existed between the world-wide reputation of Emperor Haile Selassie and the state of affairs within Ethiopia must strike most forcibly any person interested in the country. He was widely regarded as an absolute monarch with semi-divine status. This was far from the case. He always had to contend with a number of conflicting power groups—the Church, the central and provincial aristocracy and the army. He kept his position by balancing these forces and by playing them against each other, at which he was very competent. But the imperial position, in spite of all efforts at centralization, was never really strong enough to ignore them. They were all incorporated into the administrative structure and all remain relevant politically in the mid-1970s.

Underlying the political situation has been a socio-economic system that can only be described as feudal, having as it does all the major elements of the feudal societies of western Europe and of Japan. The basis of political power remains land and in the early 1970s the government gave land grants to supplement or replace salary, using this as an integral part of the administrative technique. A common feature in twentieth century Ethiopia has been the total lack of interest of each Government and all power groups in changing the land system that has been the basis of their authority. Certain superficial reforms have been enacted—the setting up of a Ministry of Land Reform, the introduction of an agricultural income tax—but these have been essentially still-born and have not affected most peasant farmers. Their position remains more or less what it was fifty or 500 years ago—exploited and over-taxed, and at the mercy of frequent famines.

The power groups that have been incorporated within the Government by the Emperor, or have forced themselves upon him, have come precisely from the landed aristocracy. Where outsiders, imperial appointees, have been used, they also have been brought into the system by judicious land grants and by advantageous marriages. This applies not just to officials of the traditional administration in the provinces but also to those in the newer institutions created in the interests of centralization: the Parliament, the bureaucracy and the army. To avoid the dilution of power there has been no encouragement of a genuine national bourgeoisie: rather, foreign capital has been brought in and utilized almost exclusively by the landed elite to support their own position and status.

Opposition to the ruling elite has been considerable and nearly continuous. It has ranged from small-scale attacks on individual landlords to substantial peasant revolts with nationalist overtones that have lasted for a decade or more. The exploitative nature of the system has also fuelled intellectual dissent, especially from the students, and brought about substantial discontent among the ordinary soldiers and the small urban proletariat. In 1974 this culminated in a spontaneous upsurge of popular feeling against a Government that was clearly unable to cope; for the first time the demands for massive and widespread change produced the real possibility of restructuring the socio-economic basis of Ethiopian society.

This book attempts to analyse some of the causes of the 1974 crisis and to identify the power groupings that have relevance in Ethiopian politics. These involve not only the central administration and the landed aristocracy, but also the various groups and individuals that have opposed the Emperor and the Government, in the revolts that have taken place or been attempted especially since 1941. Very little work has been done on analysis of class structures in Ethiopia, and this can only be a preliminary effort to identify some of the major traditional classes as well as some of those that have come into being since the Second World War. These new forces are now beginning to make their political presence felt and are bound to play a vital political role in the future.

CHAPTER ONE

Historical Introduction

It is a cliché to say that a country cannot be understood without reference to its past. Equally it is a truism, and the aim of this chapter is to provide a brief outline of Ethiopia's last 300 years, to trace the development of some of the problems that became critical in 1974. There is not however an attempt to present a comprehensive picture.

In the first half of the seventeenth century, a permanent capital was established by the Emperor Fasilidas at Gondar, in partial response to a century of disaster. The medieval Ethiopian empire collapsed in A.D. 1529 when a Moslem leader, Ahmed Gran, Sultan of Adal, won a decisive victory over the then Emperor. For the following fourteen years his forces pillaged across the empire. Only with Portuguese aid could the Ethiopian army ultimately defeat and kill Gran. But the Portuguese brought their own problems. Their attempt to convert Ethiopia to Roman Catholicism created havoc; civil war broke out over a succession crisis that was reinforced by religious dissension. Though the successful Emperor, Susenyos, was also converted to Catholicism, opposition was so strong that in 1632 he finally abdicated in favour of his son Fasilidas. This marked the end of Portuguese influence in Ethiopia and it had the effect of encouraging the empire's already strong xenophobia.[1]

The foundation of Gondar marked a new approach to government. Throughout the medieval period, between the thirteenth and sixteenth centuries, the Emperors tended to circulate around the Empire, and despite having favoured camping sites, the "capital" was thus highly mobile. This provided a number of benefits—the simplification of tax-collection and facilities for feeding the enormous court and army that surrounded the Emperor and his administration. These advantages disappeared with a static centre.

This loss was not foreseen; nor did it become apparent for some time. At its inception Gondar produced a new flowering of architecture and art which was to persist for a hundred years. It also appeared as a successful and conscious attempt at reuniting Church and State. During the previous fifty years the Portuguese missionary effort, concentrating on conversion at the highest level, had the effect of dividing the throne from the Orthodox Church. When Fasilidas, who was firmly Orthodox, succeeded, he was very conscious of the need to respond to his people's overwhelming rejection of the imported faith. So the imperial enclosure at Gondar was surrounded by churches. In all some forty-four were built there, as well as the residence of the *Abuna*—the head of the Ethiopian Church who was always a Coptic Christian from Egypt[2]—and of the *Ichege*—the abbot of Debra Libanos monastery, head of the monks of the empire and chief administrator of the church.

There also the great nobility surrounded the Emperor, holding the traditional offices and perquisites of power. For in terms of government and administration little had changed from the medieval period, except the mobility of the central Government. Administration was carried out primarily by two types of officials, though distinctions between them frequently disappeared. There was the hereditary ruler or chief whose position derived from imperial appointment. In time these appointed positions were passed from father to son, at least so long as the successor demonstrated his submission to the Emperor by producing the appropriate amount of tribute and raising local levies on imperial demand. In most other respects such a ruler would be autonomous except when the Emperor actually passed through his territory on his tours.

The second type of official was appointed more directly by the Emperor, and given control of substantial areas and impressive titles. His function was similar to that of the hereditary chief, namely, the production of tribute and military service on demand. But being an appointee of the Emperor it was easier to move him around—this perhaps was the only significant difference. It was an important control. One Portuguese observer in the sixteenth century claimed that one man ploughed, another sowed and a third reaped, so often did the Emperor shuffle his governors.

Both types of chief suffered additional methods of control. The Emperor insisted on their frequent and sometimes permanent presence at court; local administration was thus frequently in the hands of their deputies. In the sixteenth century the levels of appointment were often based on the amount offered as a gift to the Emperor by the potential appointees and aspirants to the nobility. This provided considerable revenue for the royal treasury and its continuation was originally an economic imperative; there is little doubt that it persisted long beyond the sixteenth century.

Another traditional check was through marriage alliances. For all that the Orthodox Church frowned on polygamy, the Emperors themselves indulged in multiple marriage and kept concubines. This facilitated not merely political alliances but also gave the ruler the means to ennoble certain families in order to weaken the position of hereditary chiefs, as well as providing opportunities for the more ambitious of the princes as well. Such factors were mitigated by imprisoning the many male relatives of an Emperor in mountain prisons—such as *Amba* Gishen during the medieval period, and *Amba* Wahni during the Gondar empire.[3] The attraction was two-fold. It kept the royal princes in isolation; and it kept alive a pool of candidates, so that the succession of the House of Solomon was assured.[4]

Primogeniture was not invoked. Membership of the lineage of Solomon was the all-important criterion. Potential imperial dignity passed to all the descendants of an Emperor: this may be compared to the *rist* system of land ownership where all descendants of a founding father had a claim to a share of the land. The actual division of the shares depended, however, on authority and power. In practice, like so much of the administration, it worked well only with a strong Emperor.

The economic power of the imperial throne was also affected considerably by these factors. The theory, based on the *Kebra Nagast* and the *Fetha Nagast*[5] was that all the land in the Empire belonged to the Emperor, who had the right to distribute areas of it in return for military or other services. In practical terms this absolute ownership had been whittled away long before by irreversible grants to the Church, and to individuals; and it was only in the newly conquered lands that the Emperor's control was complete in theory even if limited in practice by practical considerations. It was here that the Emperor could make fresh grants to the faithful followers; because this was an essential part of an Emperor's function, there was a built-in necessity for expansion. The ability to grant new land was critical for the retention of the support of the nobility; in times of weakness, the lack of such powers frequently worsened already difficult situations.

There were in essence two main types of landownership and control. *Rist* land, which was heritable and practically inalienable, belonged to the individual lineage, to which all descendants of that lineage had a claim. This was the main system of ownership in the highland Amhara-Tigre provinces. People who owned land in this way were freeholders; they would owe certain taxes or services to the Government or the governor but the land was theirs or at least their family's. The other method of land control was *gult*. *Gult* land was land on which the Emperor granted the usufructory rights to an individual, with especial reference to the taxes and obligations due on the land. Essentially the position of a *gult* owner was the same as that of an imperial governor, except that the *gult* owner could collect the tribute imposed on the land for his own use and not for imperial use. In other words the Emperor gave away certain of his rights over land to another, not in perpetuity, but for life or until such time as the Emperor decided.

A further variety of *gult* was that granted to the Church, *Semon* land. Because the Church was a perpetual corporation it was easy for such grants to become permanently attached. Occasionally permanent grants might also be made to an individual and his heirs. The name given to this was *rist-gult*, that is, inheritable *gult* rights. Although such rights were not often made to individuals, in practical terms a *gult* owner could frequently pass on his rights to his son with merely technical agreement by the Emperor—or in times of a weak Emperor, without actual permission. In this connection it should be emphasized that a *Gult Gej*—ruler of a *gult*—was a vital factor in the imperial administration. He was the local judge and chief law officer, the commander of the local troops when they were called up, and he collected the tribute due to the Emperor if there was any. The *gult* rights and services he enjoyed can be seen as a way of providing a salary.[6]

The system was largely confined to the major peoples of the Empire, the Amhara and the Tigre. Although there were other groups under imperial rule, these were the most important throughout the period of the Gondar empire. Historically the Ethiopian Empire had centred on Axum in Tigre during the second to eighth centuries A.D.; this was followed by the ascendency of the Agau peoples of Wag and Lasta. Not until the thirteenth century did Amhara supremacy appear. It has been essentially unbroken ever since.[7]

Although for the sake of simplicity the Amhara are usually treated as a unit, in practice the divisions between the inhabitants of what are now the provinces of Gojjam, Begemeder and Shoa are considerable and each values its own history and independence. Nevertheless one is justified in thinking of the Empire of Ethiopia as an

Amhara empire and today, to a great extent, also as a Shoan one. Within the Amhara groups, political supremacy has fluctuated—the medieval imperial family was from Shoa—but from the seventeenth century onwards the centre was Gondar in Begemeder. As Gondar declined both Shoa and Tigre became practically independent and it was partly due to this that the seat of power moved about in the later nineteenth century ending up with Menilek of Shoa, whose family have held the throne ever since.

A common feature of these fluctuations was the Amhara-Tigre rivalry that has persisted. It is true that overriding this has been a common imperial past, a common culture and religion, and unity against Islam. Internally, however, this has been fragmented by political and linguistic divisions. The northern province, and southern Eritrea as well, spoke Tigrygna which is closer to the liturgical language of the Church—Ge'ez—than is Amharic. Equally there was considerable resentment over Amhara rule. In fact, in spite of the links, Tigrean history displayed a steady growth towards independence, which culminated in the reign of Emperor Yohannis IV (1871–89). At the same time as Tigre was building up its strength Shoa was doing likewise. There again the process culminated in the success of Menilek, who followed Yohannis as Emperor. Both these cases are examples of centrifugal forces that grew strong enough to take over the Empire.

It must be emphasized again that the historical unity of the Empire was spurious in that it was only directed outwards. As in all feudal societies the political element was anything but unitary. This of course increased the importance of the myth of Solomon over and above the binding force of the Christian Church.

The specific circumstances behind the change from an Empire, centralized on Gondar in the seventeenth and eighteenth centuries, to a collection of virtually independent feudalities are still somewhat obscure. As mentioned above, *gult* rights were not heritable except in exceptional circumstances. These exceptional circumstances, however, occurred rather frequently. The first three Emperors of the Gondar period appear to have been strong enough to control *gult* distribution, but after the death of Emperor Iyasu the Great, murdered in 1706, the situation deteriorated steadily; by the late eighteenth century the independent position of the great nobility was firmly entrenched and remained so. It is however important to realize that even in these circumstances the nobility, for all their independence, tended to revolve around the imperial throne and to concentrate on the struggle to control it. There was still enough prestige, if little real power, attached to the position; and from about 1780 onwards the history of the Empire is a catalogue of struggles between members of the great nobility to control the Emperor and thus gain control of his land-granting and title-granting powers. It was in part a struggle to gain legitimacy for their activities, for they themselves could and did grant lesser titles; but throughout the period, with minor exceptions, their own titles were either ratified through the Emperor or in certain cases passed down on an heritable basis.

In one sense the whole administrative system was geared to collapse at times when the Emperors were themselves weak. In the medieval period there is no doubt that the frequent movement of the Emperors acted as a cohesive force. This disappeared with the foundation of the static capital, which allowed no real check on activities in the remoter parts of the empire. Gondar also encouraged a withdrawal by the Emperors. Formality flourished; the Emperors were seen in public only once a year and they frequently conversed with others exclusively through interlocutors. Their remoteness encouraged the latent centrifugal forces in the Empire. Paradoxically this remoteness and sacred quality, while it weakened imperial control, was also perhaps the prime reason for the survival of the institution. There was a holiness in the Church-supported throne which, for all the indignities heaped upon it, did keep its character. The mystique of the house of Solomon remained a potent theory and even affected Islamic and pagan Oromo—the Galla[8]—whose eruptions also played a major part in weakening the empire.

These weaknesses of control and the rise of the powerful feudal families, supreme in their own fiefs, first became absolute in the mid-eighteenth century. The appearance of *Ras* Mikael of Tigre at the court of Gondar marked the real end of imperial control. One genealogy of his is instructive in this context.[9] His father was a "great prince who ruled all Tigre" and his great-grandfather, who married an emperor's daughter, was also a "ruler of all Tigre". Further back, Mikael had other ancestors who were princes of Tigre in the fourteenth century.

It is clear that *Ras* Mikael's supremacy in Tigre was not arbitrary. It was based on his traditional hereditary rights, reinforced by the fact that as *Ras* of Tigre he dominated access to the empire's main outlet to the sea, Massawa. While there is considerable doubt as to whether he had any control of Massawa itself, Mikael was certainly in a position to acquire many more firearms than anyone else, and this position he used to provide himself with an effective armed force. Similarly his descent gave him considerable potential in terms of *rist* claims—which were inherited through either parent—and which obviously provided him with the economic basis for his power which did not diminish even after his defeat at the battles of Sabakusa in 1771 where he was forced to withdraw from the Gondar scene.[10] Tradition maintains that although in his seventies at the time, he was too powerful to be removed from Tigre. He was merely sent back there and continued to rule for another ten years. Certainly his son, *Dejazmatch* Wolde-Gabriel, was able to inherit most of his power.

Another major factor in Mikael's rise to power at Gondar was his position as the leading Christian lord. He was brought in by the Queen Mother during the reign of the Emperor Ioas (1755–69), to counter-balance Ioas' Oromo relatives who were under suspicion for their "barbaric and Islamic" tendencies. It is at this time in fact that the problem of the Oromo, who had first attacked the empire two centuries before, impinged on the central political life of the empire.

Until 1771, Mikael was highly successful in checking Oromo influence at court though in the process he had Ioas assassinated in 1769 and was responsible for placing the next two Emperors on the throne. It is significant that Mikael always acted through an Emperor. At a time when he was clearly powerful enough to have placed himself on the throne, he made no attempt to do so. He contented himself with being the kingmaker. It is also worth noticing that his defeat in 1771 was caused not by increased imperial power but by his own advancing years and by the combination of some of his Christian Amhara rivals with the Oromo lords. The imperial position was, in political terms, becoming irrelevant to the struggle to be the "mayor of the palace".

The origins of the Oromo people are uncertain but it seems most likely that they came from southern Ethiopia, around Lake Abiya (Margherita). In the sixteenth century they moved out of their heartland looking perhaps for land. Whatever the dynamic, it was a formidable one. Their expansion was short and violent. Within a period of about fifty years they had overrun most of what is now southern Ethiopia,[11] and were settling far and wide within the borders of both the Ethiopian empire and the Sultanate of Adal to the east. Even after the period of expansion was halted by the Emperor

Sertza Dengel, and the empire managed to re-incorporate large
areas along the eastern scarp, the effects lingered on.

One long term effect was on the trade of the Empire. During the
medieval period the empire had expanded south to cut across and
control all the trade routes running through the Moslem Sultanates
of the Sidama peoples. There is little doubt that a great deal of the
wealth of medieval Ethiopia came from these trade routes. The effect
of the Oromo movement was to cut off the trade and it was not until
the foundation of the Oromo kingdoms in the Gibe areas of the
southwest in the first half of the nineteenth century, that trade
began to pick up again. It appears to be no accident that the age of
the *Mesafint* coincides with the expansion of the Oromo into these
areas.[12] In the earlier part of Gondar's history the empire still had
contacts with Enarea and the kingdom of Kaffa[13], for Iyasu the Great
campaigned in Enarea. During the course of the century the Oromo
drove westward into this area, and into Wollega further north,
effectively wrecking such contacts.

The Oromo tribes who played the largest part in the political
affairs of the Gondar empire were not these groups, but the Yejju
and Wollo Oromo, who settled along the eastern escarpment in the
later sixteenth century and who gradually became incorporated, if
loosely, within the Empire. While we lack evidence for this, it seems
that it was done through imperial appointments. The settlement of
the Oromo naturally affected their culture and their adaptation to the
situation involved some intermarriage between the Oromo nobility
and the Gondar Court. Conquest may have played a part in some
areas, for further south the expansion of Shoa in the early eighteenth
century was started by the request of the Emperor for one Shoan
Amhara, Negasse from Menz, to help a Moslem ally of Gondar against
Oromo incursions. Following on from this, most of the Oromo of
northern Shoa were overrun by the Shoan Amhara expansion during
the next hundred years. This process was much helped by the inter-
tribal rivalry among the Oromo.[14]

In whatever way these tribes were incorporated, by the second half
of the eighteenth century the Yejju Oromo were playing an important
role in political affairs. Indeed from about 1780 the Yejju chiefs
were essentially paramount, or at any rate *primus inter pares* among
the nobility of the empire. The first such family to reach high
office was that of *Ras* Ali "the great", who was *Ras* of Begemeder
and Amhara in the 1780s. The governorship of these areas remained
exclusively in the family for the next seventy years. With the aid of

their Oromo cavalry, which were more or less invincible on the open plains, they thus held control of Gondar and the person of the Emperor who resided there. In the mountain areas, free of the cavalry threat, other great Amhara and Tigre nobles preserved their independence and at times—particularly in the earlier years of the Yejju supremacy—were able to interfere in Gondar as well. For all their efforts the Yejju chiefs were never able, and indeed would not have dared, to take over the empire. They always acted through an imperial mouthpiece. Not only were they not of the Solomonaic line—though they were married into it at times—but they were tainted with Islam, albeit nominally converted. Their conversion was always doubted and the Yejju chiefs were closely connected with the important Wollo line of Oromo chiefs, most of whom did remain Moslem and who at times also exercised much power in Gondar. In the time of *Ras* Ali "the little", in the mid-nineteenth century, two of his uncles, who were also his guardians, were both Moslems—and their father, Imam Liban, had been considered the most important Moslem leader in Ethiopia. It has recently been shown that in the 1830s there was some talk of an alliance between these Oromo and Egypt under its expansionist ruler Muhammed Ali.[15] This came to nothing but it helped to keep the Christian Amhara/ Tigre groups firmly set against any possible Yejju emperor.

Indeed the period of the Yejju supremacy—called the *Zemene Mesafint*, the Age of Princes—is a continuous story of wars and battles, as the great nobility of Tigre, Semien, Lasta and Gojjam fought the Yejju and each other, and allied and married into each other's families. In the process they exhausted their provinces. In 1852 a minor chief of Qwara, in the province of Begemeder, who had important connections with the Christian nobility of that province, set out on a brief and extraordinary career of conquest that enabled him to be crowned as the Emperor Tewodros in 1855; and by the end of the following year all the areas of northern Ethiopia had been reincorporated into a revived empire that included both the Yejju and the Wollo Oromo.

Tewodros is normally taken as the first modernizing Emperor with his attempts to create a personal, paid military force, to break the power of the feudal lords, to crush the Oromo and to revive Christianity.[16] It is, however, questionable whether his policies can be seen as modernization. Certainly he carried out, or attempted to carry out, reforms; but to suggest that his policies were anything

other than an attempt to re-establish traditional, imperial powers is
to be misled by the foreign commentators on his reign.

The only unusual factors in his restoration of imperial power were
the attempt to tax the Church and his use of the myth of a Saviour
Emperor; but he found it necessary to return to the concept of a
Solomonaic descent in the end. For the rest, Tewodros re-introduced
the moving capital, correctly realizing that the static nature of Gondar was unworkable at that time. His much vaunted efforts to
utilize paid officials, loyal to himself, in place of the feudal lords
must be seen in the light of the fact that the men he used were drawn
from the very nobility whose power he was supposedly trying to
break. Similarly his emphasis on his own position as supreme judge,
his attempts to take control of land distribution and to set up a
centrally-controlled army were only re-establishments of traditional
imperial powers.

In saying that Tewodros was only trying to restore, not innovate,
is not to decry his achievements; for he did restore the imperial
position and he did reinstate the Emperor as the key political
figure. He did not however attempt to alter the pattern of political
power; he did not think of altering the economic base of the feudal
structure or of alleviating the exploitation of the peasantry. His
importance lies in the fact that from 1855 there was an Emperor
again in Ethiopia. The fact that Tewodros committed suicide in
1868, with no support left to him, should not obscure this. It certainly
enabled the next ruler, Yohannis of Tigre (1871–89), to seize power
successfully and build on something more substantial.

Yohannis, like Tewodros, maintained his supremacy by military
force. This came from Tigre where he had a very strong traditional
and hereditary power base.[17] He claimed descent from a number of
the great nobility of the province, including *Ras* Mikael, the ruler of
Tigre in the eighteenth century. In the light of Tewodros' failure
Yohannis was more circumspect in his methods. There is evidence
that he thought in terms of having a number of subsidiary kingdoms
under himself as overall ruler. He created kings in the provinces of
Gojjam and Shoa; and brought four *Abunas*—bishops—from
Egypt, whom he appointed to Gojjam, Shoa, Begemeder and Tigre.
It seems likely that he intended to make kings of Begemeder and
Tigre as well. He wanted to further decentralize power, subject to his
own ultimate authority and the supply of tribute.

This approach was again fundamentally traditional even if it was
different from Tewodros. For any sign of modernization it is

necessary to look at the reign of Menilek of Shoa who, as the most powerful figure under Yohannis, was able to seize the throne on the latter's death. Although Menilek's rule was traditional in many ways, some changes of great significance were made. The setting up of a static capital at Addis Ababa, later to be linked by railway to the sea, created a genuine urban centre. A council of ministers set up in Menilek's last years, when he was incapacitated by illness, although it appeared retrogressive in view of the troubles that followed his death in 1913, was in the long run to prove significant in providing some devolution of imperial power.

In spite of these and other elements such as a hospital, a school, postal services and the like, Menilek still governed as any strong emperor of the past. He used and controlled the great nobility as his immediate predecessors had done. He centralized power to a marked degree; but he made no effort to change methods of land control—in fact he extended the system widely by his conquests to the south and west which established the present boundaries of the empire. Significantly for the future he created a Shoan hegemony to replace Yohannis' Tigre one. This has remained paramount in spite of a major challenge by the Oromo of Yejju and Wollo in the reign of *Lij* Iyasu (1913–16).

Indeed, in spite of the revived imperial power from 1855 onwards, the Oromo from these areas remained one of the most potent forces in the Empire. Both Yohannis and Menilek, while King of Shoa, found it politic to support members of the Wollo ruling house in their internecine rivalry. Yohannis' candidate, with considerable support from the Emperor was successful and was baptised as Mikael, given the title of *Ras* and made governor of Wollo. Menilek himself also found it necessary later on to give a daughter of his in marriage to *Ras* Mikael and ultimately to recognize the son of this marriage, *Lij* Iyasu, as the heir to the throne. Menilek's own marriage was into the Yejju ruling family, and *Ras* Tafari, later Haile Selassie I, also married a granddaughter of *Ras* Mikael of Wollo.[18]

It is arguable that the policies followed by both Yohannis and Menilek with regard to these Oromo was conciliatory, though Yohannis in particular was not backward in devastating Wollo at times. Equally he indulged in the forcible conversion of Moslems with the option of exile, and made it difficult for them to own land. However, whether conciliatory or not, the efforts to incorporate these northern Oromo were not very successful. The reign of *Lij* Iyasu as uncrowned Emperor (1913–16), which in one sense was a climax to conciliation, was also an illustration of its essential failure.

While there is no doubt that the suspected or actual Moslem sympathies of *Lij* Iyasu, whose father had been brought up as a Moslem, played a part in his downfall, much more relevant was the attempt, possibly inspired by his father, to destroy the supremacy of the Shoan nobility; or rather to break their hegemony over the rest of Ethiopia. The major fault of *Lij* Iyasu was in trying to do this too fast. Within eighteen months of his accession his father was crowned as King of Wollo, Lasta and Tigre with authority over the whole of northern Ethiopia. This was resented by some of the Shoan nobility who were governors in Begemeder, which was thus made subject to Mikael.

At the same time Mikael's coronation deeply worried the *Abuna* Matewos.[19] Matewos had been one of the four *Abunas* brought from Egypt by Yohannis. Two of the four had soon died but Matewos, who had been sent to Shoa, and Petros, who had gone to Tigre, survived. While Yohannis had ruled, Petros remained the supreme *Abuna*. After 1889 when Menilek ruled, his *Abuna*, Matewos, became the supreme *Abuna*. There is little doubt that Petros saw an opportunity to regain his position after 1913 and he threw his influence behind *Lij* Iyasu and Mikael. In other words a substantial part of the Church certainly did not accept the rumours of *Lij* Iyasu's Moslem proclivities. Unfortunately for Petros, Matewos' position among the Shoan nobility was very strong and in the last resort was instrumental in swinging considerable strength against *Lij* Iyasu.

In addition *Lij* Iyasu set about threatening the powers and privileges of the Shoan governors in the recently conquered areas as well. The key factor here appears to have been his dismissal of his cousin *Ras* Tafari from his inherited position as governor of Harar province; and this, coupled with the threat of further large-scale gubernatorial changes, made the great *Rases* of Menilek feel that their own positions were under attack. It was this that tipped the balance. The whole affair should be seen, not as a Christian/Moslem struggle, but as a power struggle between the peripheral non-Amhara nobility and the Shoan, Menilek-appointed *Rases* who felt their power threatened. Individual factors also entered into it; there is every reason to believe that a desire for personal aggrandisement was a major factor in the thinking of several of those involved in the overthrow of *Lij* Iyasu.

One of the essential points in this episode was the implicit, and occasionally explicit, threat of the Oromo under Mikael. In spite of generations of intermarriage, in spite of the Amhara framework that had been imposed over Wollo for fifty years and Yejju for 150 years, the Oromo of these areas were clearly prepared to follow their nobility against the Amhara. The Shoan Amhara quite clearly saw this as an Oromo threat, and they took considerable revenge in 1917 and 1918.

Menilek did not use intermarriage much as policy in the provinces he conquered to the south and west. There his approach was essentially colonialist, or an extension of the Ethiopian feudal structure into the conquered lands. The actual fighting was relatively short-lived considering the large area overrun. Between 1875 and 1898 Menilek's generals incorporated the southern and western boundaries of present day Ethiopia by a combination of overwhelming numbers and superior firepower.

As a general principle the newly conquered lands were treated in the traditional way as the personal lands of the Emperor. They were regarded as appropriated, consonant with the theory that the Emperor ultimately owned all the land in the Empire. Menilek then distributed it according to a more or less regular pattern—certain rather small percentages being allotted to the conquered chiefs, up to a maximum of a third of what they had before the conquest; the rest was either held by the crown or used to reward the successful generals and the officials subsequently sent to the areas. In other words it was used to provide for the mainly Shoan administration, and this pattern has remained unchanged ever since. The land was frequently granted not by size but in terms of the numbers of *gebbars* working on it.[20] The principle that taxation rested on the land rather than on the people thus tended to disappear in these areas; and the services owed by the *gebbars* were very onerous.

It is difficult to be precise over such services as they varied from place to place. On the peasant landowners of the north, as opposed to the *gebbars* of the south whose position was worse, the exactions due to the local governor or *gult* ruler may be summarised as follows: a tithe on crops, and taxes on production and livestock, as well as customary dues of honey, animals and produce at certain times—the great religious festivals, weddings, funerals and the appointment of new officials. In addition to this were the various unpaid, labour duties of the corvée system that were owed to the governor either in his official capacity or as a *gult* ruler. This involved the cultivation of state lands and the transport of the produce, the building of houses and fences for the governor, looking after his mules, providing wood and flour for his residence, carrying baggage and feeding officials passing through the area, transporting their tithes and taxes to the storehouses and repairing such stores, carrying the army's baggage and acting as a militia in wartime, or as prison guards, and the building and repairing of churches. There is no estimate as to how much time such activities took up but in some cases one day's work in three was demanded.

In the south restrictions on the services owed by the *gebbar* were to all intents and purposes non-existent. British consular officers in the area before 1935 painted a horrifying picture of exploitation, centred around the slave trade which it was claimed had depopulated huge areas of the countryside. The administrative basis was one in which the governors, who changed fairly frequently, used their appointments to extract the maximum from their provinces. Grants of *gult* in these areas, although technically non-inheritable, frequently were inherited in the years after the conquest. It was not unknown for soldiers or officials transferred away from these areas to retain the value of their *gebbars'* services even in their absence.

Mention should also be made of the fortified garrison towns set up by Menilek as centres for the administration of the southern provinces. These were normally under the command of a separate officer responsible directly to the Emperor. They served as military strongholds in the early years and were thus more or less exclusively Amhara-inhabited. As they have remained the administrative centres ever since, modern towns have tended to be Christian Amhara centres and have projected the image of a colonial power holding its subjects down. This has been reinforced by the use of local chiefs as rulers in small localized areas. Indirect rule at this low level is a concept that is strongly entrenched in the Ethiopian polity, and it was widely applied in the conquered provinces.

Indirect rule on a larger scale was used in a few areas of particular difficulty, remoteness, or where immediate surrender had occurred. The Sultanate of Aussa in the Danakil desert was too remote to deal with; so also was the Sultan of Beni Shangul in the west. Both were allowed virtual independence subject to an annual tribute. The same held true for the Sultan of Jimma and the chiefs of northern and central Wollega who all surrendered to Menilek's armies without a fight. It was not until the immediate pre-war years or in the aftermath of Haile Selassie's return in 1941 that these areas were more fully incorporated into the administrative system. It is however noticeable that the former ruling elites have continued to be used more widely than elsewhere.

It is true that especially at the higher social levels a certain amount of assimilation did take place between the Amhara and other groups, mainly through intermarriage. This was however limited and operated differently in different areas. In the south, the whole administration militated against genuine contacts. There was little effort to spread Amhara culture or the Christian religion in any positive way, though of necessity a certain minimal use of Amharic became quite common. In the north exploitation was based less on ethnic differences, except in the relatively small areas inhabited by Oromo and other minority tribes in the north and north-west, and more on social distinctions. This did not however really affect the degree of exploitation.

Both the failure of assimilation and the type and degree of exploitation have been, and still are, instrumental in sparking off many peasant revolts. The history of Ethiopia is full of such revolts although their significance has been obscured by the emphasis of observers on the importance of the nobility as leaders. It is true that the leaders of sizeable revolts were nearly always members of the local nobility; but this merely reflects the structure of the society. It does not imply there was no peasant unrest. A typical pattern was for a dissatisfied local noble to put himself at the head of, or be co-opted by, a peasant revolt already in operation. Both elements used each other, but the vital factor was the peasants' depth of resentment not the ambitions of the nobility. This applied not only in the north but also in the provinces conquered by Menilek.

One area usually adduced as an example of an assimilated province is Shoa, partly because of the presence of the capital city, Addis Ababa, for the last eighty years. On closer inspection there is little evidence for real assimilation. From the seventeenth century the Shoan Amhara princes were expanding southwards and over-running the plateau areas that the Oromo had taken earlier. The first stage in this process came to a halt in about 1800; and the limit of this early Amhara expansion exactly marks the dividing line between Amharic and Oromo speakers in Shoa today. Later expansion under Sahle Selassie, King of Shoa (1813–47) and his successors, took over the areas further south around what is now Addis Ababa. In spite of unbroken Amhara rule since then and the influence of an enormous urban centre, and much recent emphasis on the use of Amharic as a national language, the people of the area still have Oromo as a first language and have, in all essentials,

retained their own culture. It can only be concluded that even under
the most favourable circumstances the commitment of the Amhara
towards genuine assimilation has been neither real nor successful.

It is useful at this point to look a little more closely at the historical
and theoretical bases of the two institutions which still made up the
political centre of the Ethiopian State until the changes of early 1974—
the Monarchy and the Church; though it is as well to remember that
the theory and practice were certainly poles apart at times and
never more so during the period of the *Zemene Mesafint* when,
at one point, there were five crowned Emperors living in various
parts of the central provinces. Yet even then the imperial mystique
did not fail. The concept of the Solomonaic line, although it only
appears historically as a fully-fledged story to justify the usurpation
of a prince of Tegulat in Shoa in the thirteenth century, remained
very vivid. When in the later nineteenth century three Emperors
seized power consecutively—Tewodros (1855–68), Yohannis IV
(1871–89) and Menilek (1889–1913)—all were constrained at some
point to find genealogies to link them to the House of Solomon. It
is true that Tewodros for a time used an alternative approach—
identification with a Saviour Emperor called Tewodros—but this
did not last long. An earlier usurpation in the eighteenth century
indicates the strength of the myth as well. *Ras* Yostos who seized
the throne (1711–16) is supposed to have said as he fell ill and was
deposed; "I have ruled as well as any man can do who is not of the
house of Solomon".[21]

It is the *Kebra Nagast* which enshrines the legend of the line of
Solomon and both it and the *Fetha Nagast*, which dates roughly
from the same period, provide the documentary and Biblical supports
for the throne. The *Fetha Nagasta* was the traditional law code and
uses extensive biblical quotations to underpin the God-inspired and
supported position of the Emperor. In a sense the size and wealth
and power of the empire was irrelevant to such a throne, based on
God and tradition. The parallel with Byzantium is striking and
valuable. Indeed theocracy is perhaps the best word to use in
describing the imperial system. Religion was a major pre-occupation
of the Emperors and a main function for the throne was support
for the Church. Certainly in this lay the basis for the Christian
population's reverence for the throne.

The careers of Tewodros and Yohannis clarify this. Tewodros'
life was deeply involved with religion. Especially in his earlier years
he identified Ethiopia with orthodoxy—it has been argued that in

such a multi-national and religious society there was no other path to re-unification.[22] No other institutions existed outside the throne and the Church. Equally it can be said that the root cause for Tewodros' failure was his inability to persuade the Church to finance him. His attempts to do so merely alienated the Church, which kept public support while he lost it. Yohannis was more successful in maintaining Church support. Both were, on the whole, intolerant of missionary activity and made strong efforts to convert Moslems. Yohannis was however responsible for getting four *Abunas* from Egypt, an unheard-of number; and he did not get involved in the same quarrels as did Tewodros, nor did he imprison and cause the death of an *Abuna*, as Tewodros did to *Abuna* Selama.

As this suggests, one aspect of sovereignty was the guardianship of a Church which in turn legitimated the Emperor through the formal ritual of the services and the coronation ceremonies. It seems that the Church seldom interfered either to help or hinder the overthrow of a sovereign directly but at times there is no doubt that a failure of orthodoxy contributed to the downfall of an Emperor. Susenyos (1607–32) found himself obliged to abdicate because of his Catholic conversion. Iyasu I (murdered in 1706) and Yostos (deposed in 1716), were both suspected, on scant evidence, of leaning to Catholicism. In the deposition of *Lij* Iyasu the role of *Abuna* Matewos was clear-cut though his attitude was not shared by the whole Church.

The other vital attributes of the sovereign were those pertaining to any "heroic society": leadership in war and the rewarding of service. An Emperor's function was definitely military in traditional terms. The seventeenth and eighteenth century chronicles make this very clear. Year after year the armies marched—somewhere. If there was nowhere to go or no one to fight the Emperor would go off on one of the great ceremonial hunts which were always important enough to be noted. Iyasu I was apparently averse to bloodshed; nevertheless he led yearly expeditions until his twenty-ninth year and carried out many large hunts after that. It is notable that a large number of people who objected to the return of Haile Selassie in 1941 did so because he had fled the country in 1936 rather than die fighting at the head of his troops. Even today older men still express their disgust at this.

As regards the granting of rewards the Emperor remained paramount. In most cases they took the form of land, usually *gult*, and titles. The theoretical position concerning imperial land control is to be found in the *Kebra Nagast* and the *Fetha Nagast*; but perhaps the clearest exposition of it comes from a proclamation by one of the Yejju "mayors of the palace" in the earlier nineteenth century:

> The land belongs to God; man can be no more than the usufructuary . . . Holders of lordly estates and holders of great fiefs (let me say unto you that) there is no hereditary right of suzerainty . . . I am the lord of the land . . . I alone allocate at my pleasure . . . I bestow rank and office.[23]

It is of course true that this proclamation illustrates the power of the Yejju leader and the weakness of the Emperor at that time; nevertheless it also shows perfectly the theoretical imperial position.

The importance of titles cannot be overstated. The Amhara people have very strong patterns of deferential behaviour and the granting of titles became a key element in this. It is interesting to note that it does not appear to matter too much who grants a title— a number of men still use titles granted by the Italians between 1936 and 1941; though usually, but not always, they were confirmed by the Emperor on his return.

A function related to this was the giving of feasts. The traditional imperial *guebbars* given by Menilek at the New Year at Maskal, Genna and Easter Sunday were enormous affairs, lasting over three days and requiring all the resources of the palace to be mobilised as well as the Emperor's presence. The palace guards and servants, clergy, citizens of Addis Ababa and the nobility took their places in due order. During each day between about ten and fifteen thousand people were fed. "Informants talk about the grandeur of the occasion, and of the wealth Menilek must have had to be able to feed so many people; they complain that the good old days seem to be gone for ever."[24] This was in fact the real and visible sign of the great man. If he could not feed his followers in the style to which they were accustomed then they dropped away. This was perhaps not so relevant to the Emperors, but among the mirror-image courts of the provincial nobility such factors were vital.

The other major institution was the Church, which not only sanctified the throne but had immense importance in its own right, especially in the northern provinces which were more or less Christian.

This was not entirely due to the strength of the Christian ethic. It was equally, if not more, dependent upon the great wealth of the Church. It was traditionally maintained that the Church had been granted a third of the land of the country in the thirteenth century.[25]

While there is little doubt that this figure was an exaggeration there is also little doubt that the Church does probably own about a quarter of it; and this does tend to be some of the best land in the country.

Church land is also practically inalienable because the Church is a perpetual corporation. The land is organized around particular churches and the major obligation laid on the land is the provision and support of a priest and of the church services. Within this limit the land can be *rist* owned, the church having what amounts to perpetual *gult* rights over it. While it is impossible to calculate the actual size of church lands until a genuine land survey is made there is no doubt that the great monasteries are extremely wealthy with lands and estates all over the country.

The Church's whole attitude was an essentially static one. Politically it did little except support the status quo, although it did possess and use the right of sanctuary and mediation in disputes. Its static nature also comes out in the lack of missionary activities. Conversions were usually carried out as and when the Emperors decided, not at the behest of the Church. In the southern areas conquered by Menilek some conversions took place, but most of the churches built in these provinces were for the military personnel or for the

ETHIOPIA IN THE 17th AND 18th CENTURIES

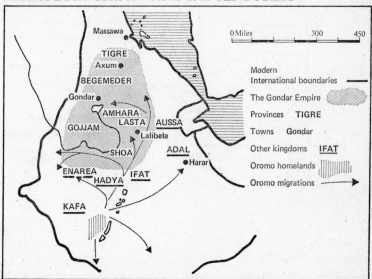

new Amhara settlers from the north, and virtually no efforts were made to missionize after the conquest when conditions would have been easiest.

The most striking aspect of the last three hundred years of Ethiopian society is its stable nature and its continuity. The real practical strength of the system lay not in the mystique of the House of Solomon nor in the religious sanctions of the Church, important though they were. It lay in control of the economic base of the Empire—land. For a variety of reasons trade never succeeded in supplanting land as the dynamic of the society.[26] It is important to realise that this situation still has not changed today. The medieval land structure and that of today remain in all essentials the same. Details of obligations on the land have changed at times, new nobility have emerged to some extent, especially in the southern provinces, and the power of the emperors *vis-à-vis* the nobility has fluctuated. On no occasion, however, was any attempt made to alter the hierarchical feudal structure arising out of control of the land.

All the supposedly modernizing Emperors of the nineteenth century used the old methods of control—frequent gubernatorial changes, marriage links, feudal obligations and the continued maintenance and expansion of the imperial lands. No real efforts were

ETHIOPIA IN THE 19th CENTURY

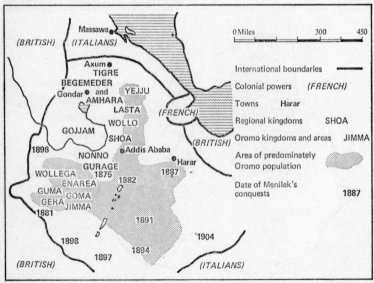

made to assimilate the Oromo or the other non-Amhara groups. They used only the Church, which failed to operate outside the highland Christian areas, and the myth of Solomon as the means of holding their disparate Empire together. It was impossible for the Emperors to attempt to break the feudal ties which underpinned it all. They had to fight hard enough to hold on to the limited amount of centralization that they could salvage from the great feudal nobility. To do more in the shape of disestablishing the local hierarchies was to expect something of which they were incapable. As a result, when *Ras* Tafari Makonnen became the Emperor Haile Selassie I in 1930, Ethiopia was to all intents and purposes in a situation very similar to that of three hundred years before.

PART ONE: POLITICAL POWER STRUCTURES

CHAPTER TWO
The Traditional Elites

The traditional elites were both secular and religious. Taken as a whole, the most important was the nobility. For the sake of simplicity, the nobility may be subdivided into three groups. The greatest were those of the royal line and their immediate relatives, and the major provincial families, usually one to each province. These were the princes—*mesafint*. Next in rank came the officials, both from the court and the military—*mekwanint*. Finally there were the lesser nobility, the local gentry—*balabat*.

The Amharic terms are not quite as exact as this implies, and have come to have more than one meaning in normal usage. Strictly speaking *balabat*, which means one who has a father, should be applied to the whole of the nobility; and *mekwanint* should only apply to one holding an appointment. In fact *mekwanint* has really come to be applied to any non-royal noble and his family. *Balabat* continues to be applied to the local gentry as well as the local nobility, but it is also attached to those who hold positions of authority at the lower levels of the provincial administration.

Distinctions between these divisions are also much more complex than this suggests. The hierarchical nature of the society was carried to extremes within the nobility. The complexities are almost impossible to unravel, based as they are on a combination of factors that include birth, marriage, land ownership, office and even age. Inevitably there is a certain amount of disagreement over the exact status of the more distant relatives of a family. Equally, since office and therefore political power are factors, the pecking order can and does change with some frequency.

In any discussion of the Ethiopian nobility as a class, it is also necessary to remember that it never became a politically homogeneous group. It has never managed to act as a political group united against the imperial position. This is not to say that individual nobles have not done so. Indeed during the last hundred years there have been six Emperors, and of these, four came to power from positions as *mesafint* of particular provinces. Tekle-Giyorgis III (1868–71) was previously the *Wagshum*, the hereditary ruler of Lasta. Yohannis IV (1871–89) had previously been *Shum* (ruler) of Tembien and was descended from the ruling family of another area in Tigre, Agame. Menilek II (1889–1913) had been *Negus* (king) of Shoa; the province his family had ruled for over a hundred years. Haile Selassie had succeeded both his brother and his father as governor of Hararge province; and it was his removal from it by *Lij* Iyasu that was a primary consideration in Haile Selassie's participation in *Lij* Iyasu's overthrow.

It was political power derived from these provinces that was the basis to their claims; though such claims had to be buttressed by an appeal to the blood of Solomon. Until their coronations they had the potential, as members of the *mesafint*, that is Princes of the Blood, to become Emperors, but it was a potential shared with many others. It was the coronation and the Church that gave them actual legitimacy as Emperors. The emphasis in the coronation was on the religious element. "May you, by your prayers, preserve your faith unshaken and unconquerable". The oath involves the maintenance of "the Orthodox religion, the laws of the Empire, the integrity of the territories of the country . . .", in that order.[1] It was buttressed by the presentation of the sword of justice, the sceptre and the ring. Most important was the anointing with the holy oil, which together with the imperial blood of Solomon, rendered the person of the Emperor sacred, his dignity inviolable and his power indisputable.

The importance of the imperial blood had a significant effect on the nobility, and put a premium on political intrigue. Above all it inhibited the great nobility from acting together to forward the ambitions of one of their number, when all had equal claims. Over and above this, provincial feelings helped to emphasize the divisions in spite of frequent inter-marriage. Even today there is certain animosity between the nobility who come from Shoa as opposed to those who are considered to come from Tigre, Gojjam or Wollo.

In spite of these divisions, and while it may be difficult to categorize an individual within the class, it is relatively easy to classify the factors that go to make a noble. The nobility did indeed have a distinctive attitude towards others, brought about by education as well as status. For all that they were not laid down in any code, there were a number of characteristic touchstones. Of course, as in any feudal society, geared to the heroic ideal, prowess in battle could offset these factors; but this happened relatively rarely.

First and foremost were land and birth, the two being inextricably intertwined through the *rist* system of land ownership. As an alternative to *rist* ownership there was *gult* land. The distinctions between the two were important. *Rist* was heritable; *gult* strictly speaking was not. The Emperor had no control over the former except in cases of treason, and even then expropriated land normally went to a traitor's kin. *Gult* however was the grant of imperial rights over a piece of land. It was given, in most cases, in lieu of salary to an imperial appointee, a *mekwanint*. Such a grant gave the *mekwanint* the right to keep and use the taxes from the land. It should not be confused with governorship which involved passing on the taxes to the central government.

Any important governor had substantial *gult* grants made at the same time as a governorship. Thus in most cases when the governorship was granted to the son of the previous governor the same *gult* would be granted as well. Imperial *gult* grants were given directly to the greatest governors only. These *mesafints* then granted control over the areas to their followers who acted as sub-governors. Such secondary grants might also be in the form of *gult* instead of salary, but were more likely to be given in the form of straight governorships that did not involve any land grants.

The sub-governors were recruited through the *ashkar* system which provided the military basis of the power of the nobility. It was a client (*ashkar*)–patron relationship that cemented political or family bonds, and incidentally provided for a certain amount of upward social mobility. The normal practice was for a member of the *rist*-owning class to send one or more of his sons to the household of relative, friend or potential ally; preferably one who had more wealth or was of a higher position or title. The boy would enter such a household young, and at first would act as a general servant in a variety of ways. Once he had reached the requisite age he became one of soldiers of his "lord" and was used in peace-time for the purposes of establishing his "lord's" authority. This meant collecting taxes, investigating failures of payment and in general acting as the executive force.

The *ashkar* was supplied with arms, food and possibly a mule; in addition he took a percentage of the taxes collected. These were in kind until the 1920s when cash began to be used. The actual amount that an *ashkar* obtained depended upon the wealth of the lord; but all in all it came to a higher wage than could be acquired in any other way. The most noticeable omission from the rewards was land. In the northern provinces it was impossible to get a direct grant of land because all the land was already under *rist* ownership and therefore inalienable. The situation was different in the southern provinces where the conquered territories were available, and were widely granted to the generals responsible for the conquest and, in turn, to their followers.

In lieu of land, however, a governorship could be expected. This was likely to be only a small district, but the size was almost irrelevant. The most important benefit that came out of this was the *ashkar*'s establishment in the hierarchy of deference. He was also able to activate *rist* land claims. Any member of this class could find these through interlocking genealogical links (see charts on pp. 40–44); and as governor an *ashkar* either judged cases himself or was in a position to influence judgement.

With a governorship went some sort of title; and this again was significant in terms of influence and deference. The title might be symbolic, with nothing specific attached to it, but it was a very potent symbol. It established a man's importance and was for life. It could only be removed by the Emperor and then only in extreme cases. Title granting was not confined to the Emperors although the highest subsidiary titles were their perogative alone. Every major title-holder—*Ras, Dejazmatch, Fitawari* and *Kegnazmatch*—could grant titles up to, though not including, the level of his own (see Glossary). A distinction was however drawn between imperially-granted titles and those granted by the nobility, the former ranking higher. A *Fitawari* who was appointed a governor with the title of *Dejazmatch* in 1934 refused the title. This was because it was being granted by a *Ras* and his own title had been granted by the Emperor; and the *Fitawari* thus maintained that he already had the equivalent of the higher rank. Although most titles related, at least in origin, to their military function, there was also a series of civilian titles which were granted to holders of administrative posts or to people of intellectual distinction.

It is noteworthy that there was apparently little premium placed on loyalty to an individual lord. This was the case to the extent that loyalty was rewarded but no guarantees or promises were made on either side. The actual ceremony of title-giving makes this clear. The recipient was carefully robed with a special shirt and cloak and was then led before the governor granting the title. An announcement was then made before the governor's retainers and courtiers; and a sword, possibly even a rifle and a mule, were given. No other words were spoken. The recipient bowed to the ground and kissed the feet of the lord. This symbolized his acceptance of the lord at that time and his gratitude. Some loyalty was implicit in the gesture, but the whole concept of the ceremony was much more a reward for past loyalty. The act of bowing and kissing the feet did not in fact imply submission—that was shown by an appearance with a heavy stone upon the head or neck.

Without any oath or promise of continued loyalty the main thing that bound an *ashkar* to his lord was self-interest. There was an inbuilt moral stigma attached to desertion but it was not very strong. Indeed certain figures who betrayed their lords were respected for their cunning and good sense. In breaking with an Emperor it was not uncommon to obtain Church sanction, but this was less to avoid charges of immoral behaviour than to try and gain the active support of the Church. Examples can of course be found of those who did die for their lord but the emphasis placed upon them suggests that they were relatively rare.

These attitudes were clearly illustrated in the years immediately following the expulsion of the Italians in 1941. Many of the great nobility had not followed the Emperor into exile but had made a quick peace with the invaders. Both *Ras* Hailu of Gojjam and *Ras* Seyoum of Tigre were collaborators and ruled their provinces under the Italians. After the Emperor's return, *Ras* Hailu never recovered the rule of his province, though this was less for his collaboration than because he had lost it before the war for alleged misgovernment. *Ras* Seyoum was however re-appointed fairly quickly as the governor of Tigre. In neither case was there any attempt to punish them for what could have been considered as betrayal.

The only important figure who was punished was *Dejazmatch* Haile Selassie Gugsa who had ruled southern Tigre before the war. He had actually been in correspondence with the Italians before the invasion, in spite of being the Emperor's son-in-law for two years. He took refuge with the British in 1941 and was handed over to the Emperor in 1948. Since that time he has been under close confinement first in Arussi province and then in the isolated town of Gore where he still was in 1974. In 1971 he was allowed out for three days to visit his mother in Tigre when she was dying; otherwise his confinement is supposed to have been total. The reasons for this unique treatment are somewhat obscure but presumably

the fact that his marriage to the Emperor's daughter was a failure—
she died after only two years of married life amid rumours of ill-
treatment—contributed as well as the fact that Haile Selassie Gugsa
was the only major figure who actually went over to the Italians
as soon as the invasion started. Interestingly enough the main reason
for the betrayal was that he had not been granted all of his father's
former governships, but only some of them. He may have hoped
the Italians would grant them to him though there were other
reasons, among them accusations that the Emperor showed an
anti-Tigre bias.[2]

The failure to provide a strong religious sanction in matters of
fealty or to have oaths dependent upon the church is surprising in
such a strongly Christian society. The Church was never explicitly
involved in sanctioning the feudal connections though it was deeply
involved through its own landholdings. It is true that revolts might
be anathematized and certainly the Church's teaching emphasized
the necessity for keeping the hierarchy of society unchanged. The
Church was also sometimes involved in trying to bring rebels to
surrender and to stop fighting between nobles. Nevertheless the
evidence is scanty and the attitude of the Church was much more
one of non-involvement, surprising in such a state-dominated Church.

The explanation perhaps lies in the way that the society was
geared to dependency—each man owing something to his immediate
superior on the hierarchical ladder. In this the Church's teaching
played its part. This was not only seen in the movement of tribute
or in the obligations of service, whether military or civilian. It
appears even more vividly in normal day-to-day activities. The greet-
ing of a superior by an inferior is always carefully calculated with
a particular arrangement of the cloak, folded according to the rank
of the person being greeted, and the depth of the bow which is also
carefully angled according to his importance. There are also unlimited opportunities for subtle insult in these greetings, and they
are not neglected.[3]

It was then self-interest that primarily attracted and held men to
the great nobility who had something to offer. In their households,
which were minor images of the imperial court, they provided the
great feasts, the gifts and offices to gain loyalty.[4] A *mesafint* who
fell from favour himself would immediately lose a proportion of his
men because his funds were less when he was cut off from the sources
of wealth. Success would correspondingly increase the number of
followers.

Under normal circumstances the amount of money available to any of the nobility was considerable. It is true that *Ras* Hailu of Gojjam was more independent than most, but before he was removed from office in 1932 he was fined the total of 380,000 MT[5] dollars. This sum gives some idea of the wealth that could be accumulated by a governor. It came from taxes on land and trade, and from court fees. At the boundaries of all provinces and sub-provinces were customs gates, each under an official appointed by the *Ras*, which levied a toll on every animal and load that passed through. Gojjam was on a major route from the rich south-west to the northern outlet at Massawa in Italian Eritrea. It also had a rich coffee-growing area at Zeghie on Lake Tana, which was a *gult* property of *Ras* Hailu. In the *Ras*' case a great deal of his money had been transferred into property in Addis Ababa, which had made him more vulnerable to pressure from the Emperor. After his disgrace much of this property was in fact expropriated by the crown, although the family were able to keep a portion.

Control of trade was a vital factor in the politics of the period. Haile Giyorgis, for example, a major political figure before 1916, derived his power from his position first as chief of customs in the 1890s and then as chief *Negadras* of Addis Ababa. It was the wealth he obtained from these posts that gave him political importance; indeed he was reckoned to be the wealthiest person in the country.[6] A great deal of the power of *Ras* Tafari before he became Emperor arose from his control of the trade routes that ran through Harar and Dire Dawa after the railway was built, to Djibouti, Ethiopia's main outlet to the sea.[7] *Lij* Iyasu's attempt to break *Ras* Tafari involved transferring him from the governorship of Hararge. It is noticeable that after 1930 Haile Selassie was never to allow the province to be governed by anyone other than a member of the imperial family, even though Harar as a trading centre has long since lost its former great importance. Similarly Haile Selassie did always make sure that the main route to the north, running through Dessie, the capital of Wollo province, has been effectively under his control, by having his eldest son as its governor.

It is usually argued that as soon as he was in a position to influence appointments, that is after 1928, when he became *Negus*, *Ras* Tafari set about smashing the power of the great nobility. On investigation this turns out to be something of a myth. In the period 1928–35 only two of the *mesafint* were actually removed from their positions permanently. These were *Ras* Gugsa Walie of Begemeder and *Ras* Hailu of Gojjam.

Ras Gugsa Walie was of the family of the Empress Taitu, wife of the Emperor Menilek, and of the ruling family of Yejju and of Begemeder and Semien. He had also been the last husband of the Empress Zauditu before she became Empress in 1916. In early 1930 he made a bid for power, aimed at *Ras* Tafari not at the

The Royal House of Gojjam

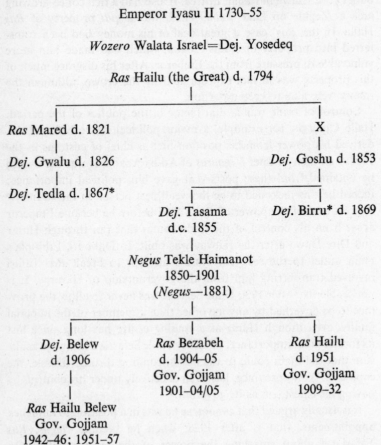

Emperor Iyasu II 1730–55
|
Wozero Walata Israel=Dej. Yosedeq
|
Ras Hailu (the Great) d. 1794
|
Ras Mared d. 1821 — X
|
Dej. Gwalu d. 1826
|
Dej. Tedla d. 1867*

Dej. Goshu d. 1853
|
Dej. Tasama   *Dej.* Birru* d. 1869
d.c. 1855
|
Negus Tekle Haimanot
1850–1901
(*Negus*—1881)
|

Dej. Belew
d. 1906
|
Ras Hailu Belew
Gov. Gojjam
1942–46; 1951–57

Ras Bezabeh
d. 1904–05
Gov. Gojjam
1901–04/05

Ras Hailu
d. 1951
Gov. Gojjam
1909–32

*The rival claimants in the time of the Emperor Tewodros.
Dej. = *Dejazmatch.*

Empress. It was unsuccessful and *Ras* Gugsa died in battle. Nevertheless so important a family could not be ignored. Two of the cousins of *Ras* Gugsa, who had certainly been in correspondence with him in 1930, *Dejazmatch* Ayele Birru and *Dejazmatch* Admassu Birru, both remained as governors of importance; Admassu in Yejju and Ayele in Semien.

The other major figure to go was *Ras* Hailu of Gojjam, whose semi-independence behind the circle of the Blue Nile had been a constant irritation for years. *Ras* Hailu was the only surviving son of Tekle Haimanot, *Negus* of Gojjam, 1881–1901; and he was directly descended from *Ras* Hailu the Great who had ruled Gojjam until his death in 1794. Hailu had only established himself with some difficulty in the first years of the century, but once established it was almost impossible to get him out in spite of his persistent defiance of imperial orders. Haile Selassie was able to fine him in 1932 but he would not have been able to remove him from his position had not the *Ras* involved himself in a plot to free the ex-Emperor *Lij* Iyasu and thus laid himself open to charges of treason. Indeed at the time of this plot *Ras* Hailu's son was about to marry one of the Emperor's daughters in an attempt to make the *Ras* more amenable to imperial control.

In spite of the fact that *Ras* Hailu had also been indicted for misgovernment nearly all his sub-governors were kept on after his removal, even though quite a number of them were close relatives of the *Ras* and equally guilty of this extortion. One of the first things that the Emperor did after *Ras* Hailu's removal was to assure the lesser governors that they would be kept in their respective commands, an edict that produced a favourable reaction among the population of the province as a whole. The appointment of *Ras* Imru as the new governor of the province was not as well received, for he had no connections with the province, and therefore he faced considerable difficulties.

Ras Imaru [sic] also told me of the difficulties he had and was still experiencing with officialdom of Gojjam and Agaumeder, particularly Agaumeder, as its remoteness from government influence at Debra Markos made defiance of his orders possible. Its people are steeped in the old traditions and evil customs of Mediaevalism—slave trading and owning, official bribery and highway robbery. *Ras* Imaru seemed surprised to meet with so much obstruction. He had been misled by the Emperor (he did not say this) who had led him to believe that the whole country was suffering under the tyrannical rule of *Ras* Hailu and would welcome him, Imaru, with open arms. This was of course not the case, rather the reverse .... I knew he had had great difficulties, a new unknown reformer surrounded by *Ras* Hailu's officials who wanted neither him nor his reforms.[8]

Ras Hailu survived until 1951 although he did not recover his province after the war, being too compromised by his relationship with the Italians, and still distrusted for his pre-war performance. However his family kept control of the governship in the post war years. His nephew, *Ras* Hailu Belew was governor from 1942–46 and again after 1951. In the 1970s the people of Gojjam look back to his period of government as the last time that they were properly governed.[9]

In place of *Ras* Hailu in 1932, Haile Selassie put *Ras* Imru; and in Begemeder to replace *Ras* Gugsa Waile he installed *Ras* Kassa. Neither of these could be described as being outside the traditional run of governors, although both were relatively enlightened figures, especially *Ras* Imru. They were in fact both closely related to the Emperor, and thus members of the Shoan *mesafint*. *Ras* Kassa, in terms of strict primogeniture, which did not apply, had a better claim to the throne than Haile Selassie. It is said that in 1916 he formally waived his claim and swore allegiance to his cousin in an oath that he and his family have continued to regard as binding.

It was not a new type of governor that Haile Selassie installed before the war, although there were a number of changes. It was the substitution of men that the Emperor could rely on—close relatives, Shoan *mesafint* and others bound to him by ties of marriage. By 1935 the majority of provinces were secured in this way, although the arrangements did not always work out satisfactorily. But none of the pre-war appointments can be considered as non-traditional except in so far as the appointment of a Shoan *Ras* to govern Gojjam, for instance, was a departure, and there were plenty of precedents for such attempts in the time of Menilek and earlier. This was a feature of the Emperors' perennial efforts to control the provincial *mesafint*.

The pattern of the organization of local government was similar, although it was not normally controlled by the Emperor directly. Sub-governors were drawn from the immediate family of the provincial governors or from loyal retainers of the *rist*-owning class.

Like the *mesafint*, these *balabats* can be traced back over generations through their genealogies. While some of the details may be suspect, especially in the earlier generations, there is no doubt that they are in general accurate. The reason for this was the necessity for remembering details upon which land claims depended. As a result a specialist group of what might be described as professional genealogists arose; and they are still much used in court cases over land today. This professionalism was especially necessary because the family relationships that were relevant to land claims were complicated by the fact that claims could be made through both the male and female lines.

A good example of the way this worked can be seen in Tigre, though it applies to all of the northern and central provinces. The political history of the province in the period before the Italian invasion revolved around the attempts of three or four branches of the major family to build up their power in the aftermath of the death of *Ras* Mengesha in 1906 who had ruled all Tigre after the death of the Emperor Yohannis IV. One branch of the family, that of *Ras* Sebhat, lost all chances early on when the *Ras* was killed in battle by his cousin and rival, *Dejazmatch* Gebre Selassie, in 1913. The remnants of his family, however, came under the wing of another contender, *Ras* Seyoum, who used various members for administration in the sub-province of Agame. From then on, until both *Dejazmatch* Gebre Selassie and *Ras* Gugsa Araya died in the early thirties, they and *Ras* Seyoum were involved in constant political machinations to influence the central government to grant one of them overlordship of the whole province. In fact, given the rivalry, Emperor Haile Selassie was able to prevent any one becoming totally supreme in the province (see chart on p. 38). After the war the only available survivor was *Ras* Seyoum and after an abortive effort to put in a Shoan governor, he was duly confirmed as the governor of the whole province and remained as such until his death. It is relevant to notice that he was succeeded by his son *Ras* Mengesha who remained governor until mid-1974.

The changes that took place at the highest levels of the provincial hierarchy did not inhibit the survival of locally important families, most of whom claimed connections with one or other of the greater lords. This survival was to be expected because these lesser families were considerable landlords and were able to keep their property. Because of their importance in any given area they were automatic choices for the various official positions that were available, and

PART OF AGAME

ILLUSTRATING THE OFFICES HELD BY THE DESCENDANTS OF WO. AWLAGNIA
(see pp. 40–42)

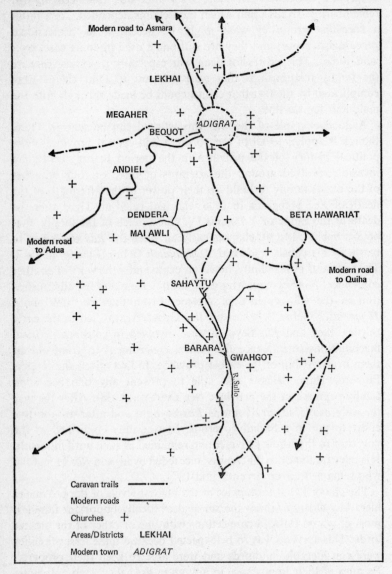

Modern road to Asmara

LEKHAI

MEGAHER

BEQUOT

ADIGRAT

ANDIEL

DENDERA

MAI AWLI

Modern road
to Adua

BETA HAWARIAT

Modern road
to Quiha

SAHAYTU

BARARA

GWAHGOT

R.Sullo

Caravan trails	—·—·—
Modern roads	———
Churches	+
Areas/Districts	LEKHAI
Modern town	*ADIGRAT*

they were also of the class that provided *ashkars* to the greater nobility.

The lowest official position, and at the same time the most vital, was the office of *chika shum*, which is a complex office subject to various and confusing interpretations by foreigners. One of the difficulties in describing the office of *chika shum* and other local administration posts is because they did vary from area to area. Nonetheless there are certain broad characteristics that are common to most provinces; the differences tend to lie in the method of appointment rather than in the duties carried out.

First and foremost it must be remembered that the *chika shum* came from the *balabat* families, whether he was appointed, elected or succeeded by inheritance—election was extremely uncommon. In the vast majority of cases there was a sufficiently important local landowner who could be chosen without difficulty. In the northern provinces the office was frequently hereditary though not necessarily within the direct father/son relationship. In fact it went with the family's *rist* holdings; and thus was equally likely to go to a cadet branch of the family or to an older person such as an uncle.

The attached genealogies from Tigre show the close connections that existed between the holders of these offices; and they also illustrate the class of the appointees. In this particular case all the families are descended from a prominent woman of Agame (a sub-province of Tigre) in the seventeenth century. *Woizero* Awlagnia was the daughter of *Ajimat* Haftegiorgis, a supposed son of the Emperor Galawdewos (1540–59). By virtue of the wealth of her father and also by her own three marriages to prominent local figures, *Woizero* Awlagnia acquired for herself extensive *rist* lands all over Agame, but especially in the area around Adigrat. The districts mentioned are small; often little more than self-contained valleys in the mountains, and they are relatively close together (see map on p. 36). It is clear that each group of descendants, roughly speaking, localised their own claims in a particular area, and managed over the years to build up control of the largest landholdings even where they did not have such a position from the beginning. Political power and thus appointments followed on from this. *Woizero* Awlagnia had at least three children and, among their descendants, this kind of pattern can be found in nine families.

It is noticeable that within the families that are descended from *Woizero* Awlagnia there is a marked lack of titles. These people, although very much of the *balabat* class, were at the lowest level of

The Ruling Families of Tigre Province

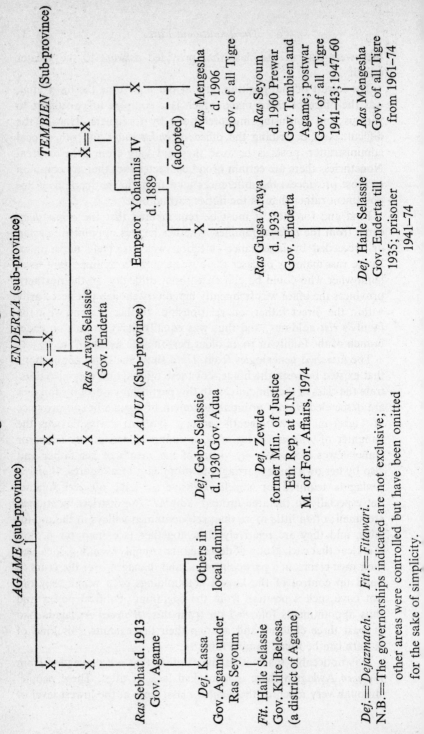

Dej. = Dejazmatch.   Fit. = Fitawari.

N.B. = The governorships indicated are not exclusive; other areas were controlled but have been omitted for the sake of simplicity.

the administrative hierarchy and the positions that they obtained and held on to were those of *chika shum* and *danya* (judge) of the small districts or parishes. Their political pull was, by and large, minimal and they were unable to acquire higher positions easily. This incidentally suggests that the amount of upward mobility within the class was very small. The next level of governors and official positions—*meslenie*, *woreda* and *awraja* governors (use of *woreda* and *awraja* governors is anachronistic here as these are post-war titles, but the areas were comparable)—came from the various branches of the ruling house of Agame, Tembien and Enderta (all *awrajas* of Tigre) which were interlinked. The most important figures in these families would be classified as *mesafint*, but the majority come under the heading of *mekwanint*. The descendants of *Woizero* Awlagnia always remained as *balabats*.

These genealogies make it clear that the traditional methods of selection at all levels of the provincial hierarchy have remained unchanged—in Tigre at any rate. This is perhaps a slight exaggeration as the administration surrounding the provincial governor has become centralized under the Ministry of the Interior; that is the governor's secretary, the provincial director and some other appointments. Some of the *awraja* governors have also been appointed from outside. Tigre however has had a very high percentage of local figures appointed as *awraja* governors. Of the *awraja* governors between 1944 and 1966, 72 per cent came from Tigre itself, and 28 per cent from outside.

This percentage is high even among the highland provinces, though Wollo with 68 per cent local appointees is not far behind. No figures are available for Begemeder. In Gojjam some 52 per cent of the *awraja* appointments come from the local *mekwanint*—though this figure should be treated with caution due to the problem of discovering the origins of several governors.[10] The inhabitants of Gojjam are Amhara and are thus less easy to distinguish than those in Tigre; furthermore the royal house of Gojjam lost considerable power with the fall of *Ras* Hailu Tekle Haimanot, and this led to the imposition of more central, that is Shoan, control especially in the aftermath of the plots of the 1940s and 1950s. Even allowing for this the family of *Ras* Hailu has remained extremely significant. Indeed most of the appointments from the *mekwanint* of Gojjam come from his family. In Wollo, in spite of the fact that *Negus* Mikael lost his position and power in 1916 and died in prison, the influence of his descendants has remained paramount at the levels

Chika Shums of Gwahgot, Barara and Info

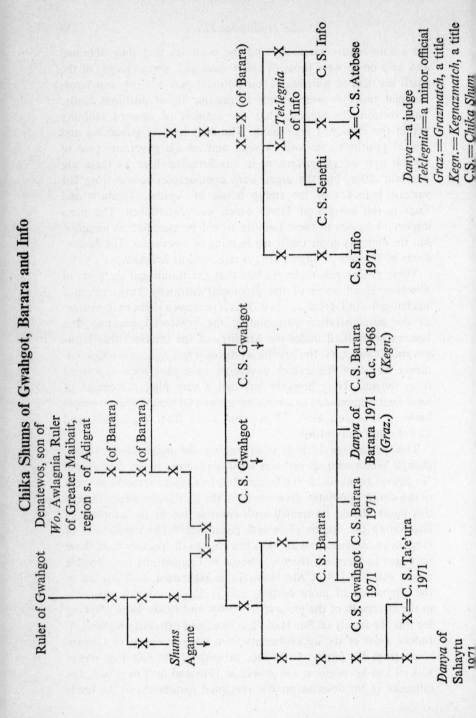

Denatewos, son of *Wo.* Awlagnia. Ruler of Greater Maibait, region s. of Adigrat

Danya = a judge
Teklegnia = a minor official
Graz. = *Grazmatch*, a title
Kegn. = *Kegnazmatch*, a title
C.S. = *Chika Shum*

Chika Shums of Sahaytu, Bequot and Megaher

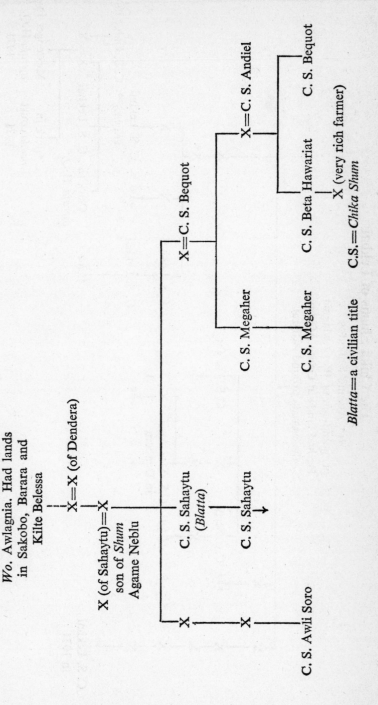

Zewoldemedhin, son of *Wo.* Awlagnia. Had lands in Sakobo, Barara and Kilte Belessa

Blatta = a civilian title   C.S. = *Chika Shum*

The Chika Shums of Lekhai

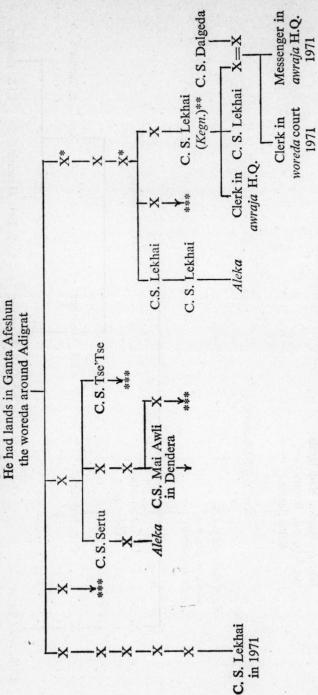

Ato. Atsemo Kalkutos
gt. grand-son of *Wo.* Awlagnia.
He had lands in Ganta Afeshun
the woreda around Adigrat

* married into the family of the *Shum* Agame
** *Kegnazmatch*
*** various other descendants all classified as wealthy farmers
Aleka = The head of a monastery.   C.S. = *Chika Shum*

of *awraja* and *woreda* governorships. Part of the reason for this in Wollo has been the fact that the governor since the 1930s has been the Crown Prince, and he is the son of the Empress Menen and thus the great-grandson of *Negus* Mikael. He has emphasised this hereditary aspect which has strengthened his position in the province.[11] In Begemeder, although no figures can be calculated, the collateral descendants of the Empress Taitu, a member of the ruling family of the province, have continued to hold on to important positions; though the greatest members of the family, who are to be classified as *mesafint*, have been used for positions outside the province.

Exceptional among the highland provinces is Shoa, as it is the centre of the Empire and provides the largest percentage of officials in all positions. Not surprisingly the percentage of *awraja* governors drawn from the province is the highest—83 per cent. Most of these come from a limited number of families such as Moja, Addisge, Bezu (see genealogies on pp. 238, 268) and the descendants of *Negus* Sahle Selassie, the founder of the present royal line. These families have also been used to provide loyal appointees in similar positions in the other provinces—people who could be sent anywhere. *Dejazmatch* Yemane Hassan (Moja) has, since 1941, been successively Director-General of Wollega province, Governor of Azebo-Raya *awraja*, Director-General of Tigre, Governor of Borana *awraja*, Director of Tigre province, Member of the Senate, Deputy Governor-General of Gojjam province, and in the Senate again. *Dejazmatch* Sebsibie Shebirou (married into the Addisge family) has been governor of the *awrajas* of Wolliso and Managasha, Director of Gojjam, Deputy Governor-General of the provinces of Gomu-Goffa, Gojjam and Shoa. *Dejazmatch* Tesfaye Enko-Selassie has been Governor of the *awrajas* of Guma, Azebo-Raya, Kambatta, Harar, Jem-jem, Menz and Yifat, Chebo and Gurage, and Tegulat and Bulga, before retiring into the Senate. Other examples could easily be adduced.

The prominence of these families in Shoa stems from their large *rist* holdings in Shoa province, supplemented by the grants they have received elsewhere; and from their peripheral connections with the royal line. It is worth emphasising that the genealogies are by no means complete. The significant women tended to marry often, their importance for land claims thus becoming enhanced considerably—in all the provinces mentioned above, the primary form of ownership is *rist* which can be inherited through either parent.

Some Tigre Family Connections and Official Positions Held 1941-71

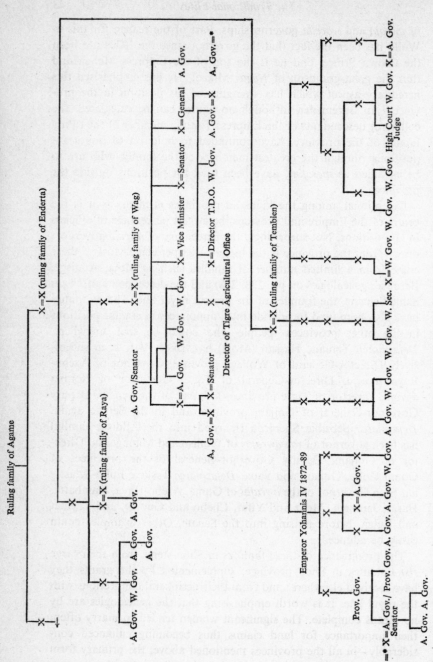

This chart only illustrates the importance of these families in local government since the war; it is not a complete record of positions held.

Areas: Enderta. Awraja Governor: A. Gov. Woreda Governor: W. Gov. Provincial Governor: Prov. Gov. Tigrean Development Organisation: T.D.O.

Female, or no office held after 1941: Y. Marriage: =. * signifies married to each other.

To obviate disagreements over land it was normal for a will to be drawn up, witnessed by priests, and handed to the godfather for safe keeping as well as for secrecy. The land could be divided as the owner wanted, but in Shoa it is fairly common for a meeting to take place in the family to decide how the shares should be divided; in Tigre this is considered somewhat shameful and is not done. This means that the most influential member of the family probably gets the major share of the lands, though other criteria may be used in the decisions; and revisions can and do take place at other times.

The importance of the godfather is underlined by the status that he has in regard to the will. Not unnaturally he is chosen for his influence and for his potential or actual friendship with the family. In Shoa particularly he is considered to be a member of the family in every way and the position is taken very seriously. Interestingly enough it is common also to wait for someone to ask to be godfather to an individual. Since the godfather can have a lot of influence with regard to the distribution of the land (and in the case of a minor without relatives can and does exercise control over the land), the position is sought after. The Emperor, for example, has an enormous number of godchildren, and has found it a very useful political link especially with the great Shoan families. Equally, of course, such families have found it to their advantage as well.

In all the highland provinces then, a substantial majority of the positions of *awraja* governor have been filled by members of the local *mekwanint*. At the lower levels of *woreda* governor, *meslenie* and *chika shum*, the *balabat* families have been almost exclusive providers, today as in pre-war times. The major effect of the post-war centralization of appointments in the Ministry of Interior has been that the actual appointment has been made at the centre; the decision as to who is appointed still comes from local impetus, dependent upon local position and importance, and is at the recommendation of the *awraja* or provincial governor.

The lowest level of governor, paid by the state, is the *woreda* governor. He controls an administrative structure and has the power to order police units into action; there is a *woreda* court, and officials from the Ministry of Finance are also normally to be found at the *woreda* headquarters as well as the other necessary officials. One of these is the *meslenie*, who is the governor's deputy. The *meslenie* has a particular responsibility for tax-collection and *shifta* control, and works very closely with the governor, having as wide a jurisdiction.

In this the *meslenie* is unlike the *chika shum*, who is confined to a small territorial area, usually the village and surrounding area. Originally the area was probably a parish but it is now normally larger and may include several parishes. Although the *chika shum* is usually unpaid, he holds the lowest government position.[12] He is also however the representative of the village and the area, which gives him something of a dual loyalty, at least in theory. The *chika shum* acts as an arbiter in local disputes—if they cannot be settled then they go to the *danya* or to the *woreda* court—and as the organizer of the tax collection. He is in general responsible for the village to the *woreda* and to the *awraja* governors. Unlike the *woreda* governor he has no control over the police force, though like the *meslenie* he can use the *nech-libash*, voluntary policemen, who are also servants or retainers of a sort to the *chika shum*, though their actual status varies from province to province.

An important part of local administration is the judicial system at the level of the *awraja* and *woreda* courts, and lower down with local judges—the *atbia danyas*.[13] Below this level it is still common for the elders to try to settle disputes through customary law and their decisions are often respected by the courts. The system was set up by the Proclamation of Administration of Justice—no. 2 of 1942. It included at that date the *metekel-woreda* (sub-district) courts and the *teklay guezat* (provincial) courts, but both of these were abolished by proclamation in 1962. Although this proclamation was suspended the next year neither of these courts were given any jurisdiction in the various codes passed between 1957 and 1965 and they have therefore become inoperative.[14]

Criticisms have frequently been made of the fifteen hundred judges (approximately) who work in the *awraja* and *woreda* courts, largely on the basis of unsuitability and lack of training. Many positions are filled by outsiders from Ministries other than Justice on recommendations from some official, and without any other qualifications. This is especially true at the *awraja* level; though at the *woreda* level the personnel are often promoted court clerks. Clerks from the Ministry of Justice are also given such appointments with considerable frequency without any regard to their training or educational status. The positions are not particularly well paid, though the variations are large—a *woreda* court judge gets between Eth.$80 and Eth.$150 per month depending upon the area.

One of the chief complaints against the judges at this level is corruption, reinforced by delays that militate against the poorer plaintiff, and by resentment of the impersonal procedures. The following quotations from a government-sponsored report of 1969 underline these points:

> Deliberately or otherwise, public officials take months to decide minor questions and years to settle major disputes . . . it costs people much more money than they can afford to get anything done in many of the government offices, because one has to pay almost every official if one is not to be kept waiting for hours or days to see an official. This is especially the case in the administration of justice . . . corruption of a serious sort is reported to be rampant among local policemen, *chika shums* and *atbia danyas*, who thus do not prove worthy of the trust placed in them. Arbitrary decisions and fictitious charges against poor peasants were mentioned as not uncommon; there seems to be no act of dishonesty and of hidden oppression of which these lower level bureaucrats cannot be accused . . . . The characteristic solution to these problems . . . is to avoid or at least minimize contact with these public agencies, especially the court and the police, for they create more problems than they solve. As much as possible, the farmers manage their own administrative affairs: disputes are handled by specially convened conciliation meetings. Verdicts are willingly accepted and compromise is easily reached. The system is simple, but appears to be very fair, inexpensive and yet efficient—features that the ordinary villager feels that he cannot find in the court.[15]

These problems are compounded at the lowest level by the fact that the *atbia danyas*' duties are much more than those of a neighbourhood judge.[16] Indeed their jurisdiction in civil cases is in doubt and they are often bypassed—a procedure that reduces their income. The *atbia danya* has to serve summonses on those required to attend court, to establish boundaries and value land for taxation purposes, to apprehend criminals and to act as an agent for the Ministry of Finance in the collection of taxes. His position, while it may not be particularly judicial, is certainly influential. It may be emphasized that these men are still by and large the original appointees of 1949 or their relations; and that the functions that they exercise today are identical to those that were exercised by these same men, or their fathers, as *balabats* before the 1947 Proclamation.[17]

Imperial control of the judiciary is exercised through the imperial right to appoint and remove judges at will. Theoretically this is

controlled by an article in the revised constitution. "(Judges')
appointment, promotion, removal, transfer and retirement shall be
determined by a special law governing the judiciary." (Art. 14). No
such special law has yet been passed even though as long ago as
1962–63 a commission was set up to draft one following a parliamentary request. Its report was never submitted to Parliament
so the Deputies started to draft a law themselves. There was an
immediate response to this and it was announced that the Prime
Minister's office was actually in the process of drafting the legislation
at the time. The Deputies therefore dropped their project; however
the draft has still not appeared from the Prime Minister's office.

It is impossible to be dogmatic about the duties and powers of
such officials as they vary from place to place even in the northern
areas. The Government implicitly encourages this as the pay of the
woreda governors and *meslenie* varies widely—the range appears
to be from Eth. $80 in parts of Tigre to Eth. $300 in Eritrea. Control
over the *chika shum* also varies according to area; some are appointed
by the *woreda* governors, some however are in the gift of important
landowners or the owners of *gult* lands. A few, particularly in
southern Eritrea, where a communal system of land tenure is in
operation, are elected by the villagers. Communications also play
an important part in assessing how much independence any individual *chika shum* may have. In areas remote from the *woreda*
capital the *chika shum* obviously has a lot of room for manoeuvre,
and his servants have correspondingly greater duties. In places
where the roads are adequate the *woreda* governor can more easily
use the police force and thus pre-empt the *chika shum* to a great
degree. Areas where the *chika shums* are virtually independent have
gradually reduced in number but there are still many in the remoter
parts of the highlands. The traditional system of land-tax which
still operates in Begemeder, Gojjam, Tigre and the *awrajas* of Wag
and Lasta in Wollo province also depends upon the *chika shums* or
danyas who are responsible for the actual assessment in the villages.[18]

Generally speaking the pattern of the administration is the same
in the southern provinces, though it may vary in detail—an *awraja*
governor in the southern provinces can change *woreda* governors
around without prior authorization; this could not be done for
example in Tigre. There are however significant distinctions in the
operation of the system and the personnel. These differences are
based on the fact that Wollega, Illubabor, Kaffa, Gomu Goffa,
Sidamo, Arussi, Bale and Hararge were only conquered at the end

of the nineteenth century. After the conquest most of the land was expropriated; it went not only to the important generals but also to ordinary soldiers and lesser officers, many of whom settled in these provinces or were appointed to some position or garrison duty there. Not surprisingly, since it was the Shoan empire of Menilek that made the conquest, the administration of these territories fell almost entirely into Shoan Amhara hands. At first this varied as some of the areas which submitted were left more or less untouched; after the war however they were all incorporated into the structure of Government from the centre. Nevertheless the predominance of Amhara elements in the provincial administrations has persisted. In contrast with the predominantly local figures at the *awraja* level in the northern provinces the reverse holds true for the south. The figures for *awraja* governors between 1942 and 1967 are Wollega— 26 per cent local and 74 per cent outsiders; Illubabor—20 per cent and 80 per cent; Kaffa—29 per cent and 71 per cent; Sidamo— 19 per cent and 81 per cent; Arussi—10 per cent and 90 per cent; Hararge—26 per cent and 74 per cent.[19] These should be treated with some caution as the percentages for outsiders also include those Amharas who have in fact settled in these provinces. However insofar as the majority of the population in the provinces is non-Amhara, the figures do indicate the predominance of non-indigenous people. It should also be noticed that the figures include appointments from groups other than Amharas from Shoa. In Illubabor, for example, a significant number of appointments are of Gojjamis settled in the province since the 1880s, or rather Gojjamis who have been landowners there since that period (31 per cent).

Where appointments are of local people they come from the southern *balabat* families. In general these are the descendants of the former rulers of the areas, for these families were allowed to retain up to one third of their land after the conquest; in practice *siso* land was usually less than this, but it was enough to allow the families to keep their pre-eminence in the districts. Even descendants of such strong resisters to the conquest as the Royal House of Kaffa have been allowed, or have been indispensible enough, to fill some posts.

The same holds true for the *woreda* governors. It is nearly impossible to acquire figures for *woreda* appointments. It would seem however that some 70 per cent of the *woreda* governors in the southern provinces are of Amhara origin,[20] and thus by definition are landowners. Some, certainly, are descended from the original

settlers; others are more recent immigrants who have been given
government land in these provinces as a reward for military service
and the like. It might seem invalid to regard the longer term settlers
as outsiders; however the persistence of the conquest mentality of
Amhara governors and the character of the administration precludes
the identification of these settlers with the local people. Since the
war there have been no real changes in the operation of the system,
although certainly such things as slaving have disappeared; the
origins and strength of the revolt in Bale (see Chapter Seven) support
this conclusion.

At the village level the official is the *chika shum* again, though
other names may be used. Here the use of local people varies from
area to area. In Kaffa, for example, the Kaffa chiefs were left largely
in control at the village level. To some extent this was inevitable as
the Kaffa people were not prepared to live in the same villages as
the Amhara. This is still much the same today.[21] In many areas
of the south the people are, however, nomadic or semi-nomadic and
the settled villages were set up as Amhara centres and have remained
so. Consequently the *chika shums* are also most frequently Amhara,
even though there may be many other local people living in these
villages today. By and large it appears that where there was a
tradition of administration in an area, as in the kingdom of Kaffa,
the Sultanate of Jimma, parts of Wollega and in Wollamo, the
village chiefs were retained. In areas where there was large scale
Amhara appropriation of land, Amharas were substituted at the
village level. Inevitably Amhara *woreda* governors have also tended
to favour other Amharas as *chika shums* as well. Once again communications play a part in this, especially in the south-west which
is severely lacking in roads and the administration is spasmodic
or non-existent. A recent writer on the Majangir, a tribe in the south-
west, says that except where the government has established a centre
at Tepi the tribe has continued to function almost without outside
interference of any kind; even efforts to stop internal fighting or to
collect taxes have so far had little effect.[22]

A further point should be made in regard to the administration
of these southern provinces. Particularly at the *awraja* and *woreda*
levels, but also where outsiders are appointed as *meslenie* and
chika shum, the use of appointments as a form of exile has had
appalling effects on the attitudes of the governors; and this has
been reinforced by the general antipathy between the Amhara and
the people under their control. While this situation obtained most

severely before the war it has by no means vanished since. Some of the greatest landholdings have been acquired since the restoration. The best known example is that of *Ras* Mesfin Sileshi who, in his tours as governor of Illubabor (1942–46) and Kaffa (1946–55), succeeded in building-up holdings that are popularly supposed to be the largest in Ethiopia. If this is the case then they certainly must be substantial for in Hararge province one individual has managed to acquire 900,000 hectares in the same period. It is certainly true that whatever the size of *Ras* Mesfin's lands he is regarded by many of his tenants as being a difficult landlord to deal with; and there have been many complaints against his methods of acquiring land.

One estimate for the extent of the *Ras'* land is for his estates in Kaffa and Illubabor—50,000 *gashas*.[23] There are other landowners who have acquired smaller though still substantial estates. In the province of Sidamo this has happened extensively, as it is a province that has been much used by the government for *madeira* grants. Cases can be adduced of men who have acquired up to 5,000 *gashas* (200,000 hectares). Such men run what can only be described as small private armies of servants, who force sales of property to them. Such people of course inevitably have the final say in appointments to *woreda* governor in the area where they are important, and also control the positions of *meslenie* and *chika shum*. Few try to argue with his nominations, and those who do are in no position to do so a second time. Other examples could be quoted throughout the southern and western provinces.[24]

The point to be emphasized in all these areas is the continued reliance upon the traditional personnel whose power is based on land. In the southern provinces the pattern has been distorted by the conquest but the Amhara settlers have stepped into the place of the former *balabats*. Since these settlers were originally members of the armed forces and the conquered lands were distributed in accordance with rank, at a time when rank was almost totally dependent upon status in the traditional hierarchy, the size of the original estates related to the position held by the recipient in the Shoan landowning classes. The newcomers in the south thus set up a class structure similar to that obtaining in the north, and with the same personnel. The only previous inhabitants who retained their landholdings to any extent were the former rulers. The granting of *siso* land thus perpetuated the previous hierarchy, although at a lower level than before. It might also be noted here that the grants that are still given by the government in the 1970s are essentially based upon the same attitude. *Maderia* land is granted for meritorious service, in the armed forces or in the civil administration; since recruitment to these depends, in the higher ranks, very much upon status in the traditional hierarchy it is clear that the system is to a large degree self-perpetuating.

There is one element of participation by the traditional elite of the southern provinces which should be mentioned. This is in the religious organization, which in these areas tends to be independent of the government in a way that the Christian Church in the highland provinces does not. In the south the Church has made little or no attempt to proselytize and the traditional "paganism" has been left more or less untouched, as has Islam which is widespread especially in the south-east. Islam, of course, has its own organization and particularly through the Islamic courts maintains a strong hold which parallels, and to a certain extent undermines, the Government administration.[25] Similarly spirit-cults in Kaffa and Arussi have been so organized that they have, to a great degree, allowed for the side-stepping of the government. For example, the leaders of two of these cults operate what are, to all intents and purposes, independent organizations (see Chapter Eight). Part of the reason for the post-war growth among their followers as well as increasing support for Islam should be put down to the fact that some of the people in these areas do see them as something opposed to Amhara control. This control is of course firmly linked with the Church which, while it has done little missionary work, has accompanied the conquest, and because of the Christianity of the vast majority of the administration has been clearly identified with it.

This is even less surprising when the Church is itself considered. The Ethiopian Orthodox Church is another of the institutions in Ethiopia that possesses its own legitimate authority, independent of the imperial power. Like the imperial authority this came from two sources, religious as well as feudal, for the amount of land owned by the Church has become enormous over the centuries. This also encouraged the formation of a strong hereditary element within the Church, especially since marriage is a necessity for ordination. Heredity is not lacking in the monastic section of the Church either as it is not uncommon for elderly people to enter a monastery after the death of their spouse; or even for an elderly married couple to enter a monastery and a nunnery at the same time.

It is true that the links between the Church and imperial power always remained close and the Emperor has always been the head of the Church and in many ways has controlled it. Yet historically the consecration of the *Abuna* was a ceremony that only the Alexandrian Patriarch could carry out. This most effectively provided the spiritual legitimacy and thus an independence of the secular power. Even so, it worked to the imperial advantage. The *Abuna* was always a foreigner until the consecration of an Ethiopian Patriarch in 1950, and therefore found it difficult to exercise his authority in a country where he did not know either the liturgical or the day-to-day languages, and where he did not control the clerical or monastic administration. This was in the hands of the *Ichege*, traditionally the head of the monastery of Debre Libanos and always, of course, an Ethiopian.

At first sight this weakness in the position of the *Abuna* would seem to be an insuperable obstacle to any independent Church position; especially since one of the recognized jobs of the Emperor was to convene and control councils discussing purely theological questions. In fact Emperors who ignored the independent authority of the Church did so at their peril. The examples of two early seventeenth century Emperors, who converted to Roman Catholicism, are exceptional, and do not significantly alter the general tendency. More recently, in the mid-nineteenth century, the Emperor Tewodros' problems were compounded by his attempts to tax the Church and his imprisonment of the *Abuna*. The fall of *Lij* Iyasu in 1916 was made the more likely by the attachment of the *Abuna* Matewos to the Shoan nobility. Significantly *Lij* Iyasu was never sanctified by the coronation ceremony.

The centre of the Church's spiritual control over the imperial power is in the coronation ceremony. The ceremony is a religious and liturgical one that can be carried out only by the *Abuna*. It is the sanctification of the individual as a descendant of the dynasty of Menilek Ist, eldest son of King Solomon by the Queen of Sheba, and thus of the royal lines of Israel and the house of David. It is above all the investment of the Emperor with a religious aura. At the actual crowning the Patriarch prays for the crown to be a halo of holiness and glory and adds "May you, by your prayer, preserve your faith unshaken and unconquerable." The oath is made on the Bible to maintain the Orthodox religion and the sword of true justice is given to protect the Church and to serve Jesus Christ. Then there comes the anointing with the holy oil which provides the actual consecration by God through the Patriarch. "It is not a seemly thing to revile the king, for he is the anointed of God."[26]

Perhaps the clearest exposition of this attitude comes from the royal chronicles, for the monks who wrote them invested the Emperors with hagiographical aspects. Although only one of the Emperors was ever canonized—Lalibela, whom tradition reveres as the builder of rock churches at the town in Lasta named after him—the hyperbole in the descriptions of the rulers can best be seen as hagiography. Even in the chronicles of Menilek II the religious element is ever present. Menilek's escape from the Emperor Tewodros' prison fortress at Magdala is surrounded with an aura of the supernatural. The victory over the Italians at the battle of Adua in 1896 is brought about by St. George and because Menilek's goodness made women and monks brave, as well as the men.

Since it was the Church which provided the legitimacy of the "Elect of God", one of the titles of an Ethiopian Emperor, the authority of the Church was ultimately untouchable by the secular power. The *Kebra Nagast*, although it makes much of the imperial position, makes more of the priesthood:

> . . . And a priest, who hath in him understanding, rebuketh the king concerning the work that he hath seen; and that which he hath not seen God will enquire into, and there is none that can call Him into account. Moreover the people must not revile the bishops and priests, for they are the children of God and the men of His house, for which reason they must rebuke (men) for their sins and errors. And thou, o priest, if thou seest sin in a well-known man shalt not hesitate to rebuke Him; let neither sword nor exile make thee afraid.[27]

In return for this legitimacy confirmed upon a Christian ruler, and by implication extended to the nobility as well, the Church as a whole benefited largely. The most obvious reward came in the building of churches, a traditional function of the great and one that was never neglected. Although land was theoretically in the hands of the state, the Church acquired very substantial amounts from early times. Grants inevitably became permanent whatever the intentions of the original donors, though this perpetuation was less to the Church as a whole than to the individual churches and monasteries that were the recipients of the grants.

Churches are not entirely dependent upon their lands for their keep. Each Church is also supported by the community at large,

especially at times when the church needs repair, with either labour
or materials. Baptism and burials are accompanied by payments
and although church weddings are not necessary they are paid for
when they occur. An individual church or monastery also frequently
holds the rights and perquisities of justice over its *gult* area, and the
resulting income is considerable. Furthermore all Church income is
held for the use of the Church and is not handed on to the central
authorities; this is a right that has been confirmed in all the proclamations connected with land or tax since the war.

TABLE 1.

Number of *Gashas* of Measured Land Owned by the Church

| | Source | |
Province	Central Church Treasury	Ministry of Land Reform
Arussi	3,126	9,696
Gomu Goffa	1,051	777
Kaffa	1,460	1,992
Shoa	12,311	11,907
Wollega	2,583	2,489
Wollo	1,430	1,074

*Source: Ministry of Finance and Central Church Treasury, and
Ministry of Land Reform Land Tenure Surveys:* quoted in Lawrence
and Mann "F.A.O. Land Policy Project".

(It is significant that for Tigre, where it is obvious that the Church
owns very large lands, there are no figures available.)

Naturally enough the Church is extremely wealthy, but its exact
wealth is impossible to calculate. The extent of Church land is
unknown in spite of the Ministry of Land Reform's attempts at
classification. It is significant that figures supplied by the Central
Church Treasury in Addis Ababa and figures drawn from the Land
Surveys seem to bear little relationship to each other (Table 1).
The figures given in 1961–62 by the Central Church Treasury produce
a total of 29,563 *gashas* of measured land for all provinces except
Begemeder, Eritrea and Tigre; and Tigre has one of the highest
concentrations of monasteries and churches in the country.[28] In
addition there is the amount of unmeasured land to be taken into

consideration. Here the only estimate available is again from the
Central Church Treasury for 1961–62, this time for only six provinces—30,425 *gashas*.

TABLE 2.

Land tax and tax in lieu of tithe paid to Church revenue 1961–62 from measured and unmeasured lands

(figures from Ministry of Finance and Central Church Treasury)

Arussi	128,263
Bale	25,921
Begemeder	No figures available
Gomu-Goffa	75,812
Gojjam	105,851
Hararge	90,705
Illubabor	61,726
Kaffa	50,667
Shoa	636,128
Sidamo	81,183
Tigre	394,258
Wollega	93,990
Wollo	236,664
Total	1,981,168

Quoted from Lawrence and Mann, *op. cit. Figures in Eth.$.*

Similar problems arise in trying to find out the actual revenue that
the Church obtains in a year. It is known that in 1961–62 the revenue
from land-tax and tax in lieu of tithe amounted to nearly Eth.$2
million from all provinces except Eritrea and Begemeder (Table 2).
This figure however is incomplete and does not allow for sums held
by the individual churches. Consequently it would seem that there
are no reliable estimates to be made for Church land or land revenue;
and the same holds true for other forms of income for which no
estimates can be made at all, reliable or otherwise. It seems probable
that the Church does not in fact own the full one-third of the country
that it is credited with, though in the only area where an accurate
attempt has been made to estimate Church holdings, albeit a very
small area, the calculation worked out at almost exactly one-third.[29]
Even without exact calculations it is important to realize that the

great monasteries in particular have very considerable lands. To take the province of Tigre, there are six major foundations. St. Mary of Sion at Axum, Gunde Gunde on the eastern edge of the escarpment, Enda Medhane Alem at Makalle, Enda Selassie at Adua, Debre Damo and Abraha Atsbeha. All of these own substantial estates and not only in the areas around them. They all have lands in every part of the province and further afield. St. Mary of Sion, for example, received a grant of one hundred *gashas* in Shoa from the Emperor recently. A similar list of wealthy foundations could be drawn up for the other central, Christian provinces—Gojjam, Wollo, Begemeder and Shoa, though not for the more recently conquered southern and western provinces where the Church is hardly established, and which remain largely pagan or Moslem. A study of the distribution of other churches and monasteries points up the number of foundations which are far in excess of the needs of the people.

One reason for the number of religious foundations was that it was considered a necessary part of the function of the nobility and the emperor to found new churches as well as giving land to existing ones. The Church in return supported secular policies and the political status quo. This support involved the use of excommunication and the freeing of a rebel's followers from their allegiance, as well as more generally encouraging the peasantry to pay their taxes. Nevertheless the Church's attitude towards the nobility was sometimes ambiguous, for numbers of the local priests came from the peasant class and sympathized with the overtaxed farmers. The right of sanctuary was often granted, certain areas being set aside for this purpose, and reconciliation rather than anathematization was frequently carried out. The latter was an effective weapon when used, however. In the attempted coup of 1960 one of the rebel's major mistakes was their neglect of the Patriarch. His excommunication of those involved played a vital part in their failure to gain more support from the army units which might otherwise have followed the rebels. In 1930 when *Ras* Gugsa Walie rebelled, his excommunication as a rebel by the Patriarch proved a much more effective move than the *Ras'* accusations that *Ras* Tafari had become a Roman Catholic, because the accusation was not supported by any equivalent religious figure. Ultimately it was not surprising that the general attitude of the Church was one of supporting the regime. Not only was the Church totally involved with the landowning system and the recipient of enormous grants, it was also subject to

the imperial authority, which was the arbiter of doctrinal disputes
and the fount of the highest posts.

A look at the hierarchy makes this clear. At the head was the
Abuna. Historically there was normally only one *Abuna*—Bishop—
at any one time though this has changed considerably during Haile
Selassie's reign. After the election of the first Ethiopian Patriarch
in 1950, *Abunas* were appointed for each province in 1959. Until
1950 the Patriarch was always a foreigner whose *raison d'être*
was really to provide for ordinations which only he could carry out.
This, on occasions in the past, led to the incumbent carrying out
mass ordinations, including children, in order to ensure the availability of priests during the long period that it might take to get a
new *Abuna* from Egypt.

In terms of the power of the Church the position of the *Abuna*
was in most respects symbolic. Much more important was the
imperially-appointed *Ichege*, head of administration of the Church.
The duties of the *Ichege* involved the control of both the monastic
and priestly sections of the Church and was operated through a series
of officials who were appointed by the Emperor.[30] These were the
Liqe Kahenet, heads of the Churches of a province, and the *Aleka*
who were in charge of the larger Churches and monasteries. These
officials reported directly to the *Ichege* and provided him with an
important power base; this also applied to the Emperor since he
had the final say in such appointments. Their functions were as
much lay as ecclesiastical, for they were concerned with the administration of the monastic and Church lands and with justice in them.
They also had the status of considerable landowners by virtue of
their control of these lands; and they were frequently appointed to
office on the same basis as the high state officials were—family and
wealth.

There were five other officials at the top of the Church hierarchy
whose appointment depended on the Emperor. Second was the
Neburaed of Axum, who held both secular and religious power
over Axum which was considered a holy city. Although it carried
high prestige the status attached was somewhat confused because
it could be given to either lay or ecclesiastical personages. The four
other positions provided the four chief judges at the court. They
were the *Qeshate*, the Emperor's confessor, the *Aqabe sa'at*, keeper
of the hours, that is, the organiser of the ecclesiastical calendar;
the *Liqe Debterra*, chief of the *debterras*; and the *Liqe Mamiheran*,
chief of the learned men of the Church. These men might have

enormous power by virtue of their contact with the Emperor. The imperial confessor for example has at times wielded considerable influence, or at any rate has been thought to do so. The major recent figure who has been in this position was *Abba* Hana Jema, who was Haile Selassie's confessor and keeper of the private purse until he was killed in the attempted coup in 1960. His close connections with the Emperor went back to 1928 and, just before the Italian invasion, he was the guardian of the ex-Emperor *Lij* Iyasu, a position in which it was obviously necessary to have someone completely trustworthy. *Abba* Hana was always thought to have had great influence upon the Emperor and there is no reason to suppose otherwise. One who has the imperial ear as confessor is bound to have importance even if it is only in ecclesiastical matters.

Lower levels of the Church are not, however, under such control as the foregoing would imply. Certainly Government control of the higher ranks of the Church has increased just as Church influence on Government decisions has steadily decreased. But the Church is far from being a unified administrative structure in spite of the post-war changes—the definition of the various types of Church land; the establishment of a Central Church Treasury and the abolition of the jurisdiction of the Church Courts over temporal matters. Many heads of monasteries still continue very much in their own way and the comment of one *Aleka* in Lasta is symptomatic: "What has the Patriarch ever done for me that I should do anything for him". Nor is it true that all the required income from individual churches reaches the central treasury; and many churches, or rather their *Alekas*, retain judicial functions over temporal affairs within the area of Church lands. The Government has indeed hardly tried to interfere with this practice and perhaps does not seriously want to do so. It is in fact a parallel with the way in which the individual churches distribute the land at their disposal.

This semi-independent status is reinforced at the lowest levels of the hierarchy. The lowest office is the deaconate, which is theoretically open to all. However the necessity of marital status as a qualification for the priesthood inevitably led to the growth of priestly families. It is after that training as a deacon that a boy has the opportunity to continue with the required education, get married and be ordained. Other alternatives were to embark on the far longer course to become a *debterra*, or to enter a monastery. In a priestly family he could also help his father to farm the land that his office brought him. In such a case continuance of the ecclesiastical office meant continuance of landownership—a chance not to be missed.

There is a wide variation in the amount of training that is demanded of a priest, a *debterra* or a monk. That of the *debterra* is extremely arduous, involving as much as twenty years of study in the religious chants, dances and in the grammar and poetry of *Ge'ez*, the liturgical language. An unofficial element in this education is magic and the control of spirits. *Debterras* can often gain a substantial income from the sale of protective amulets and from other dealings with spirits, for involvement in the *Zar* cult is common.[31] This, however, is merely a sideline. *Debterras* are best known for their learning and have frequently been used as counsellors and governors, deriving status from the respect given to erudition.

The training necessary for a monk is, by contrast, almost non-existent. Recruitment comes mainly from the deaconate and the priesthood; the latter being eligible after the death of a wife. It is also not unknown for older laymen to enter the monastic life for personal reasons. The monastic life is organized with a minimum amount of regulation and there are few specific rules. Even the quantity of prayer depends upon the individual, though he is of course expected to follow the Church's rules for fasting. Nevertheless organization is loose enough for both the eremitical and the monastic systems to co-exist in the same monastery. Monks at the monastery of Debra Damo in Tigre, famous for its rope climb entry, sometimes get themselves lowered down to caves in the sheer cliff-face of the *amba* on which the monastery stands, to become hermits for a time. It may be until death or only for a year. Conversely missionary work is not unknown, though it is not common, and monks have no hesitation in acting as advisers to political figures or in re-entering the world to act as confessors.

The element of the Church most in contact with people is the priesthood for it is only the priest who has continuous contact with the ordinary peasant. He carries out the services, baptises, marries (when required, which is not often, for the luxury of getting a divorce from a supposedly indissoluble church marriage is not something most peasants can afford), buries and hears confessions. Priests also act as elders in disputes over affairs in the parish, being fitted for this not only by their position of spiritual guardians but because they are themselves farmers through the Church lands. It is often suggested that this in fact makes the priesthood a unique part of the local scene, and indistinguishable from its parishioners.

This is however not really the case. The priest is usually one of the larger landowners by virtue of the Church lands that he personally farms and, through his interest in the Church lands as a whole, often one of the two or three biggest landowners. His status, besides reflecting his own education, limited though that may be, reflects the status of the Church as a whole as well as the status of the particular church which is the focal point of the parish—the smallest unit of Government and the judiciary, at least in the highland Christian areas.

The priest thus has a place in the secular hierarchies because of his land-owning position; and the head of any Church, whether he is an *aleka* or not, plays an important role as a governor of Church lands and in some areas of other lands as well. He is owed deference by his parishioners and the teaching of the Church underlines this strongly. The traditional law code, the *Fetha Nagast*, makes the point clearly by quoting Romans, Chapter 13:

> Let every soul be subject unto the higher powers. For there is no power but of God: the powers that be are ordained of God . . . Wherefore ye must needs be subject, not only for wrath, but also for conscience sake. For this cause ye pay tribute also: for they are God's ministers, attending continually upon this very thing. Render therefore to all their dues: tribute to whom tribute is due; custom to whom custom; fear to whom fear; honour to whom honour.[32]

And tribute, custom, fear and honour belong to the Church as much as to the State. In this sense the Church is clearly an integral part of the feudal system of Ethiopia. It is true that Haile Selassie has made certain changes that have been aimed at reducing its independent status. Of those mentioned the most significant was the cutting of the control of the Alexandrian Patriarch. This set up an autonomous Church, more under imperial control—at least at the higher levels where the Emperor, by the revised constitution, approves and confirms episcopal appointments. The present patriarch, Theophilus, is also a progressive figure and has made considerable efforts to modernize certain sections of the Church— encouragement of Amharic in place of *Ge'ez*, the opening of a theological college at the university, a training school for the priesthood at Lake Zwai and the encouragement of a pressure group, *Haimanote Abew* to help update certain sections of the liturgy. He has also made efforts to break the Ethiopian Orthodox Church's traditional isolation by making far more contacts with other churches and by joining the World Council of Churches.

None of these attempted reforms have yet had much effect on the mass of the clergy in the countryside. Most of the 20,000 or more churches and monasteries and the 170,000 clergy are in a position, by virtue of their almost independent landholdings, to ignore any such ideas. The Church may not be as strong as it was but it still requires, and gets, strong support in the Christian highlands. Nor is there much evidence that the majority of the clergy have any real desire to change the usually conservative nature of the Church in the provinces. From the imperial point of view such an attitude has much to recommend it, providing that in the last resort imperial control is accepted as it usually is. One small qualification should be added. In the crisis of February/March 1974 some churchmen did follow the many other groups in demanding a pay rise, pointing out that their salary was infinitesimal. This was in fact granted; but it only affected those who worked at the Church's headquarters in Addis Ababa, and was not meant to apply to the provincial priests, nor to the Church administration as a whole. Nevertheless the idea of any members of the Church going on strike is symptomatic of a considerable change in the attitudes of some of the clergy at least.

CHAPTER THREE

Modern Government

The central aim of any government is, above all else, efficient control; Haile Selassie's has been no exception. From the beginning of his reign in 1930 he endeavoured, with considerable success, to re-establish the imperial control that the Emperor Menilek exercised. In the traditional sense he has been a great centralizing monarch. This has been the underlying thread of all his reforms and changes. These have ranged over a wide variety of fields, but the greatest efforts have been directed to the most vital areas of finance, internal control and defence. Social services have not been stressed, as a comparison of budget figures (page 163) for the respective Ministries shows. The only exception to this has been the education sector, perhaps because of the necessity of staffing the centralizing agencies of the Government.

A substantial part of Haile Selassie's reputation as a modernizer rests upon the changes that he has made in the operation of the Government. There is now a structure that was entirely lacking when he came to power; an elected Chamber of Deputies, Ministers and a Prime Minister, and a constitution introduced in 1931, revised in 1955 and again in 1974. All this, particularly the constitution, has created an entirely new dimension in the Ethiopian state, a dimension which was emphasized in the crisis of early 1974 and led to demands for a constitutional monarchy. There is however no doubt that Haile Selassie had little thought of this when he granted the 1931 constitution "unasked and of Our own free will".

Its primary function was to lay down the principles of imperial control. It did, in fact, reflect the political aims of the Emperor at that time—executive control over local and central government, administration, the army and the judiciary. The constitution placed virtually no limitations on the imperial powers and, more significantly, mentioned none of the limitations that actually operated in practice. The fact that the greater nobility as well as the local lords were both incorporated, by appointments to the Senate, emphasized the Emperor's need to try and keep them under his eye in Addis Ababa, and so lessen their direct control in the provinces. On the other hand the Deputies were chosen by the aristocracy. The Emperor was in no position to interfere too much in the local administration of the provinces, or to bypass the local powers.

In the circumstances of the 1930s it mattered little what the terms of the constitution were. The machinery for its implementation did not exist and although it was often quoted, particularly after the restoration in 1941, it had no effect upon the actual Government of the country. The Parliament was never more than a body of minimal importance; its value being in the association of the nobility, both great and small, with imperial activities which were thus more readily acceptable to the country at large. Given the strength of support that the nobility could still call upon this was certainly vital to the Emperor. Since the Emperor was actually in a weaker position *vis-à-vis* the nobility in the 1940s it might be expected that Parliament would be a little less subservient in this period; and that was in fact the case, although other factors obviously contributed to this as well. In the period between the Land Tax Proclamations of 1942 and 1944, opposition, both in and out of Parliament, forced considerable changes mainly relating to exemptions for lands owned by the Church and the nobility. In this sense the actual fact of a Parliament as a place where the nobility could get together was significant.

The constitution was revised in 1955, again with the assistance of the great nobility, members of the Church hierarchy and other important figures, and the influence of these groups on the final text was enough to limit some of the Emperor's powers laid down in the preliminary stages. The changes were mainly concerned with tying the Emperor's emergency powers to constitutional approval but he was left with extensive control, including control of the Armed Forces, wide emergency powers, foreign policy and the courts as well as "the duties to take all measures that may be necessary to ensure, at all times, the defence and integrity of the Empire; the safety and welfare of its inhabitants, including their enjoyment of the human rights and fundamental liberties recognized in the present Constitution." (Article 36).[1]

The most important change in the Revised Constitution concerns Parliament. It set up a Chamber of Deputies to be elected by universal adult suffrage, the first such election having been held in 1957. However, it would be a mistake to regard this as being very significant in terms of broadening the social make-up of the institution. Qualifications for candidacy are strict. Nomination requires a minimum of fifty signatures on a petition, payment of a deposit of Eth. $500, a literacy test as well as the conditions for nomination—being a resident and owning a minimum of Eth. $2,000 of movable property. These qualifications make it perfectly clear that candidacy is therefore restricted to a small group of influential landowners, to relatively wealthy Amharic speakers, for the conditions automatically eliminate most people in the empire.[2]

In addition, the costs of fighting elections are considerable and have to be found by the candidates themselves—one estimate ranges between Eth. $500 and Eth. $10,000 with an average around Eth. $2,000.[3] For the countryside this limits possibilities to the landowners or their nominees, though in the towns it does allow for more flexibility. This is not always immediately apparent. In an analysis of the membership in 1965 it was found that landowners made up only the second largest group after former civil servants which three-quarters of the Chamber claimed to be.[4] This, however, conceals the fact that a high percentage of those who said they were former civil servants were former *Woreda* governors or similar, and were appointed to these positions because they were local landowners. Another important group in terms of influence among the former civil servants were teachers, whose education gave them the incentive to stand; though in the majority of provincial cases they were also nominees of local dignitaries.[5]

TABLE 3. **Parliamentary Candidates, voters, etc.**

Year	Nos. of candidates	Nos. registered	Nos. voted	Percentage of new MPs
1957	597	3·5 million	2·5 million	—
1961	940	4·5 million	4·0 million	—
1965	1,308	5·1 million	3·2 million	65
1969	2,000	5·2 million	3·6 million	68
1973	1,500	7·0 million	4·4 million	58

In this connection there is normally little campaigning in the western sense of the word. The difficulties are too great, considering the transport problems that face the candidates in a rural constituency. Campaigning is carried out by attempts to get endorsements from the local notables on a personal basis—meeting them at church

ceremonies, at court, or going around to their houses. It is vital
for future Deputies to make extravagant promises and commitments.
If elected, they have little influence on the central Government
and most of these promises cannot be redeemed. As a result a high
percentage fail to get re-elected although in fact most do try, for
the salary is an important inducement.

Parliament, until 1974, remained essentially a consultative body
using little power of its own. It is true that it had sometimes shown
its teeth and it seemed to take a certain delight in using its powers
to call ministers and various other officials before it for questioning.
These expressions of its own will did, however, come very much in
the areas that might be expected from a body that was composed
essentially of landowners. In this connection it is as well to note
that both Deputies and Senators may be classified as generally
representing the same interests. There is a certain distinction in that
the Senators are perhaps greater landowners and under greater
imperial control by virtue of having been appointed; they also tend
to be more important figures and therefore to live in Addis Ababa.
The Deputies' importance is local rather than national and in theory
is founded on a partly independent power base. Although there has
been Government intervention in certain elections, there is no evidence of anything systematic.

The actual cases in which Parliament has interfered in legislation
have been few and the most important of these has been its opposition to the Agricultural Income Tax Law of 1967 and its attempts to
alter the situation of tenants.

In 1966 the Ministry of Finance produced a draft proclamation
for a reform of income tax.[6] This was a sweeping measure covering
all forms of income that were already taxed—salaries, rent from
lands and buildings not used for agriculture and income from
businesses and other occupations—and revising them upwards. In
addition, and more controversially, an entirely new schedule was
proposed for a tax on agricultural income. At that time land taxes
were collected according to the Land Tax Proclamations of 1944 and
1951; and they were paid at three standard rates according to the
fertility of the land, and according to whether they were measured
or unmeasured lands (the bulk being unmeasured). The new schedule
in the draft proclamation provided for a tax on the income derived
from the harvest, that is to say, on produce and not on land. This
was not to take the place of the land tax and the tax in lieu of tithe
but to supplement them.

The proclamation laid down the new schedule at rates which were to begin at Eth. $1·50 per annum for incomes not exceeding Eth. $300 and rising eventually to 40 per cent for incomes of Eth. $150,000. As this tax came into operation, the tithe was to be gradually reduced. Furthermore, unused land was to be taxed at the same rate as adjoining land and another tax was to be introduced on all sales of animals and animal products. Assessment was to be carried out either through tax documentation, where this applied, or through estimates by the Income Tax Authorities. It was significant that no details of how the estimates were to be made were laid down. There were also to be appeal commissions set up on a local basis—to consist of the district governor, a judge nominated by the provincial governor and three elders selected by the local inhabitants.

TABLE 4.

Revenue from Land Tax, Tithe and Cattle Tax

	Land Tax	Tithe	Cattle Tax
1956–57	5·0	9·4	0·2
1957–58	4·8	9·6	0·2
1958–59	4·8	9.3	0·3
1959–60	4·1	8·3	0·2
1960–61	5.0	10·1	0·2
1961–62	5·2	10·3	0·3
1962–63	4·4	8·9	0·4
1963–64	5·4	10·5	0·2
1964–65	5·6	10·5	0·3
1965–66	5·9	10·4	0·35
1966–67	6·3	10·6	0·2
1967–68	5·7	1·6	0·3
1971–72	6·0	1·5	0·7

Source: Statistical Abstracts, and Budget estimates.
Figures in Eth. $ million.
Published figures and the Statistical Abstracts do not always agree.

One aim of this proclamation was to obtain more revenue. This is not surprising if one looks at the figures for Government revenue received from the land taxes and the cattle tax (Table 4). In theory it was apparently hoped that such a tax, being new, would not be subject to the traditional exemptions. The Ministry of Finance's estimates for the increase in revenue that might be expected ranged up to Eth.$100 million. The other published aim of the proposals was to end "the system of privileged exemptions". There are a wide variety of these based upon the diversity of land tenure systems (see Chapter 4). The larger landowners in particular benefit from these and from the traditional divisions of taxable land into fertile, semi-fertile and poor. It has been easy for a landowner to arrange to pay the rate for poor land; in any case there are wide variations in the crops grown on fertile land. Coffee land, for example, is taxed at the same rate as any fertile land in spite of the fact that income from coffee is around ten times more than the income from any other crop. Furthermore in three provinces—Tigre, Begemeder and Gojjam, and in two districts of Wollo, Wag and Lasta—the land tax was, and is, assessed as a tribute on the province as a whole, and worked out at a special rate. The Church also has special exemptions including not paying the education and health taxes.

Parliament's reaction to the original form of the proclamation was marked and when it was finally passed it was a very different bill. The only part that remained untouched was the schedule for the tax on produce. The tax on unused land had been dropped completely. The tithe was immediately abolished, and in drawing up the details for the estimation teams the Deputies provided for a local not a central basis. Each team was to consist of three members, two elected by the local residents, and the third to be a local official, with an attendance fee to be paid for each meeting.

These changes make clear the traditional attitudes of the Deputies. The refusal to accept the tax on unused lands was in the interests of the larger landowners, many of whom possessed large, undeveloped areas. Equally these large estates often had parts classified as idle that in practice were not so. A tax on unused land, however, would have involved attempts to measure production on the ground. The Ministry of Finance's witnesses to the Parliamentary Committee had made the point that cutting out this tax would encourage landowners to let land lie fallow or drop out of production. In this connection it is hardly surprising that the Deputies followed this up by taking out the proposed tax on the sales of cattle and animal products.

The additions over the question of assessment which established control at the local level obviously provided landowners with the opportunity for packing the teams with their own nominees—much in the same way as they were able to influence parliamentary elections. As the appeal commissions were already biased towards local control this meant that the entire administration of the tax was effectively in the hands of the local notables who were in theory to be the ones who would pay the most tax. In these circumstances it is hardly surprising that the revenue from the tax has been much less that originally anticipated—the estimate for 1971–72 was only Eth.$17 million.

The one change made by the Deputies that should, at first sight, have benefited the tenants was the immediate abolition of the tithe. In fact this had very little effect. The Ministry of Finance had argued that immediate abolition would merely affect Government revenue; for the people involved, the tenants, would not be informed by their landlords. This has certainly been the case in many areas. Landlords still collect the tithe and keep it for themselves. In addition it seems that many landowners in fact paid neither the tithe nor the new tax for a considerable time because of the length of time taken over the new assessment. It should be noted though, that the tithe, according to the 1971–72 budget estimates, remained at Eth.$1·5 million.

Similar efforts were made by the Ministry of Land Reform and Administration in 1968 when it introduced two draft proclamations to "Provide for a Tax on Unutilized Land" and more importantly a revision of the landlord-tenant relationship. The Ministry's original draft proposals did attempt to remove several of the traditional privileges of landlords—eviction at will, share-cropping at up to 75 per cent of production and, in general, total control of tenancies without restriction,[7] and to remove the undoubted advantages for large landowners, of keeping substantial areas in a theoretically unused state; neither measure received much support from the Deputies.

In spite of the bias of Parliament towards the landowning class, both in the Chamber of Deputies and the Senate, debates on these proposals have at times been acrimonious. There were a few Deputies who were against the landlord-tenant proclamation because they believed it did not go far enough. Genuine supporters of this viewpoint, however, numbered no more than fifteen.[8] A number of others who supported them did so in order to appear more radical or because of the interests of their constituents, but they remained happy in the assurance that the measure was unlikely to pass. There was indeed a strong feeling among the Deputies that the Government was not anxious for the measure to be passed anyway. A number of

Deputies believed that this would have been done long before if either the Government or the Emperor had been really serious about the proposed reforms. Such views were of course only expressed privately, and the most serious element in the opposition came from the class-conscious, landowning section, the great majority of both Senate and Deputies.

The Emperor has made a number of public pronouncements about land reform, one of the most forthright in 1961:

> The fundamental obstacle to the full realisation of the full measure of Ethiopia's agricultural potential has been, simply stated, lack of security in the land. The fruits of the farmer's labour must be enjoyed by him whose toil has produced the crop. The essence of land reform is, that while fully respecting the principle of private ownership, that landless people must have the opportunity to possess their own land, that the position of tenant farmers must be improved, and that the system of taxation applying to land holdings must be the same for all. It is our aim that every Ethiopian should own his own land, in implementation of this principle.[9]

However, the fact that he could perhaps have done more to push the measures through does lead to a suspicion that he has not been as concerned as he might have been—or rather, that he has been prepared to allow the certain opposition there was from the landed interests to effect a rejection of the reforms, a rejection that also was in his own personal interest as one of the largest landowners in the country.

Then, in 1974, Parliament suddenly took it upon itself to act in a far more militant way. Resentment over the Government's failure to deal with the famine was sharpened by a series of rebuffs by the then Prime Minister, Aklilu Habtewold. Although Parliament played no part in Aklilu's downfall, after it there was a constant series of extremely outspoken debates in the Chamber of Deputies over corruption, land reform and a number of other issues. It is evident that the crisis galvanized the Deputies in particular into taking a fresh look at their position in the state, and into trying to establish their power *vis-à-vis* the new Prime Minister, *Lij* Endalkatchew Makonnen, and his Council of Ministers. Since one aspect of the new situation was the promise of constitutional reform, the Chamber was obviously set on emphasizing its claims in what is expected to be a constitutional monarchy with Ministers responsible to Parliament. In the process of doing this it made some radical suggestions about land reform and in May was warning the new Government that this must be carried out before it was "too late for a peaceful solution".

In this sense the crisis of early 1974 has been a part of the process of the devolution of imperial power that has been occurring as the Emperor aged. It has not been a planned part. During the 1960s the Emperor partly by default and partly because of the sheer impossibility of controlling the bureaucracy directly allowed Aklilu Habtewold, Prime Minister from 1961–74, to build up a very strong position. It needed the twin catalysts of a disastrous famine and very rapid inflation, plus the support of the military, to over-throw him in February 1974.

Aklilu's position as Prime Minister did however come out of a logical growth in the power of the Ministers. The origin of the ministerial system dates back to the early part of the century, to the reign of the Emperor Menilek II. In 1907–08 when Menilek was suffering from the effects of his first stroke, which occurred in May 1906, he decided to appoint a number of Ministers, presumably to act as a stabilizing force should he become incapacitated, or rather to define the powers of certain individuals and lessen the likelihood of divisions should he be unable to carry on. There is now a total of nineteen Ministers and a Prime Minister. Together, these make up the Council of Ministers.

This body did not exist before 1935 when the status of Ministers as Ministers was low. Foreigners who had dealings with the Ministers of this period were highly critical of them, for the Ministers were nearly always absent from their Ministries, in attendance on the Emperor at the Palace. Even when they were present nothing could be done without imperial approval and, furthermore, there was no administrative machinery to carry out any instructions even if such were issued. If it could be said that the Ministries had any relevance, it was to Addis Ababa and its immediate vicinity only.

Their position only gradually improved. In 1943 it was laid down that the Ministers could transact State business, prepare draft laws and submit the budgets of their Ministries—with the limitation that all these had to have the Emperor's approval. They could also make appointments to positions below that of director-general; vice-ministers and director-generals remaining in the Emperor's gift. In 1955 the regulations concerning the Ministries were formalized and elaborated but no fundamental changes were made until the Order of 1966.[10]

This last order was significant because for the first time the Council of Ministers was given the power to be more than advisory: "Our Ministers shall, after discussion in Council, make decisions concerning all matters brought before them". However, this is qualified by the next sentence: "All decisions on matters of policy shall be submitted by Our Prime Minister to Us". Furthermore, the Prime Minister's power was increased by the fourth clause: "4a. Our Prime Minister shall be appointed and dismissed by Us. b. All other Ministers shall be proposed for appointment to Us by Our Prime Minister and thereafter duly appointed by Us. c. All other Government officials above the rank of Assistant Minister shall, after consultation with the appropriate Ministers, be proposed for appointment to Us by Our Prime Minister and thereafter duly appointed by Us". Ministers were also allowed to transact state business, to enter into contracts and agreements, within the limits of their budgets.

This, coupled with the inevitable growth of the bureaucratic machine, obviously made the Council of Ministers something much more than an advisory body. In practice, however, imperial control remained considerable. Even though the Emperor made speeches encouraging the Ministers to act more independently,[11] he obviously did regard the Ministers more as a body to co-ordinate and deal with the administrative questions that had become too numerous for his own personal supervision. It should be emphasized that this limitation of imperial approval was not necessarily binding on any particular Minister whose power might have been much greater by virtue of his personal position.

Once again the events of 1974 enforced a new situation. Although everything was done in the name of the Emperor it is clear that the change of Ministers was forced upon him and the responsibility for it did not rest with him. From the moment it took office, the new Council of Ministers, subject to the various pressures from the Armed Forces and other power groups, acted largely in isolation from the imperial wishes. They have been able to call upon the bureaucracy built up over the years to start on constitutional and other reforms, and to initiate programmes without having to rely on imperial support or agreement. This part of the process of devolution had not looked as though it would take place until the Emperor died. Indeed, without the crisis providing a moment when Aklilu could be attacked with good prospects of success, it is probable that it would have had to wait until then.

Nevertheless, the new Ministers appointed in March 1974 were not very different from the former ones. Many of them, including the new Prime Minister, *Lij* Endalketchew Makonnen, come from the great nobility, and thus possess a traditional legitimacy of power, as well as land from which the power derives. Others have married into the extended Shoan royal house—this being one of the traditional ways of binding an individual to loyalty. These men, like some others whose traditional legitimacy is based on smaller provincial land-holdings, have tended to be essentially dependent upon imperial favour for their actual position as Ministers. That is, they have been at the mercy of the Emperor for promotion or the reverse; they were seldom as dependent upon him for their lands or wealth, as these in most cases were inherited. The spreading tentacles of connection have been clearly indicated by Clapham who manages to get 70 per cent of the Ministers between 1941 and 1966 on a single genealogical table.[12]

There are exceptions to this. A few individuals have been picked out by the Emperor and pushed up into high positions. This again has been a traditional feature of the Ethiopian political scene—there have always been the occasional royal favourites. The most notable individual totally dependent upon the Emperor in the years since 1941 was Wolde-Giyorgis Wolde-Yohannis. He was an Amhara from Bulga in Shoa, and of humble origins, his father being a leather-worker. He came to Haile Selassie's notice long before the war and rose to become a director of the Ministry of the Pen as well as the Emperor's secretary. During the war he was constantly at the Emperor's side and on his return in 1941 he became Minister of the Pen and held the position for fourteen years until 1955. For six years (1943–49), he coupled this with the Ministry of the Interior and after that with the Ministry of Justice.

It was from this position as Minister of the Pen that Wolde-Giyorgis derived his importance; for this was the Ministry that transmitted all the imperial orders. It was also a position that allowed virtually unlimited access to the Emperor himself, and to a considerable extent controlled the access of others to the imperial presence. This was augmented by utilizing the Ministry of Interior's powers of appointment over provincial offices to provide a steady source of patronage for potential supports. Furthermore Wolde-Giyorgis was well aware of the importance, indeed the necessity, of having an efficient information service and his positions helped him to set up a highly competent service that was unique and greatly feared.

There is no doubt that the key to Wolde-Giyorgis' continued power was his hold on the Emperor's confidence. It apparently even survived a very presumptuous suggestion in the early 1940s that he should be allowed to marry the Emperor's eldest daughter, Princess Tegnagnework.[13] One reason behind this request was the fact that Wolde-Giyorgis needed something like an advantageous marriage to provide an independent power base. Without it he depended at this time on his position, which in turn was completely at the Emperor's mercy. Once his support became shaky, or disappeared, as it did in 1955, none of his erstwhile followers were prepared to help him and there was nothing to fall back on. He was in fact given the job of governing first Arussi and then Gomu-Goffa, both of which appointments are often considered as a form of exile. The moment any such positions were given him he was finished as a serious politician; and so it proved, for he was unable to resurrect his influence.

The Minister to whom the Emperor gave most support after the fall of Wolde-Giyorgis was for 13 years Prime Minister, Aklilu Habtewold. Aklilu is from a Shoan Church family and became deputy Prime Minister in 1957 and Prime Minister in 1961, a position he held until February 1974. To a large extent he achieved this through the intrigues of his elder brother, Makonnen, who had been a long-time supporter of Wolde-Giyorgis before being instrumental in getting him out of the Ministry of the Pen in 1955. Makonnen was killed in 1960 and his influence at the centre of events was inherited by Aklilu. Aklilu operated in the same way as Wolde-Giyorgis, through individuals who received his patronage.[14] His position was, however, more secure in practice—he mixed better with the Shoan aristocracy, who thoroughly disliked Wolde-Giyorgis (a feeling that was mutual). This gave him a wider base of support. Nevertheless, he was, like Wolde-Giyorgis, dependent upon the Emperor and could be dismissed at any time.

In practice the Emperor was prepared to let him stay in power. It is possible that he felt that Aklilu had so deeply entrenched himself in the bureaucracy that it would be too difficult to remove him. On the other hand his defence of the ex-Prime Minister in March 1974 and his attempts to stop him and other ex-ministers being arrested suggests that Haile Selassie still supported them. His replacement, at a time of crisis, was significantly *Lij* Endalkatchew Makonnen, son of *Ras-Bitwoded* Makonnen Endalkatchew who had been a Prime Minister in the 1940s, and the leading member of one of the

most important Shoan noble families. In this sense the fall of
Aklilu and his replacement can be seen partly as an aristocratic
reaction against imperial favourites. Certainly, although *Lij*
Endalkatchew has been a Minister on and off since 1961, he was
an important member of the faction that opposed Aklilu's pre-
eminence.

The change in the method of Government that occurred between
the 1940s and the 1960s can be seen in the distinction between the
positions that Aklilu and Wolde-Giyorgis held.[15] Wolde-Giyorgis
was Minister of the Pen and this automatically ensured a close
liaison with the Emperor. By definition strong opposition from the
aristocracy might have been expected and this is what happened.
Aklilu operated through the Prime Minister's office which was not
subject to direct imperial rule and thus through a less closely super-
vised bureaucracy. This allowed for the creation of institutions of
Government independently of the Emperor. The possibilities inherent
in this did not however become explicit until Aklilu's fall, for he
remained very much an imperial appointee.

Even though there has been a marked increase in the power and
extent of the bureaucracy, it does remain a question as to how far
this can really be considered as significant for development when
so many of the personnel are well-connected. It is undoubtedly true
that the key requirement for a job is the connections that an applicant
brings with him—and this is true for all levels of administration. This
is not meant to imply that an unconnected individual cannot get a
job. As in the imperial system of appointments, there is room for
individuals from a wide range of backgrounds. Ministers operate
their own groupings of people from their own areas, of private
clients, of their relatives and friends. Given the general propensity
for intrigue, it is always useful for a Minister to have individuals whose
sole loyalty is to the Minister himself, and for this the unconnected
person is more likely to be effective.

Modernization may perhaps be thought to operate within such
a centralizing agency as the Ministry of Finance. Indeed it is true
that the very concept of the Ministry's powers does mark a break
with the past. The traditional method of taxation was to order tribute
from a local governor, who was responsible for collecting at least
enough to fulfil the imperial demands. There was little check on the
surplus that might be collected at the same time—it was not until
after *Ras* Hailu of Gojjam had been disgraced and arrested that it
was possible to obtain allegations of his overtaxation (in 1932). The

amount that the imperial treasury actually received however, depended upon a number of factors, including the relationship that
the local lords had with the Emperor, the strength of the imperial
power, the closeness of the area to the capital and the amount of
trade that went through the province.

The latter was the most significant in terms of actual cash—this
was why Haile Selassie's control of the great trade route that ran
through Harar and/or Dire Dawa was so important to his assumption
and retention of power. All the non-trade taxes were collected in
kind. Furthermore substantial areas were granted as *gult* for a
governor's salary, and from these very little would go to the imperial
treasury. The money that the government had at its disposal came
directly from the taxes on trade through Addis Ababa and from
imperial commercial dealings. These ranged from the sale of mono-
polies and concessions, to various commercial farming and trading
ventures. Another angle was imperial money lending; this was very
important under Menilek, and the importance of controlling these
loans was an essential political factor in the troubles of 1908–16.[16]
As the legal heir to Menilek the Empress Zauditu got control of
them in 1916; they were in turn taken over by Haile Selassie in
1930 and they were a useful factor in helping control the greater
nobility in the thirties and after the war. Within this "system" there
was no room for a budget as spending was done at the behest and
direct order of the Emperor; for the same reason any independent
Ministry of Finance would have been totally superfluous.

After the war the need for more revenue and the establishment of
a bureaucracy had the effect of regulating the financial distribution
and it was turned over to a finance Ministry. A new series of taxes
was instituted during the 1940s; these were both direct and indirect.
It is however noticeable that Ethiopia has made relatively little
use of taxation as an instrument of development policy. The dominant sphere has remained indirect rather than direct. For example
direct taxes only comprised 15 per cent of the revenue schedule in
1965/6 and 21 per cent in 1971/2. The increase of direct taxes
as a proportion of total tax returns has also only been marginal—
23 per cent in 1951 and 27 per cent in 1972. Most taxation revenue
thus came from the indirect taxes such as salt, tobacco and alcohol,
and the customs duties which are widely applicable to everyone
but affect the poorest sections of the community most seriously.
The only taxes that are in theory specifically aimed at the wealthier

sections of the community are the direct ones on income and particularly on land.

Income tax was introduced in 1943 and has been revised on several occasions since, the latest revision being in 1967 when the schedules were changed and an income tax levied on agricultural produce. The relative weight that is given to these schedules and to the other direct taxes can be seen below.

TABLE 5.

Direct Taxes 1971/2 Budget Estimates

Applicable to landowners:

Income tax Schedule D	17,000,000	
Land Tax	6,000,000	
Tithe (abolished in 1967)	1,500,000	
Rural Education Tax	5,500,000	
Urban Education Tax	5,500,000	
Health Tax	6,000,000	
		41,500,000

Not applicable to landowners:

Cattle Tax	700,000	
Income Tax Schedule A	35,000,000	
Income Tax Schedule B	7,000,000	
Income Tax Schedule C	41,000,000	
		83,700,000
		125,200,000

Figures in Ethiopian dollars.

Only one third is thus directed towards the wealthiest sector of the community. Even this is highly misleading, for the greater part of Schedule D, as the Ministry of Finance itself admits, comes from the farmers whose income is below Eth.$300—the bottom rung of the schedule. Furthermore the tithe is an officially abolished tax and the rural education tax is frequently not fully collected (see Table 7). It should also be noted that the percentage share of land tax and tithe (the taxes most applicable to the landowners) has shown a steady decline in relation to the total tax revenue and the direct tax revenue, though obviously this is to a limited degree made up by the imposition of Schedule D.

TABLE 6.

Land Tax and Tithe as a percentage of:

	1958	1962	1966	1972
a Total Tax Revenue				
Land Tax	3·78	2·35	1·12	1·01
Tithe*	7·3	4·82	2·09	0·25
b Total Direct Taxes				
Land Tax	16·67	9·76	8·77	4·79
Tithe*	32·20	19·99	16·44	1·19

* *legally abolished 1967.*

This cannot be seen as a normal phenomenon considering the great agricultural potential of the country and the fact that over 90 per cent of the population are engaged in agricultural activities.

It should also be noted that the tithe was never really borne by the landowner, but by the tenant. Even before its official abolition the landlord would normally gain considerably on the assessment. The tenant set aside one-tenth of his crop to offset the tithe to be paid by the landowner. The tax, which was actually in lieu of tithe, was assessed at the rate of Eth. $35 per fertile *gasha*. The value of one-tenth of a crop from a fertile *gasha* would almost always be vastly in excess of the tax to be paid to the Government. So the landowner could be sure of a handsome profit on the transaction. Of course after the abolition, the tithe could merely be collected by the landowner and nothing handed on to the Government.

Very little has been done to try to remedy this situation although Income Tax Schedule D has been incorporated, some part of which does bear upon the wealthier landowners, at any rate in theory. In other ways there is little change to be seen. This is not to say that the Ministry of Finance does not represent a different approach to Government in that there is now a centralized tax-collecting department of the Government. No longer, with the exceptions noted, are the provincial nobility actually responsible for collecting the land taxes. The Ministry has its officials in every province and many districts. The aim is still, however, the collection of revenue as an

TABLE 7.

The Education Tax 1967/8

Province and Araja	Estimate	Collection	Difference
Arussi			
Argagugu	51	49	—2
Chilalo	177	155	—22
Ticho	90	79	—11
	318	283	—35
Bale			
Dolo	16	Not reported	—16
Elkerer	—	Not reported	—
Fasil	78	Not reported	—78
Genale	67	Not reported	—67
Webe	27	Not reported	—27
	188	Not reported	—188
Begemeder			
Wogera	72	Not reported	—72
Chilga	30	Not reported	—30
Debra Tabor	99	Not reported	—99
Gayint	52	Not reported	—52
Gondar	58	Not reported	—58
Semien	79	Not reported	—79
Libo	75	Not reported	—75
	465	Not reported	—465
Gojjam			
Agaumeder	47	31	—16
Bahrdar	53	15	—38
Bichena	49	10	—39
Damot	78	25	—53
Debre Markos	89	53	—36
Metekel	26	18	—8
Motta	43	1	—42
	385	153	—232

The Education Tax 1967/8 (*continued*)

Province and Araja	Estimate	Collection	Difference
Gomu-Goffa			
Gardula	47	33	−14
Geleb	7	7	
Gemu	72	61	−11
Gofa	32	28	−4
	158	129	−29
Hararge			
Chercher	88	82	−6
Dire Dawa	23	20	−3
Garagurcha	16	6	−10
Gursum	64	48	−16
—	22	22	
Harar	151	109	−42
N. Ogaden (2 *Arajas*)	36	19	−17
S. Ogaden (3 *Arajas*)	—	—	
Wobera	75	56	−19
	475	362	−113
Illubabor			
Bunno	86	75	−11
Gambella	—	—	
Gore	92	61	−31
Mocha	26	14	−12
	204	150	−54
Kaffa			
Gimira	18	14	−4
Jimma	134	125	−9
Kaffa	42	42	
Kulo Konta	29	27	−2
Limu	102	84	−18
Maji	13	10	−3
	338	302	−36

TABLE 7. The Education Tax 1967/8 (*continued*)

Province and Araja	Estimate	Collection	Difference
Sidamo			
Arero	18	18	
Borenna	4	0·5	−3·5
Deressa	61	59	−2
Jemjem	56	58	+2
Sidama	135	130	−5
Wolamo	127	128	+1
	401	393·5	−7·5
Wollega			
Arjo	37	30	−7
Asosa	46	22	−24
Gimbi	87	79	−8
Horo	66	58	−8
Kelem	65	64	−1
Leka	50	41	−9
	351	294	−57
Wollo			
Lasta	26	14	−12
Yejju	39	31	−8
Other *Arajas*	500	453	−47
	565	498	−67
Shoa			
All *Arajas*	1,161	1,120	−41
Tigre			
All *Arajas*	211	210	−1
Eritrea			
Tax not levied	—	—	
TOTALS	5,220	3,894·5	−1,325·5

Source: *Ministry of Finance.*
All figures in 000 Eth. dollars.

end in itself. It should be added that the new Government in 1974 committed itself to important social and financial changes to provide a more equitable approach to taxation.

This attitude comes out very clearly in the relationship of the

Emperor with the Ministry of Finance since the war. Essentially, the system that obtained after the war was the traditional one, approval of spending came from the Emperor alone. Recurrent expenditures were granted by imperial order. The Ministry of Finance was thus the imperial treasury, the institution responsible for payments according to imperial instruction. There was no budget, except for the one year 1944–45, and that was retrospective. The controlling Ministry was the Ministry of the Pen which transmitted the imperial orders. In fact in immediate post-war years there was no Minister of Finance.

It was not until 1960 that the Finance Ministry evolved under Yilma Deressa (Minister 1960–69), along with the growth in the power of the other Ministries as a whole, into a more independent bureaucratic organization. In some ways Yilma also allowed his subordinates considerably more independence of action than many of the other Ministers, and showed perhaps a greater willingness to employ the educated graduates necessary for such a bureaucratic system. Nevertheless, by no means all of the highest officials of the Ministry could be classified as adequately educated. There were various balances and it was relatively easy for a Minister to gain credit for promoting educated personnel while still retaining un-obtrusive checks upon them, or utilizing the more traditional sectors of the Government machinery to block any real changes—something at which the Emperor excelled. The Finance Ministry did work hard to provide more revenue, and with considerable success; but the exemptions of the wealthy were not seriously threatened and the attempts to acquire the legal amounts of tax from them have been almost uniformly unsuccessful. Equally, the Ministry, in the nine years of Yilma's control, became a highly personalized organization. The criteria for appointment and promotion were as much support of the Minister, or the Minister's patronage, as competence.

The Emperor is, of course, fully aware of the importance of finance. There has been the continuation of a traditional system of authorization by imperial order which indicates very clearly that, for all the changes in the Ministry of Finance itself and the establish-ment of a Ministry of Planning (this only retained the status of a separate Ministry between 1966 and 1969 after which it was in-corporated into the Prime Minister's office), the Emperor was determined to hold on to an imperial element of financial control, which amounted in total to about 12 per cent of the budget. In practice the Emperor could also affect and authorize the expenditure of much larger sums than this—few would have dared to try and oppose his wishes in such matters.

The situation was thus similar to the other institutions—a modernized bureaucracy, not very efficiently run, paralleled, and frequently undercut, by more traditional powers. The personal nature of the way allocations were made remained a central feature. Yilma was a highly important Minister, not just because of his own status, or because of his significance as the leading Oromo in the Council of Ministers for many years; he also had the Emperor's ear in financial matters. To gain funds it was necessary to convince either the Emperor or Yilma—for even if the rest of the Ministers were in agreement it was possible for either to block the required funds in some way or other. Personalities and individual pressures remained the vital elements in matters of finance in spite of all that the younger educated officials in the Ministry could do.

This raises the point of whether the events of early 1974 have changed this. Within limits there has obviously been an effect, for nearly all the older, long-serving Ministers who had worked with Aklilu were removed. The new Council of Ministers consisted essentially of highly educated, younger technocrats. This must not be over-emphasized for the malaise within the Ministries goes far further than the Ministers themselves. It will require many more far-reaching changes to effect any real revolution in the methods of administration.

The combination of the traditional, tempering and controlling the modern, has been similar in the Ministry of Interior's organization of the provinces. Some limitations on this have already been noted in the previous chapter. Another projected reform that related to this was first started in 1973. The origins of this go back to a draft proclamation for the "Establishment of Self-Government" in 1962, which presented a plan to establish councils in each *awraja* to be composed of three members from each *woreda* or a single representative from each *metekel-woreda*. The representatives were to be elected by the inhabitants and the councils were to have control of roads, health, education and to have the right under certain rather difficult conditions to remove the provincial governors, or rather to pass votes of no confidence in them; they were also to have the right to impose additional taxation providing that the Ministry of Finance accepted such taxes as being necessary.

In 1966 a Local Self-Government Order was published. In the intervening four years considerable changes had been made. Some

of the provisions most offensive to the landowning elite were removed. The right to remove the provincial governor vanished as
did the right to raise additional taxes. The councils were put under
the supervision of the provincial governors and the number of
representatives was cut to two per *woreda*. Although staff were
transferred in order to implement this, the order was in fact rejected
by Parliament on the grounds that it encouraged separatist tendencies and that it was attempting to put into the hands of the provinces development projects that were the responsibility of the central
government. A further reason was the dislike of the whole idea of
elective council members.

However the idea was not dropped[17] and it was eventually decided
to implement the watered-down version during the year 1973–74,
though only for seventeen *awrajas*. The Emperor referred to the
project in his speech from the throne when opening Parliament in
1973:

> Thus for the first time this year a system of local administration
> is going to be in force in seventeen *Awrajas* in accordance with
> plans drawn up to enable the Ethiopian people to reap the benefits
> of modern administration, to enable them to participate in
> activities directed towards the development and guidance of their
> own communities, and for making a new system of public ad-
> ministration which promotes the cause of development easily
> accessible to the people. This will not only be in conformity with
> the socio-economic standard of living attained by our country
> but would also help in promoting the cause of local government
> by fully mobilizing the financial and manpower resources of the
> people. The new system of local administration is planned to
> embrace the whole country in the next few years.

In past circumstances it could be expected that this would go the
way of other projected reforms in the provinces. As it is organized
it will be under the governor-generals, and in any case there is no
doubt that the councils will, in spite of the uprush of democratic
procedures in Addis Ababa in 1974, continue to represent the views
of local elders and landowners and have little immediate effect on
the local people. Democratization remains impossible while the
conjunction of land and power remains as the fundamental basis
of control in the country, and while the system is geared to per-
petuating the rights of the landowners.

Assessment of the possibilities of changing this, made more urgent by the outburst of peasant unrest in anticipation of land reform in the first half of 1974, depends upon appreciation of the commitment of the new Government to it, and on the strength of the pressures for it. It should be remembered that a number of those in the new Council of Ministers are substantial landowners including the new Prime Minister. It may also be noted that the whole idea of this reform has been cynically received by a considerable number of Deputies and by many in the selected provinces, who are convinced that this was meant to be a method by which the central government would avoid putting finance into the development of schools, roads and health clinics.

The third most vital ministry, besides Interior and Finance is that of Defence. It is hardly surprising that the armed forces have been modernized. Before 1941 there was no effective central army. The troops who fought the Italians were composed of levies called-up by, and under the control of, the individual governors of provinces plus the small imperial bodyguard that had modern training. Haile Selassie, having begun to train his own bodyguard before he became Emperor, sent a number of officers to study in France in the 1920s and engaged a Belgian Military Mission in 1929. This mission continued to train the Imperial Guard after his assumption of the throne in 1930. The Holeta Military Academy was also set up before the war, in 1934. However, the number of troops and officers who had received European training by 1935 was very small.

After the restoration and as a part of his centralization programme the Emperor persuaded the British to finance and organize a Military Mission to train and equip ten infantry battalions as well as a regiment of artillery and one of armoured cars. The British also supplied key personnel for a number of years. At the same time many of the patriots were formed into territorial units to neutralize them and to keep a check upon arms in the countryside. The Imperial Guard was also reconstituted under pre-war graduates of the Holeta Academy.

After the British mission finally withdrew in 1951, the United States assumed the position of main military advisers though others have also been used—Swedes, especially in the airforce; Norwegians for the navy; Indians to run the second military academy set up at Harar in 1958, and to train the reconstituted Bodyguard of 1961; and Israelis for the police commandos and various other security units. With the very generous U.S. military aid (a total of U.S.$187 million has been given over the years 1946–72) the size of the armed forces has been substantially increased.[18] During the 1960s the territorial forces were also reorganized and increased to a total of 10,000 at any one time. In addition the Police Force has been enlarged, improved and augmented by special emergency and commando units.

The most important method of holding the loyalty of the military and especially of the officer corps has been the distribution of land, which brings them into the ruling elite, although many in fact come from it already. Statistics are difficult to come by, but an analysis of the cadets at the Harar Military Academy in 1959–60 provided the following breakdown. Upper class, 11 per cent; middle class, 53 per cent; "poor" or lower class, 21 per cent; peasant class, 3 per cent; no reply, 13 per cent.[19] Another classification carried out for the cadets of 1970–71 broke down the categories as follows. Landowning (upper class), 21 per cent; other landowning, 55 per cent; landless peasant, 20 per cent; unknown, 4 per cent.[20] There are certain difficulties in interpreting these figures as the class breakdown, especially for the earlier analysis, is by no means clear. It would seem that the term "middle class" in fact included those who owned at least small amounts of land; if so this would provide a figure of at least 64 per cent coming from the landowning classes. For 1970–71 the comparable figure is 76 per cent—this includes all landowners however small, but not tenants who are included in the 20 per cent of landless peasants. From these figures it is clear that well over 50 per cent of the Harar intake come from the landowning classes as a whole, and it would appear that the number is rising. It should be remembered that there is another academy at Holeta so that these figures do not necessarily apply to officers as a whole. Since the foundation of the Harar academy, Holeta has been reserved for short-service commissions and for promoting non-commissioned officers.

Another factor that has helped loyalty has been direct imperial patronage which has operated for particular officers. That is, the Emperor has promoted outside the general administrative system of the army on the grounds of loyalty, merit, athletic success or whatever. Similarly marriages have been arranged for senior officers to set up links with various groups. It may be noted that, with some exceptions, the greatest nobility have been kept out of the Armed Forces, though one of the Emperor's daughters was married to General Abiy Abebe, and one of his grand-daughters is married to General Naga, the former commander of the 3rd Division. The Emperor also kept a sharp eye on officers and moved them around to prevent them building up power bases. This, however, is easy to overstate. In nineteen years up to 1960 there were only two Commanders of the Bodyguard; and since then there have only been four.

One of the most important elements in holding loyalty has been the negative one of encouraging dissension among the various elements of the Armed Forces and in particular the army. The importance of this was demonstrated in 1960 when it was army units that were responsible for crushing the Bodyguard's attempted coup. In the same way the other parts of the Armed Forces have been built up as potential counter-weights—the Police and the Territorial Army. That the regime is fully conscious of the dangers of discontent in the Armed Forces is shown by the speed with which demands for pay increases have been accepted. An obvious example was in 1961 when the demand had to be met by cutting back the pay of civil servants; a move that was hardly popular but not particularly dangerous.[21] Again in 1974 pay rises were granted twice to try and hold the loyalty of the Armed Forces and the Police.

It is significant that in 1974 this was not sufficient. This was essentially because the pressure was coming from those outside the normal traditional lines of control. It came from the ordinary soldiers and NCOs plus groups of radically minded younger officers. They were able to take advantage of the crisis to push for sweeping reforms, and it was because of this that a Government with a mandate for real reform appeared.

With this exception, and with the partial exception of 1960, Haile Selassie has managed to keep the mass of both officers and men loyal or at least acquiescent. They have been used largely in the maintenance of internal control and this has been especially important in the 1960s and 1970s with the appearance of two major national movements in Eritrea and Bale, besides the continuous peasant disturbances. In fact the events of the early part of 1974 testified to the position built up by the Emperor. He was still being seen as a necessary unifying factor by the majority of the Army in May— to that extent his methods had been successful.

One further point should be stressed. In the last few years various units have come to be in a semi-regional situation as a result of their long periods of duty in particular areas; the 3rd Division in Hararge province, the 4th in Bale and the 2nd in Eritrea. To a considerable extent the commanders of these forces whether they have had official positions in the provincial administration or not, have tended to build up their own supporters within their divisions and within the provinces. This applies to some degree to the men. In the crisis of 1974 some of the demands put out by the various units were signed by the "Ethiopian Army of the North"—the 2nd Division in Asmara—and "The Army of the East" in Harar. This underlines the possibility of regionalization should the authority of the central Government break down totally. In the last few years there has also been a growing use of the territorial army under the authority of the Governor-Generals of such provinces as Wollo, Bale and Gojjam, and this emphasizes the danger. In a future crisis it is not impossible that the splits that have been encouraged among the troops and the different units may produce a movement towards regional or national activities rather than loyalty to a central Government—though the Army's unity in 1974 has been impressive.

Another Ministry that has been influenced, at first sight, by concepts of modernization is that of Education. This is an area that Haile Selassie has regarded very much as his own—he was for many years his own Education Minister. Certainly substantial changes can be noted both in quantity and attitudes, though not in the aims. Education, as the Emperor saw it, was primarily a factor in centralization, a method of providing an educated administration under imperial control. It has also been used to help in the Amhariza-tion of the Empire and to provide a national language and culture to replace some of the strong regional and ethnic affiliations that are found in Ethiopia. For the first of these reasons the educational system has expanded side by side with the administration as the economy and bureaucracy enlarged. It has not however increased commensurately with the needs of the population, nor has there been any evidence of a governmental desire for it to do so.

In theory Ethiopia had a basis on which to build in the educational sphere unparalleled in Africa—a substantial, stable and literate culture for over two thousand years. This was provided by the Christian hierarchy (and to a lesser degree the Moslem hierarchy, especially in the Moslem centre of Harar before the Shoan conquest) in its religious schools. Until this century such schools were the only available institutions of learning. Literacy was confined to the ecclesiastical products of these schools although the children of the nobility were often educated in monasteries for a time as part of their general training as members of the elite. In general, however, those who went to the schools went on to enter a Church or Monastery.

The skills of literacy were employed either there or in the services of the governing class, as in the drawing-up of land charters, official documents and similar activities. It was noticeable that the facility did not spread very far for the Church schools were by definition for the recruitment of the Church. No attempts were made to extend the privilege of literacy, for the Church agreed with the secular power on the necessity of limiting educational opportunity. It should also be mentioned that to many foreign observers the education of the clergy, in general terms, left a great deal to be desired, much of the learning being by rote and hardly to be dignified with the word "literacy". This may have been an exaggerated picture but it contained a great deal of truth.

No effort was made to provide an alternative educational system until the early years of this century. Menilek II made a preliminary move in the direction of providing a system that would be of some use in the modern world when he founded a school in Addis Ababa, the same year that Haile Selassie's father, at Menilek's instigation, set one up in Harar—1908. There was then a gap, but at the end of the 1920s when *Ras* Tafari became *Negus*, and especially after his crowning as Emperor, a number of schools were established, not only in Addis Ababa, but also in the provinces. All of these were primary schools and the instruction was either in French or English.

It is clear that the aim of this expansion both in Addis Ababa and in the provinces was to provide not the beginning of nationwide literacy but a small cadre, educated to fit into the more modern administration that was becoming necessary. The impetus came from the Emperor and there is no doubt that it was seen by him as a part of the centralization process; as a method of reinforcing imperial control. This holds true even for those sent abroad, of whom there were 248 before the war. Numbers of these were killed during and after the Italian invasion, but the charge that the Italians systematically massacred the educated has been disproved.[22] About fifty of the survivors became high officials after the war, but there was no general use of educated personnel as opposed to loyal graduates. This is shown by the fact that at least another fifty survived the war but were not used at the higher administrative levels.

The Emperor's general attitude was underlined by his use of educated personnel before the war. They were not put in charge of ministries but only utilized at the Director-General level. Their job was to try to organize, certainly not to innovate. Innovation was the prerogative of the Emperor alone. Several observers at the time made it clear that none would try to act without the imperial instructions. This was in spite of their own traditional importance— in most, though not all, cases. The majority of this group in fact came from the landowning classes and they never succeeded in throwing off the influences of their backgrounds; nor were they in sufficient numbers to influence the even more traditional attitudes of their non-educated contemporaries or seniors.

This general approach persisted long after the war. The system was to provide for small groups that could be educated and relied upon to follow orders as well as importing a flavour of modernization. In 1950 there were still only 200 Ethiopians studying abroad; fifteen years later 42 of these had reached the rank of Assistant Minister or above; and another 65 were holding important positions in such fields as law, engineering, medicine and education. Once again not all were used in spite of the chronic shortage of trained personnel. The objectives were summed up by a Director-General of the Education Ministry:

> Our traditional education had as its primary aim the teaching of religion and morals, while the aim of our educational system during the pre-war period was essentially to teach foreign languages. The first decade of the post-war period can be characterized as a period in the sense that knowing a foreign language was not sufficient. One had to learn the modern techniques of government and administration in order to cope with the demands of the time. Today [1964], the need for more professional people, like engineers, medical doctors, educators, agricultural experts and military scientists is the motivating factor in educational ventures.[23]

In other words it was the education of specialists as the Government inevitably became more complex and elaborate; but there was no suggestion that education should be expanded to meet the needs of the whole population, or indeed nothing to indicate that the whole population could have any need in this direction.

This should not be exaggerated. Education has in fact expanded greatly since the war, even if it is an expansion in relative rather than absolute terms. In this sense the educational system has had its own momentum and this, coupled with the ever-increasing bureaucracy, has propelled the advances. However, given this basic approach to the idea of education it was not surprising that the first post-war efforts should be aimed at higher education, then at the secondary system and finally at the primary sector.

The origin of university education dates from the foundation of five colleges in the decade 1950–60. These have all since been amalgamated into the Haile Selassie I University, and a Theological College has been subsequently added. The total enrolment for 1973–74 reached 6,450 students, with a freshman programme containing 2,791—400 over the planned figure. This is a considerable increase from the 827 students who were attending the various colleges in 1959–60. All in all the University has had over 3,000 graduates and another 1,500 have graduated overseas. Under this increased pressure the average expenditure per student has dropped from Eth.\$6,000 per annum to about Eth.\$3,000 per annum. It is partly for this reason that a new programme of expenditure (for Eth.\$15 million) to improve living conditions has been launched. More significant in the long run is the introduction of new courses in land-reform and rural science education for 1973–74.

The increase in higher education is paralleled by increases in both secondary and primary education (see Tables 8, 9, 10). These figures

TABLE 8

Enrolment in Government schools 1955–69

	Primary and Junior Secondary (Grades 1–8)	Secondary (Grades 9–12)	Expenditure on Govt. Sch.
1955/6	109,368	3,624	
1956/7	135,749	4,815	
1957/8	150,892	6,739	
1958/9	158,005	8,144	
1959/60	170,460	8,919	
1960/1	195,618	8,533	
1961/2	195,619	10,794	
1962/3	220,953	12,366	
1963/4	248,325	15,513	
1964/5	277,778	19,954	Eth.\$25·9 m.
1965/6	307,710	22,935	Eth.\$31·8 m.
1966/7	343,043	25,545	Eth.\$37·8 m.
1967/8	377,130	29,025	Eth.\$41·5 m.
1968/9	430,876	35,005	Eth.\$52·7 m.

Source: Statistical Abstracts.

TABLE 9

Enrolment in all schools 1963–72

	Primary Grades 1–6	Junior–Sec. Grades 7–8	Secondary Grades 9–12	Secondary Special Sch.
1963/4	313,240	21,121	11,927	5,497
1964/5	347,770	24,697	15,637	7,337
1965/6	378,750	28,812	21,623	5,150
1966/7	409,710	36,480	23,832	6,674
1967/8	452,457	44,777	26,690	8,067
1968/9	513,981	56,918	31,943	9,559
1969/70	590,445	63,215	42,487	8,968
1970/1	655,427	73,121	53,236	9,389
1971/2	721,500	83,000	61,900	8,600

Source: ECA Summaries of Economic Data. Ministry of Education Report on the organization of education in Ethiopia 1971–72, and 1972–73, Addis Ababa, June 1973.

TABLE 10

School* enrolment by provinces 1968/9

	Government	Others**	Total
Arussi	20,209	3,607	23,816
Bale	7,561	1,342	8,903
Begemeder	26,597	1,711	28,308
Eritrea	60,781	34,895	95,676
Gomu-Goffa	10,422	913	11,335
Gojjam	26,714	1,148	27,862
Hararge	29,854	9,145	38,999
Illubabor	17,336	281	17,617
Kaffa	16,285	2,590	18,875
Shoa	75,811	17,271	93,082
Addis Ababa	62,092	39,078	101,170
Sidamo	28,082	8,848	36,930
Tigre	21,660	5,855	27,515
Wollega	30,720	13,605	44,325
Wollo	25,512	2,918	28,430

Source: Statistical Abstract 1969–70 Addis Ababa.

* Primary and Academic Secondary Schools.
** Mission, Private and Church Schools.

do however conceal some serious shortcomings within the system. The increase in student enrolment has not been accompanied by a comparable growth in classroom units or teachers. For example the relative increases in 1968–69 were 13 per cent, 3·3 per cent, and 9·7 per cent. This failure to integrate expansion has caused over-crowding particularly at the early primary levels, as well as a very bad pupil-teacher ratio—a ratio that has been steadily worsening in both Government and non-Government schools. In 1961–62 there were an average of 33·3 students per teacher and 36·6 per classroom. By 1967–68 there were 39·1 per teacher and 45·1 per classroom. The situation was worse in the government schools; in the latter year there were over 50 students per teacher. In fact this conceals the overcrowding that occurs in the first two grades. In 1968–69 there were 184,000 in grades one to two and 198,000 in grades three to six. Classes of several hundred are not unknown. This overcrowding is undoubtedly most severe in the primary schools and yet there is considerable pessimism at the rate of expansion. One Minister privately remarked in 1971: "At the present rate of growth it will take to the end of the second decade of the twenty-first century before all primary age children are in school".

One feature that reduces the problem of overcrowding slightly is the drop-out rate. This is very high—in the period 1960–67, for grades one to six, in Government schools, it was 66 per cent, and in non-Government schools it was even higher at 79·8 per cent. Part of the reason for this is that over half the Government primary schools do not go as far as grade six but stop at lower levels. Furthermore there are difficulties of attendance in the face of parental opposition or indifference and especially over costs. Education is technically free, but there have been significant hidden charges in the cost of buying uniforms (which are compulsory), examination fees, books and other teaching aids. Many parents, with the best intentions, are unable to afford these charges, small though they may appear to be.

Another problem in the primary sphere is the unequal distribution of schools. Only the two major cities of Addis Ababa and Asmara are even relatively well served. In other areas there are very few Government schools. The main difference is between urban and the rural areas—though in terms of numbers being educated it is balanced to an extent by the Church schools, which are mainly in the rural areas. The opportunities also vary considerably from pro-vince to province. Even where schools are available the facilities may be inadequate, except perhaps in the new schools put up with the assistance of the Swedish International Development Agency, which has been responsible for 200 buildings which have the merit of being modern and new. But outside the major urban centres, the majority of primary schools have little in the way of modern teaching equipment, and many are without basic furniture and current expenditure extends little beyond the salaries of the teachers.

At the secondary level the pattern is very similar, namely a considerable growth in the enrolment figures without a corresponding growth in the facilities. This is especially true of the junior secondary level (grades seven and eight) where to a great extent the schools have been created by local pressures and by local efforts, and have not gained much from recognition by the Ministry of Education. Even at the secondary level in the Government schools, of which in 1969 there were forty-three, pressure of numbers has resulted in shift teaching—in several cases three shifts a day are used. This helps to produce the lack of facilities that bears particularly heavily on the secondary schools.

There is no chance that the Teaching Training Institutes will be able to cover the shortage of teachers for a long time. Before the withdrawal of the Peace Corps Volunteers in 1970, foreign teachers made up about half of the total secondary school staff. At the same time a number of Indian teachers resigned as well. The latter withdrew partly because they were dissatisfied with conditions, as they were paid at the same level as the Ethiopian staff and not at the much higher rates for other foreign contract teachers. In 1969–70, the Indian Government finally negotiated better terms for them and as a result they were priced out of the range of the Ministry. As a result of this shortfall the Ministry of Education was forced to explore the possibilities of trying to recruit from Ceylon, the Phillipines and South Korea; and more significantly, to begin seriously to investigate the possibilities of using the mass media as a real alternative to the shortage of teaching staff. Since 1969, when the first emergency radio teaching programmes were put out, many of the teething troubles have been solved and a comprehensive estimation of the possibilities worked out.

The curriculum for both secondary and primary levels has been under heavy fire on a number of occasions. The criticisms are concerned with matters such as concentration on academic subjects without adequate vocational training. Subjects are taught in logical fashion according to strictly laid-down rules. Whatever is contained in the syllabus for a semester's course must be covered. Rote learning is commonly insisted upon; the subjects are firmly compartmentalized. All subjects are planned irrespective of regional, cultural or linguistic differences. The most notable case of this is the use of Amharic, which is the official language of the empire. Its use in the school system has been spreading in recent years—partly in response to provincial pressures against the Amhara, which has led to an increased attempt to provide cultural centralization. In 1963 Amharic was made the medium of instruction in the primary schools and in 1970 the junior secondary schools followed suit. One of the Teacher Training Institutes switched over to Amharic in 1971 and it seems possible that this policy will be extended. However, the immediate effect on the secondary and university levels has been a lowering of standards and the discovery that the students find further education harder—for these are areas where English is used for instruction. So far this policy has not had the desired success. Pressures from other language groups, for example, the movements in Bale and Eritrea, have forced the government into allowing other language broadcasts over Ethiopian radio. There has also been a resurgence in Oromo among University students which suggests that the policy is strongly disliked even by those who have been most exposed to it.

The most telling of the criticisms is perhaps the objection to the concentration on academic themes, the assumption that all students will progress through the system to become bureaucrats; and this in a country where 95 per cent of the population is engaged in agriculture or related topics. The curriculum is laid down by specialists, often foreigners, who have little or no knowledge of the rural scene, and often little or no knowledge of the classroom either. Many of those involved in curriculum planning have not even been teachers. This applies to both secondary and primary syllabuses. It is true that about a quarter of the secondary schools are comprehensive in the subjects offered. There are also other institutions that allow for alternatives—the percentages are approximately: Teacher Training, 8 per cent; Public Health, 2 per cent; Commercial, 8 per cent; Technical and Vocational, 6 per cent; Agriculture, 2 per cent; others, 6 per cent; leaving 68 per cent in the academic field.

The fallacies in this situation have long been recognized and commented on. In 1971–72, the first steps were taken at a major education sector review and a decision in principle was taken to make the primary curriculum fit an essentially agricultural country. It was proposed that a new curriculum be devised to include basic agricultural techniques, essential education in the areas of health and hygiene, and technical training suitable for agricultural communities.[24] This however met with substantial opposition on a number of grounds. Many teachers felt that it would lower academic standards. More telling was the complaint that it would affect the non-Amhara peoples of the empire adversely. The proposal was that after the first four years there should be an examination that would include Amharic. This was felt to seriously prejudice the chances for non-Amharas at an unreasonably low level. The furore that the review caused was in fact one of the elements that went to make up the 1974 crisis. The new Government found that it had to think again and it may be some time before much progress in curriculum revision is actually made.

Overlying all these problems has been finance. Education is financed by the education tax (on land), by voluntary contributions, by the Government and by foreign aid. These contributions to the education budget are roughly divided so that the first two categories in theory cover the expenditure on primary education while the rest goes to secondary and higher education. This has not worked in practice. The education tax returns are static (or even falling) and will continue to do so. Nor in fact has the amount normally collected covered the budget requirements, and the difference has been made up by the Government. It should be noted that part of the reason for this lies in the inefficiency of the collection system and the difficulty of extracting the tax from the landlords (see Table 7). This illustrates the amount of shortfall that may be expected. It also brings out another difficulty, that in cases where there are local problems, or revolts, the tax is simply not collected, as in Bale and Begemeder, or only partially, as in Gojjam. The amount of shortfall is not always as large as in 1967–68, but it was Eth. $1 million in 1962–63 and Eth. $0·6 million in 1964–65.

Local communities have done a great deal to make up the losses from the education tax by voluntary contributions. In fact this is really regarded by the Government as another form of taxation, for local governors have been judged on the capability they show in getting these contributions out of the people. The Swedish International Development Agency has encouraged this approach by agreeing to match the amounts raised by local communities. This has certainly been successful in increasing the number of primary schools—by approximately 200 in the last few years. It does however mean that the Government has contributed virtually nothing to this sector.

Government contributions to education through the budget have been relatively impressive. Nonetheless there have been substantial differences between requests and allotments. The percentage of Government revenue going to the education sector has remained roughly constant since 1950, although there has been a substantial increase in the amount of aid from UNESCO, the World Bank and other sources. This must be seen in the light of increased enrolment throughout the system, with which expenditure has not kept pace. The *per capita* expenditure on education stood at Eth. $145 in 1955–56; by 1964–65 it was down to Eth. $86 and has been falling since. Inevitably the quality of the education has suffered. The fall in quality does not affect all sectors equally. The emphasis has remained on producing a fairly small selection into the university, and encouraging students to leave at the sixth, eighth and twelfth grade levels. While it is true that those involved in the educational system may want to see a much expanded system it has not been Government policy to encourage this.

As so often happens in this sort of situation, matters have got out of control. The pressures for local expansion of schools or for new schools have usually come from local people, with the result that a school is often built by them and then integrated into the ministerial system after completion. This operates at the junior secondary and secondary levels as well as the primary. An increasing number of students reach the sixth grade to find that there is no junior secondary school in the neighbourhood. The pressures operating here are not just desire for education, though this can be powerful; there is also the factor that in the urban centres where most schools are, there are no job opportunities. This has helped to produce the disturbances that have become so widespread in the last few years (see Chapter 8), for the "student troubles" have not been confined to the university students. They have involved every secondary school in the country at one time or another, as well as a number of primary schools.

The development of education and literacy has thus been held back because the actual aims of educational policy and the development needs do not coincide. The same criticism can be applied to the modernizing procedures that have developed throughout the Government institutions. To see modernization solely in terms of increasing bureaucracy, schools built and arms provided, and in terms of imperial or government control, is to misunderstand the needs of the country. The underlying problems have not been tackled and the opposition to imperial and aristocratic Shoan rule that has arisen from this failure is clear and increasing.

PART II. THE BASE OF ECONOMIC POWER

CHAPTER IV

Feudalism and Land Tenure

It has already been made clear that the basis of political power in Ethiopia is land. This is underlined by the country's dependence upon agriculture, as the figures show.[1] Official pronouncements also demonstrate it.

From any point of view, agriculture is dominant in Ethiopian life. Even after the end of the present Five Year Plan, which aims at diversifying the economy, it will remain by far the largest sector of activity in terms of the number of people gainfully occupied, in its total contribution to the G.D.P., in the absolute size of increase in value of production during the plan and, finally, by virtue of its dominance of Ethiopia's exports.[2] While the Third Five Year Plan ended in 1973, there is little reason to believe that the foregoing will be any less true in another ten years time, unless the new Government really does introduce fundamental land reform.

Something has already been said of the various forms of land holding and tenure that exist in the country. This chapter will elaborate on these and attempt to categorize the systems of tenure more completely, and to investigate the effects of mechanization. The forms of tenure that are to be found are not entirely traditional or feudal in their operation. Mechanized farming has been spreading, especially in the last few years, and with it the concomitant forms of capitalism. In the normal run of events it could obviously be expected that these would expand at the expense of the traditional forms—though the argument that follows will illustrate the proposition that the effects on Ethiopian society and feudal land tenure will be far less than might be expected in changing the society. There appears to have been a growing alliance between the feudal and commercial forces that has undercut the dynamics that would otherwise operate for change within the Ethiopian state.

Ethiopia is generally reckoned to have one of the most complex systems of land tenure in the world—in one province alone (Wollo) an estimate of one hundred and eleven types of tenure has been made.

However, many of the types are only marginally different. None-theless the complexity has played a major part in hindering any serious progress towards a reform of the system. It has made the task of applying measures of reform to the whole country impossible so far, and has been instrumental in limiting the effects of reform in other fields, especially in the area of taxation. But even more serious than the various types of tenure have been the attitudes of those involved in potential reforms.

There are two basic points that must be borne in mind when discussing Ethiopian land tenure. One is the split between the Amhara/Tigre highland areas of the north and centre and the non-Amhara provinces in the south and west. The latter were conquered towards the end of the nineteenth century when new patterns of ownership and holding were introduced. Secondly, land ownership and grants were originally based upon military service. This relates not only to the conquered provinces where military settlements set up the present patterns of ownership, it also provides the basis in the north as well. That the imperial grants of *gult* and *rist-gult* were of this type is fairly obvious. It is also true of the *rist*—family ownership as well. The genealogies date back to the seventeenth-century re-organization of the northern provinces after the disasters of the previous hundred years. Thus the connections between land, military service and class have been present for a long time, and are still very relevant, lying behind a great deal of present-day Government and imperial grants.

To take the Amhara/Tigre highlands first. These comprise the provinces of Gojjam, Begemeder, and Tigre, and parts of Wollo, the northern parts of Shoa, and the southern parts of Eritrea. With the exception of the last area the major form of landowning in these provinces is *rist*. The name is given to land theoretically brought into cultivation or ownership at some time in the past (judging by the genealogies this appears to have been about three hundred years ago). All the descendants (both male and female) of the individual founder are deemed to have a claim to a share. Theoretically the land should be divided equally among all the living descendants of the original founder of the family. In this sense the land belongs to the family and the members use it in only their lifetime. No user of any piece of it may sell it outside the family unless they all agree. It is this restriction on the individual's right and the theoretical insistence on all the family members having an equal share that has led to the *rist* system being described as communal.[3]

This is, however, somewhat confusing, especially as there is a genuine form of communal tenure in Eritrea (see below). Furthermore there is a marked divergence between theory and practice. Any piece of the family land that an individual uses is regarded by him as his own; and that same land will normally go, legally, to his children on his death. The only limitation on the individual's use is the sale to outsiders, and even this does not always operate. The ways round the limitations do depend, as does the amount of *rist* that any man may acquire through his potential claims, on the political status that he wields. Land gives power and position; and they in turn provide more power. Since the interlocking of the *rist* families by marriage is so considerable, and all may claim through both parents, all four grandparents and so on, the number of potential claims available to any single person is enormous.

Most claims are not usually activated, being too remote both in time and space. However in certain circumstances, which operated more in the past than they do now, when a man becomes an official these claims will be taken up. His new position makes all the difference between success and failure. The amount of *rist* land that any one branch of a family keeps thus depends to a considerable extent upon its political position. It is unlikely that, all other things being equal, any branch will lose all its land, though an individual may lose land to another member of the extended family. It would seem in fact that in a majority of cases, *rist* does descend from father to son unhindered. The way in which the offices of *chika shum, meslenie* and similar positions, descend in this order even when they are Government appointments and not heritable, supports this conclusion.[4]

It should be noted, however, that the Government's insistence today that payment of the land-tax signifies ownership, will affect the mobility of land within the *rist* system. This is undoubtedly one major reason why the opposition in these provinces to the imposition of land tax and tithe on a calculated basis has been so strong. The Government has been able to establish the normal pattern of these taxes in Shoa and parts of Wollo, but not in Gojjam, Begemeder, Tigre and Wag or Lasta. The attitudes were summed up by the Committee that reported to the Emperor on Land tax and tithe in 1943:

Gojjam. The attempt to levy taxation in accordance with the Land Tax Proclamation (of 1942) and the Tithe Instructions has

failed . . . The people are however said to be willing to pay a
fixed consolidated tax under a system instituted by *Ras* Imru
(Governor 1932–36) . . . *Tigre*. The system of taxation prescribed
by the Land Tax Proclamation and the Tithe Instructions cannot
be enforced.[5]

Nothing has changed since this report and the provinces concerned
still pay a consolidated tax or rather a fixed tribute based on the
province at large, one that is far lower than the regular tax would
be. The knowledge that any revision of the taxes would be to their
disadvantage certainly stiffens the *rist* owner's resistance to altera-
tions in the system.

As it is, the system works to the advantage of the landowner in
a variety of ways. The useful fiction of the original founder of the
land being the owner is maintained. The Government registration
of the land is thus in a ficticious name, or rather the name of a
deceased person. This enables a substantial number to avoid paying
the taxes that *rist* owners are liable to—the health and education
taxes, and the agricultural income tax. This last was resisted so
fiercely by the Gojjamis in 1967–68 that it is not collected from the
province at all. It is obvious that the failure to measure the actual
size of lands also works towards the consolidation of the traditional
landowners, especially the larger ones, for there is little doubt that
the estimates that are used are widely out of date and favour the
wealthy; they are of course the ones who usually carry out, or
influence, the estimates. Over and above the actual area of the lands
owned, the rate of land tax is also lighter—Eth. $32 per *gasha* for
fertile land in Gojjam, as opposed to the more normal Eth. $50 per
gasha.

The *rist* system of ownership has not however maintained itself
totally unchanged since the war. *Rist* owners do pay two of the
governments taxes—health and education—though these are not
strictly speaking land-taxes. There are also signs in Tigre that *rist*
divisions have been carried out as far as possible, that is, sub-
division of lands has gone so far that stabilization is appearing.
Younger members of the family are being forced off the land by the
shortage and there has therefore been a certain movement to the
towns, especially to Asmara, and to such areas as Setit Humera where
seasonal work at high wages is available.

The class element in *rist* ownership was summed up with reference
to Eritrea in the 1940s as follows:

Resti represents much more than an economic benefit. Its derivation from an original first occupation lends it an important social significance—that of a qualification for enhanced social status. The social status founded on *resti* possessions is permanent and inalienable, more so than the possessions themselves.[6]

The situation has changed little. This social aspect is also to be found in Tigre and there relates to the *balabat* class. The use of the word *restegna* has in fact disappeared as descriptive of this class in favour of *balabat* or *mekwanint*. It is true that *rist* in Tigre is also owned far more widely than by this class alone; but distinctions are drawn between original and what may be called secondary *rist*, that is *rist* owned by relatively new families.[7] This debasement has largely occurred through marriage to those who were not originally of *balabat* class, who have thus obtained claims to *rist* land that they would not otherwise have had. The sale of *rist* has also played a part in this, sometimes with the family's permission, sometimes without; and it can, and does, lead to long and complicated law suits. But it has not stopped such sales occurring, especially in the upheaval of the Italian occupation and subsequent events, including the *woyane* revolt of 1943. This all caused considerable stress to the *rist* system in Tigre, Gojjam and Begemeder, and helped to lessen some of the restrictions.

The changes have not, in fact, gone very far and for most landowners are probably unnoticeable. They may have had to apply a lot of pressure on the central government but the fact remains that the taxes are still collected in the old way; the lowest levels of the official hierarchy are still staffed by the same people, and, more importantly, so are the higher levels which supply the safeguard against the centralizing influence of increased taxation. So far the *rist* lands of all of the *rist* families are inviolate and this still remains the key to wealth, influence and position. Lands that have been sold, if they have, are only the peripheral parts of the family's *rist*—and these are the parts that tend to be involved in law suits anyway.

The *rist* ownership system thus has remained more or less unchanged though with a movement towards a strengthening of the individual elements in it. It is, in some areas, becoming close to such genuinely individual forms of tenure as exist in the non-*rist* areas, largely in the south and west. In these provinces the equivalent of *rist*, on a class level, is *siso*. This is a type of ownership that goes by a variety of names, all of which imply *balabat* ownership. Essentially *siso* is land that belonged to the aristocracy or the *balabats* of an area before the Shoan conquest under Menilek II. All the land was taken on the Emperor's behalf by the conquering general and it was then re-divided. In theory one third was then left for the former owner to re-acquire, "though actually the proportion varied from a third to a sixth".[8] The owner of *siso* lands was exempted from land tax, although he had to pay tithe and was eligible for military service. The land was however his own without any restrictions on sale, lease or mortgage. The freedom from the land tax was abolished in 1966 and the owner of *siso* is now liable for all taxes on the land, including health and education and agricultural taxes. These lands can now be classified as *gebbar* lands, lands on which persons paying the land tax are credited with ownership by the Government.

The other major traditional form of individual landholding was *rist-gult*. This was an inheritable grant made by the Emperor to the highest nobility or members of the royal house. It involved the permanent use of all the taxes due from the area granted, subject only to military service and the flat rate payment of Eth.$3·50 per *gasha* as tithe (this was also the figure that *siso* land was liable for). *Rist-gult* grants usually covered substantial areas where there might be a variety of other tenancies in operation. The grant did not necessarily invalidate these other tenancies or rights. *Rist* rights for example remain under *rist-gult*, becoming a more or less permanent and hereditary tenancy. While *rist-gult* was inheritable, the heir or heirs were normally expected to obtain imperial authorization for their succession; traditionally this involved the gift of a mule at least. There is no doubt that *rist-gult* grants may be compared with the European fief, and they were granted on a comparably large scale. They also provided for the use of similar judicial functions (as did *siso* grants) over the area controlled. Sub-infeudation to important followers was possible and was practised on the larger grants though this was only ever done on a lifetime basis, and the ultimate rights were retained in the hands of the original grantee. This form of holding was officially abolished in 1966, the actual agricultural producers being ordered to pay land tax and thus acquire ownership, and the judicial and administrative functions of the *rist-gult* owner being removed as well. So far this legislation has had no real effect, particularly in the matter of ownership, which has remained firmly in the hands of the former grantees or their heirs. One of the worst offenders in this respect has been the imperial family and there is little evidence that their *rist-gult* holdings have been affected by this order.

A similar form of grant that was also affected by the 1966 order was *gult*. This again was an imperial grant though it differed from *rist-gult* in being non-inheritable. It was given for a period of years or for life, usually to an important provincial governor in lieu of salary. It involved judicial and administrative functions and the obligation of military service. Where women were grantees of *gult* (or *rist-gult*) substitutes were provided for this. The grant of *gult* did not of course alienate the land rights of the others on the land within the area. The value of such a grant was considerable for the grantee gained the imperial rights of tax and dues for themselves. Some had to be handed on to the central authority, but it is not clear how much and local variations existed. An instruction relating to Gojjam, put out by the Ministry of the Interior in 1943 says, "he (the *gult* owner) shall receive one-third of the basic tax after collection of the taxes and levies is effected by the peasants".[9] The principal adviser to the same Ministry however stated in the same year that only the tithe was to be handed on to the Government.[10] In general it appears that the same amount was paid as in a *rist-gult* holding— that is Eth.$3·50 per *gasha*, and that the collected land tax, tithe and other dues were retained by the *gult* owner to compensate for his official functions, which often extended far beyond the *gult* area.

It has been mentioned that *gult* was not inheritable, and it might be expected therefore that those families that obtained *gult* would not build up the kind of power that *rist-gult* fiefs could create. In practice the Emperor was seldom strong enough to stop *gult* being given to the son of the previous recipient, any more than he was usually able to prevent the son of a former governor succeeding his father. A classic example of the way *gult* was inherited can be found in Tigre province. In the 1880s the Emperor Yohannis IV who was from Tigre, created a number of *gult* properties for his adopted son *Ras* Mengasha. Yohannis died in 1889 and *Ras* Mangasha continued to hold these *gults* until his death in 1906, in spite of two periods of imprisonment under the Emperor Menilek, and in spite of the fact that he was not, for much of this period, governor of Tigre. The exact area of these *gult* grants is uncertain but they appear to have amounted to over 1,000,000 hectares in some twenty-eight districts.[11] After *Ras* Mengesha's death his son Seyoum became governor of a part of Tigre. After various machinations concerned

with the overthrow of *Lij* Iyasu, Seyoum ended up as a *Ras*, a
governor of about half of the province and in 1918 he was granted
all of his father's *gult*. This he retained until his death in 1960, even
though he fell into disfavour in the forties and for five years was
removed from the governorship of the whole province which he
had acquired in 1941. After *Ras* Seyoum's death his son *Ras*
Mengesha was made governor of the province of Tigre and was still
in this position in 1974, taking over the *gult* properties when he became governor. As already mentioned the rights held by *gult* rulers
were officially abolished in 1966. Part of the problem over land in
the provinces has, however, been slow implementation of this
reform. This is not perhaps entirely suprising because those responsible for carrying out the change—the local officials—were often
holders of *gult* rights; the change was hardly in their interests.[12]

In the context of fiefs, the status of Church land also needs to be
considered, for taxes levied on Church lands do not go to the Government but to the Central Church Treasury or the individual churches.
Originally many grants to the Church appear to have been in the
nature of *gult* and as such temporary, but such properties rapidly
became permanent. They do retain some of the characteristics in
that Church control has not necessarily inhibited the continuation
of other tenures as well. Indeed it has not been uncommon for wealthy
landlords to give their land, or some of it, to the Church while
retaining all their own rights of inheritance on it. This involves
certain services being given to the Church—such as supplying a priest,
or other necessities for church services—and also paying land tax,
tithe and education tax to the Church. Such lands are not considered
eligible for either the cattle tax or the health tax, for neither are
collected by the Church. At first sight it would seem as though the
landlords would lose by this arrangement, having to provide
services as well as pay the taxes. In practice, since the services in
particular are handed on to the tenants, it is in their interest to
transfer such estates. Furthermore the services are frequently fairly
light, and the land taxes are not always paid at the official rate.

There are many varieties of Church holdings—specific names
being given according to the obligations laid upon the land—but
the most important ones are *semon*, used as a generic term to cover
most forms of holding under Church control, and Church *gult*
which is land granted by the Government though to a church or
monastery not an individual. It was sometimes given for a specific
period; though obviously it frequently became perpetual. It was

also customary that if the land was taken back an estate of equal worth was granted in its place. This *gult* was then normally granted to individual priests or deacons to farm during their lifetime, or during their time at the Church. It might also be farmed on this basis by lay tenants. After the death of the tenant, whether priest or lay, the Church had the right to re-grant it to another priest or layman. If it was held by a layman there might well be the obligation of supplying a priest to the church; for such obligations rested upon the land not upon the individual. Alternatively, the land not being "priest land", the obligations could be in the form of supplying candles, wax or other necessities to the church in order that the services were carried out properly.[13]

Semon land is land in which the primary or reversionary interest is held by the Church; and on which the Church collects land-tax, tithe and education tax. The most important distinction with Church *gult* is that some landowners retain the right to sell or sub-lease even after transferring the land to *semon;* and *semon* land is not normally in origin a Government grant. In addition to the usual taxes that the Church collects, there may be other obligations as with Church *gult*, ranging from paying for a priest to providing for decoration for a church. In fact the combination of taxes and services on Church land should be heavier than on other lands; though it seems that in the past the avoidance of military obligations outweighed this. One further point about *semon* is that the Church's interest is perpetual.

The independence of Church lands has been recognized by the Government in legislation passed in 1942. These regulations for the administration of the Church provide for the tax payable on Church lands to be used for the maintenance of the churches. "The tax on land given to a Church for any reason and which has thus come into the possession of the Clergy, shall be paid to the Treasury of the Church, and shall not be disposed of outside".[14] This is supported by the Land Tax Proclamation of 1944 which specifically exempts holders of *semon* land from the payment of the land tax—something the Government had neglected to do in the Land Tax Proclamation of 1942. This was further underlined in 1947 when it was laid down that the supposed abolition of services on land (made in 1944) did not mean that the

contributions towards the spiritual education imparted by the Church to the parishioners, construction of churches and in general fees given for the usual spiritual protection afforded by the Church to its Christian parishioners during life and death, as well as corn and firewood for the Church and salary for the store-keeper or any such works which shall be carried out by the local population in union are prohibited.[15]

Semon land has remained largely untouched by any changes in the administrative and financial structure; and the Church has thus retained its position as a main supporter of the country's feudal institutions. Possible opposition has been bought off by exempting Church lands from any attempts to tax them further.

Another form of individual landholding that deserves some consideration is the imperial estates, which are used for the upkeep of the imperial palaces, and to provide a source of patronage. The extent of these is a closely-guarded secret and estimates are difficult to come by. There are in fact several varieties of imperial lands, depending upon the services required from the tenants. Lands allocated for the preparation of food for the imperial palace in Addis Ababa were called *gann gebb*, for example. Under this heading one account lists sixteen districts all in Shoa.[16] The Emperor also owned extensive *hudad* lands in various parts of the country from which produce was also sent to the palace or was used to support imperial deputies in the provinces. Other types of imperial lands went under the names of *woregenu, balderas* and *bet iqa* lands, and for example 566 *gashas* of *woregenu* land are listed for Shoa.[17] In addition substantial quantities of former imperial lands are now held under *rist-gult* holding by other members of the immediate imperial family.[18] As far as can be discovered their rights have been unaffected by the abolition of 1966.

The problem of the extent of imperial lands is compounded by the confusion that exists with government lands. Until recently it is clear that no distinction was made at all. Even now there is no reason to believe that the Emperor himself makes any distinction. He certainly makes grants of Government land himself, but it is not obvious whether he does it in his capacity as head of the Government, or as the Emperor (who theoretically owns all the land in the country). The Government, however, makes the distinction even if it does not or cannot, prevent the Emperor from making grants of non-imperial land. This is perhaps a necessity from the imperial point of view, for opportunities to acquire land since the war have been limited. The growth of the bureaucracy has resulted in most of the land being channelled into the Ministries of the Interior and Land Reform for the purpose of re-distribution. The Emperor has therefore attempted to conserve what is clearly regarded as imperial land.[19]

The Government itself normally makes grants under two types of holding—*gebbar* and *maderia*. Due to historical circumstances these grants have been, and are, made largely in the non-Amhara areas of the empire, in the south and west and in the other peripheral areas to the north-west. *Gebbar*[20] is the name now given to land to which private ownership has been established by payment of the land tax. It is full, private and individual ownership with no limitations as regards sale or inheritance. The owner pays land tax and tithe and the health and education taxes. It is this type of holding that has replaced *siso* and *rist-gult* under the 1966 reform which removed exemptions. Most land owned in this way is found outside the northern areas where *rist* rights predominate. *Gebbar* ownership does not of course come exclusively from the Government and it may be acquired through sale, inheritance and so on.

Maderia is land granted by the Government to its employees in lieu of salary or as a pension for a period of years or for life. It is freed from the obligation of the land tax, but health, education and income tax must be paid. Although it remains Government land the grantee may place tenants on it and do anything with it except dispose of it by sale or through inheritance. As in the case of *gult* it is possible for a son to acquire his father's *maderia*. In addition *maderia* may be converted to *gebbar* under a series of regulations which relate essentially to the rank of the grantee. The amount granted in the first place depends upon the rank as well. Historically a great deal of *maderia* was granted at the time of the conquest of the south to the soldiers involved. At that time it was not granted according to size but according to the numbers of serfs that the land contained: a soldier getting from two to five; an officer from seven to ten; higher ranks from thirty to eighty and governors whatever they required, as many as hundreds and sometimes even thousands. This pattern of grant has remained although it has been formalised by a series of orders starting in 1942. By the first of these all who served at the battle of Maichew in 1936 were entitled to receive one *gasha;* and this was followed in the same year by an allowance of a *gasha* for patriots, exiles and the disabled. In addition *maderia* owners who were wounded in the war and who did not collaborate or who were patriots and exiles, were authorized to transfer one *gasha* to *gebbar* ownership. Two years later the categories were widened further to include all who had been soldiers and civil servants prior to 1936. They also were to receive one *gasha*. In 1958 all present members of the armed forces and the police, and in 1964 all civil servants, became eligible for grants of a *gasha* of *gebbar* land. Similarly various changes have been made in the amounts that may be transferred from *maderia* to *gebbar*. For example in 1967 Captains were given permission to change four *gashas* to *gebbar* lands, and lesser ranks relative amounts down to a *gasha* for the N.C.O.s. Special further additions have also been made from time to time—there was an order in 1966 allowing members of the Territorial Army in Wollo to change certain amounts of *maderia* land into *gebbar*, the quantity again depending upon rank.[21]

There is one other order that should be mentioned and it is, in theory, the most important. This is the 1952 order declaring that any landless and unemployed person may obtain half a *gasha* of unoccupied land. The potential significance of this order has been minimized by the difficulties that the potential recipients experience. It is necessary to provide proof of landlessness and unemployment, and to have this fact registered; the land has to be found on the ground and then registered at considerable cost.[22] These procedures are impossible for most individuals who would be eligible for these grants. Inevitably potential grantees often sell their privileges to those who can afford the procedure, that is, to those who are already possessors of land. These problems are reflected in the quantities of land actually granted under the orders. For example, under the orders of 1942, 1944 and 1952 a total of 32,940 *gashas* has been granted. Of this quantity 8 per cent has gone to the landless and unemployed in the period up to 1970; and 51 per cent to the armed forces and civil servants under the 1944 order. It might be noted that in the same time span, 1942–70, the Emperor made special grants of his own totalling 15,333 *gashas*.[23]

There is no doubt that the Government has seen the procedure of giving land to the elite groups as a primary way of securing support, and to a lesser extent, as a way of buying-off the potential opposition —the former ex-student radicals who normally obtain jobs within the bureaucracy. To this end land grants have more than doubled since the coup of 1960. Of the increase some 80 per cent has gone to members of the armed forces and the police, whose loyalty is vital to the Government.[24] Another element in these grants is that the Government and the Emperor have made their grants to different categories of people. The imperial grants are concentrated at the very top of the scale and go to the generals, to those with the highest titles, and to senators. The Government grants cover the remainder, particularly the civil servants and lower and middle ranks of the armed forces. This of course has been very much in line with the personal element in the Emperor's approach to Government and the concentration, that he encouraged, on the elite sector of the landowning aristocracy from which most of these figures come.

It is notable that the failure of this approach became visible only in 1974; and it required the unique circumstances of a major famine with a very high death toll and a very fast rate of inflation to break it down. Even then the army still protested its loyalty to the Emperor although disobeying his orders. Parliament also continued, while moving against the imperial position, to act in an essentially constitutional manner and to somehow regard the Emperor personally as above the conflict. This is a considerable tribute to his methods of control and their efficacy.

There are two other forms of Government land that should be mentioned—*mengist* and *gebretel*. *Mengist* is land that is registered as Government property. It may be leased to individuals or, as most of it is, left vacant. A great deal of *mengist* land is in fact inhabited by nomadic peoples who have no claim to it in the eyes of the Government.[25] This is land that is available for grants and most of the *maderia* and *gebbar* grants of the Government come out of *mengist* land. *Gebretel* is land that has been taken over by the Government because of a failure to pay the taxes on it. It then becomes Government land and can be granted out again under *maderia* or *gebbar* holding. It is possible for the original owner to reclaim it upon payment of the taxes owed plus a fine of equivalent value. There is however a significant proviso—that the land has not already been granted to another person in the meantime. This obviously gives ample opportunity for corrupt practices and was a major cause of unrest in Bale province in the early 1960s, contributing largely to the outbreak of the revolt there.[26]

There is finally the Eritrean form of communal landholding that is unique in the country.[27] This form of holding, in which all land belongs to the village, is known as *shehena* or *diesa*. All members of the village who have a house in it have a right to an equal share of the land. This is distributed at regular intervals—usually for three years, but sometimes seven years or even occasionally for the lifetime of the individual—by the *chika shum* and a group of elders under a lottery system. In order to ensure fairness the land is graded into the three categories of fertile, semi-fertile and poor. Each person takes his share of every category so he will end up with three fields. Younger members of the village who need land or newcomers are also eligible for shares though they will have to wait for one of the redistributions. This system, of course, precludes inheritance of land or its sale, though sales can be arranged at the decision of the whole village. This is in fact unlikely as the system depends upon a sufficient amount of land being available. Any given village can only support a certain number, otherwise the shares become too small. In recent years the shortage of land has often become acute and many younger members of these villages have been forced to leave and go elsewhere—usually to Asmara.

The origins of this system are obscure but it seems likely that it was started by the Italians. It is found in an area where *rist* was formerly predominant, and it is alien to the other highland tenures. Certainly it was extended, sometimes forcibly, by the Italians; and it was under Italian influence that it spread over into northern Tigre during the war. It also appears recent from the fact that the former *restegna/balabat* families often control the distribution within the villages. The elders are drawn from the families of the original inhabitants of the village and they tend to get a first share of the fields, before the general distribution. Nevertheless these villages do have a strong sense of corporate loyalty to the village lands. Absenteeism is unacceptable and a man who goes off loses his share. Even if he returns, he will be treated as a newcomer and will have to wait until the next redistribution before he can acquire a share again. Bad farming is also quickly checked and offenders can lose their lands.

The spread of this system is difficult today as it conflicts with the entrenched positions of the *balabat* families. As far as is known there have been no cases of villages where the system has been adopted except where there were no local families of *rist* owners, or where such families had virtually died out. This largely limits the possibilities to the marginal lands of western Tigre where such families are rare. The Government has shown no interest in such tenures—indeed quite the reverse. In Eritrea the possible spread of *shehena* is now a great deal more practicable, for in considerable areas to the west of Asmara the land tenure system has been totally disrupted by the creation of fortified villages as part of the attempts to put down the guerilla movement. This has necessitated many adjustments in the land arrangements and a good deal of land has gone out of cultivation for the time being. There is, however, no sign that the administration of the province has had any thoughts about long term re-adjustments in the land owning system, although the opportunity is unlikely to recur.

This analysis of the land system has so far neglected the primary producer on most of the land—the tenant. It is difficult to be sure of the actual number of tenants in Ethiopia as neither the Ministry of Land Reform surveys nor the census have covered most of the country on the ground. The estimates for the Ministry surveys are worked out on the basis of sample studies only and are unlikely to be any more accurate than the population figures which were substantially worked out on the basis of aerial photography. The Ministry of Land Reform's figures do not check internally either; it would seem that they have both underestimated the number of tenants and over-estimated the number of landowners.[28] Nevertheless, using these figures for all the provinces (except Bale and Eritrea) there are 1,622,975 owned holdings; 1,495,939 tenant holdings; and 446,660 landless households. These figures are for rural areas only. So at a minimum, approximately 42 per cent of the holdings are tenant owned (see also Table 11). One immediate adjustment that could be made is that the Ministry's surveys do not appear to classify *rist* owners as tenants when these lands are on Church land or on *rist-gult* land. Inclusion of these as tenants would bring the percentage of tenant holdings up to at least 65 per cent, and probably nearer 80 per cent.

The rent that these tenants pay varies both in quantity and in form. Since the war there has been the spread of a monetary economy— before the war almost all tenants paid their rent in kind. It is however illustrative of the slow spread of capitalism that so many still do pay in kind today. Table 12, although subject to the same strictures as all the Ministry of Land Reform's figures, gives a general impression and minimum percentages of the various methods of rent payment. There are approximately 50 per cent of tenant holdings that pay rent on an exclusively crop-sharing basis.

The quantity paid depends almost entirely upon the landlord. The Civil Code, promulgated in 1960, did provide some guide-lines, but it does not limit the amount. There is a proviso that rent in kind is presumed to be 50 per cent of the harvest; and that it must not rise above 75 per cent where no agreement has been reached between the tenant and the landlord. It does not however forbid "agreements" to be made, if the tenant can be persuaded to pay more. On average it appears that about one-third of the tenants actually pay at least

50 per cent in kind: Gojjam, 31 per cent; Shoa, 8 per cent; Arussi, 39 per cent; Wollega, 28 per cent; Begemeder, 38 per cent; Wollo, 63 per cent. These estimates of rent provide only minimum figures for the tenants' liabilities, whether they pay in cash or crop.

Legally speaking there is no doubt that the landlord is liable for all the land taxes, and for the health, education and agricultural income taxes. In practice, however, it is the normal custom for the tenant, especially where share-cropping exists, to put aside one-tenth of his crop to cover the landlord's tithe. The rent is then paid out of the remaining nine-tenths. This shifting of the burden of the tithe from landlord to tenant took place in 69 per cent of the districts in Shoa. It was also noted extensively in Hararge, Kaffa, Tigre and Illubabor. It is true that the tithe has been abolished since 1967; but even the Government admits that it is still collected extensively, and implicitly recognizes the legality of this by budgeting it into the revenue estimates.

TABLE 11

Distribution of Tenants

Province	Rural population	Wholly rented	Part owned part rental	Total rentals
Arussi	690,600	307,764	50,724	358,488
Begemeder	1,087,200	97,848	62,232	160,080
Gomu-Goffa	583,300	249,412	21,633	271,045
Gojjam	1,344,500	172,785	95,024	267,809
Hararge	1,435,570	703,429	71,778	775,207
Illubabor	515,375	376,224	10,307	386,531
Kaffa	969,100	571,769	29,073	600,842
Shoa	3,585,000	1,828,350	573,600	2,401,950
Sidamo	1,987,590	735,408	39,751	775,159
Tigre	1,410,800	98,848	257,218	356,066
Wollega	1,064,100	574,738	49,715	624,453
Wollo	2,061,800	360,552	474,214	834,766
Totals	16,734,935	6,076,927	1,735,269	7,812,396
		(36%)	(10%)	(46%)

Source: Ministry of Land Reform and Administration: Reports on Land Tenure Surveys of Provinces.

The transfer of tax obligations is not confined to the tithe. In one district of Sidamo province it has been found that 89 per cent of the tenants actually paid the land tax for their landlords, in addition to the rent.[29] There is no reason to suppose that the example from Sidamo is unique. Indeed the whole tenure system in Ethiopia leads one to expect that these are the norm, especially on the larger estates. The land-owning class have shown themselves adept at ignoring the abolition of *rist-gult* and *gult* privileges, and the collection of land taxes and other dues by the landlord still goes on—as indeed it still does on Government *maderia* tenancies.

As can be seen in Table 12 only a small percentage of tenants still pay rent in services. These were generally rendered illegal in 1941 and more specifically by the Land Tax Proclamation of 1944: "Any other taxes, services and fees heretofore payable are hereby repealed, and the taxes hereafter specified are substituted". Since the proclamation referred to the land tax, it did by implication exempt from this provision all lands that did not pay land tax—*rist-gult*, *gult* and *siso*, *semon* and *maderia*, which between them probably accounted for a majority of tenants. In 1966 the abolition of services was carried a stage further when the special privileges of *rist-gult*, *gult* and *siso* were abolished.

TABLE 12

Rental Payments

Province	Cash only	Cash and crop	Crop	Service
	%	%	%	%
Arussi	7	1	92	—
Begemeder	30	3	66	1
Gomu-Goffa	70	6	14	10
Gojjam	24	2	74	—
Hararge	42	11	47	—
Illubabor	66	9	25	—
Kaffa	64	5	31	—
Shoa	15	3	82	—
Sidamo	84	3	13	—
Tigre	5	5	89	1
Wollega	48	12	37	3
Wollo	9	6	84	1

Source: Ministry of Land Reform: Land Tenure Surveys.

6—TDL * *

However these various abolitions have left one very large area
in which services remain as a major part of the tenure system—
the *semon* lands of the Church. There is little evidence that services
have been done away with on the large estates, or that local officials
have ceased to demand them. The services that still continue in this
way are onerous and many. They include free labour on the landlord's own farming area, usually at the most critical time of the
year, the harvest. The tenant is also expected to provide his labour
for transporting the landlord's crop; to gather fuel and herd his
cattle; to construct the *balabat*'s house, fencing and granaries; to
provide domestic service at times of festivals or special celebrations,
or, most commonly as an alternative to this, supply offerings of
grain and drink. These in particular are dictated by social custom
and they are provided to local officials as well as to landlords.
Services also apply, though to a lesser extent, on lands held from the
government by *maderia* tenure. There are often special "voluntary"
police duties attached to these. In fact the Government recognizes
and encourages the continuation of services by exempting *maderia*
lands from payment of the land tax. Under the circumstances it is
hardly surprising that services are still demanded.

Perhaps the most difficult of the dues that a tenant finds himself
liable to is the payment of fees for the renewal or acquisition of a
tenancy. This is a major factor in the generally uncertain situation
of a tenant. Although there is not much evidence as to how often
this is done, in Tigre it was practised in thirteen out of the twenty
woredas (for six *woredas* up to 25 per cent; for five *woredas* 75 per
cent of the tenants; in two it was 100 per cent), and it was common
in Hararge and Shoa. It is a system that is encouraged for obvious
reasons by the landlord, and there is no doubt that in certain areas
tenancies are virtually put up to the highest bidder.

TABLE 13

	No contracts	Verbal fixed	Verbal non-fixed	Written fixed	Written non-fixed
Begemeder	4,100	1,600	21,500	200	500
Gomu-Goffa	4,700	—	46,000	100	2,200
Hararge	23,800	700	94,660	810	4,420
Illubabor	3,450	400	75,128	150	4,875
Wollega	17,200	1,000	82,400	2,000	10,600

Source: Ministry of Land Reform Sample Surveys.

This is coupled with the failure of most landlords to provide written agreements for their tenants. In 1960 the Ministry of Agriculture was empowered to draw up model contracts for tenancies but very little progress has yet been made. It should be noted that even where written contracts do exist, a fixed period of tenure is extremely rare. This of course allows more freedom of manoeuvre for the landlord, and it has been particularly abused in recent years with the onset of mechanized farming. The lack of written leases, and leases without a fixed length of tenure, facilitates the termination of leases. It is noticeable that some of the greatest landlords refuse to give written leases, presumably for this reason. A well-known offender in this respect is *Ras* Mesfin Sileshi, perhaps the largest private landlord in the empire. Another conspicuous offender is the imperial family; it is instructive to see that on certain imperial estates the administrators have been known to refuse the tenants written leases. They have also enforced the payment of tithe as well as income tax and rent, and insisted on services on their fields. Not surprisingly it has sometimes been found necessary to keep private prisons for trouble makers.[30]

One has only to compare the legal aspects of termination of tenancy to see that the Civil Code has legislated largely in favour of the landowner. The landowner may terminate if the tenant defaults on his rent, though he has to give two months' notice. A new landlord may give three months' notice of termination without reason when he acquires the land. A case of serious illness is acceptable for termination, though six months' notice and refund of rent is required. The landowner may also apply to the courts for ending a tenancy if the tenant defaults on his obligations, whatever they may be.[31] It should be emphasized that in any court case the tenant is likely to be at a disadvantage, for those trying the case are certain to be landowners themselves. In many areas it is equally common for no notice to be given of eviction. In one *awraja* of Hararge province, "Landlords are entitled to evict their tenants on any pretext at any time before the latter have sown their plots with seeds. They may also evict their tenants after the latter have farmed or even harrowed their plots. They may also evict them at any time after harvest."[32]

It is of course true that the tenant may also terminate his tenancy, and he is supposed to get compensation for any improvements he may have made at a rate of nine times the rental value increase. It is difficult to establish how much this may be practised but figures for the provinces of Hararge, Begemeder, Illubabor, Gomu-Goffa

and Wollega suggest that it is probably rare. In these provinces, out
of a total of 304,110 tenancies, compensation was payable on only
27,450 of them—that is, only on 9 per cent. Even when compensation
is payable there are various ways to stop the tenant getting the full
value. Compensation on coffee land is usually given on the basis of
the value when the tenant leaves. If the coffee trees are young this
takes no account of the future potential growth which would greatly
increase the value.[33]

Absentee landlordism also plays a significant part in encouraging
exploitation of the tenant. This is particularly the case in the south
and west where the very big estates have been built up.

TABLE 14

Province	Percentage of Landlords absent	Percentage Land owned
Arussi	28	27
Bale	15	12
Gomu-Goffa	10	42
Hararge	23	48
Kaffa	18	34
Shoa	35	45
Sidamo	25	42
Wollega	26	28
Wollo	27	13
Illubabor	42	—

Source: Ministry of Land Reform Sample Surveys.

The average absenteeism for these provinces thus comes to 25 per
cent of the landlords owning an average of 33 per cent of the land.
Actual figures are almost non-existent; indeed there is very little
doubt that many of them have no clear idea of the extent of their
holdings. One estimate claims that *Ras* Mesfin Sileshi has 50,000
gashas (2 million hectares) in Kaffa and Illubabor, plus substantial
estates in Shoa, and Hararge.

One further point should be made. In a share-cropping situation,
even assuming the share is at 50 per cent, the tenant will receive only
half of the value and effect of any improvement in yields. Since
in many cases the rent is in fact higher the tenant will get correspondingly less for his efforts. The inducement to improve production
is thus almost minimal; especially when compared to the owner-

farmer or to the tenant with a fixed rental agreement who would be able to keep any increased production.

The Ethiopian small farmer, whether he is tenant or small free-holder, also suffers from the size and fragmentation of his holdings. In any analysis of the agricultural scene the small size of the holdings is immediately striking. Table 15 gives the size of holdings in twelve provinces (Eritrea and Bale are excluded) for a total of 3,118,914 holdings. 95 per cent of them are three hectares or less. This probably gives an exaggerated picture for the calculations were based upon measured fields and would certainly involve underestimation of the unmeasured ones. The pattern however appears to agree with other sources. The Third Five Year Plan made the point that 90 per cent of the peasant farmers had less than five hectares each and that 66 per cent farmed less than half a hectare. On top of these small farms there is an enormous amount of fragmentation, and although the amount does vary from province to province the majority of holdings are held in two, three or four parcels (Table 16).

TABLE 15

Size of Holdings

Province	up to 10 %	10 to 20 %	20 to 30 %	30 plus %
Arussi	31	29	20	20
Begemeder	70	22	5	3
Gomu-Goffa	92	6	2	—
Gojjam	54	30	10	6
Hararge	76	16	5	3
Illubabor	69	21	3	7
Kaffa	76	19	4	1
Shoa	45	27	13	15
Sidamo	91	7	1	1
Tigre	68	21	6	5
Wollega	65	24	7	4
Wollo	80	14	4	2
Average	68	20	7	5

In thousands of square metres (10,000 square metres=1 hectare).

To use the word "serfdom" in describing the situation of the Ethiopian peasant is perhaps over-stating the case, as serfdom strictly speaking applies to those who are bound to the land, which

TABLE 16

Fragmentation of Holdings

Province	1 parcel	2	3	4	5	6	7	8	9
Arussi	26	20	23	15	8	4	2	2	—
Begemeder	19	25	27	16	8	5			
Gomu-Goffa	47	32	14	5	2				
Gojjam	26	27	24	12	6	3	1	1	
Hararge	40	31	18	7	1	3			
Illubabor	28	24	20	16	7	3	1	1	
Kaffa	38	23	20	12	5	2			
Shoa	32	23	17	12	6	4	3	3	
Sidamo	65	23	8	3	1				
Tigre	16	25	20	16	7	6	4	6	
Wollega	26	21	20	13	10	4	3	2	1
Wollo	19	24	23	14	9	5	2	4	

In percentages.
Source: Ministry of Land Reform Land Surveys.

the Ethiopian peasant is not. In practical respects, however, the average tenant has little choice other than staying on the land. Despite his apparent insecurity of tenure, the average tenant has probably inherited his tenancy, for peasant mobility is limited. Part of the reason is undoubtedly that, as mentioned earlier, the pressure from society is towards keeping one's place. Church and State combine to this end. And the alternatives are hardly alluring. Other land is virtually unobtainable and when it is it tends to be semi-desert or marginal arable land, and usually far distant. When pressures become intolerable, movement does take place. In 1965–66 many thousands left Wollo province because of famine. They moved right across the highlands into Gojjam in search of new land. Most ended up in the barely usable lands of western Gojjam or across the Blue Nile in northern Wollega. The present famine in Wollo has had a similar effect, as did the previous major disaster in 1958–59, also in Wollo. But given normal circumstances the pressures on the peasant do tend to encourage him to stay rather than to move.

In the last few years a further element has been introduced into the agricultural situation—mechanization, coupled with more modern techniques and marketing arrangements. As yet this is not very widespread and has had little effect on the majority of tenants

DEVELOPMENT IN ETHIOPIA

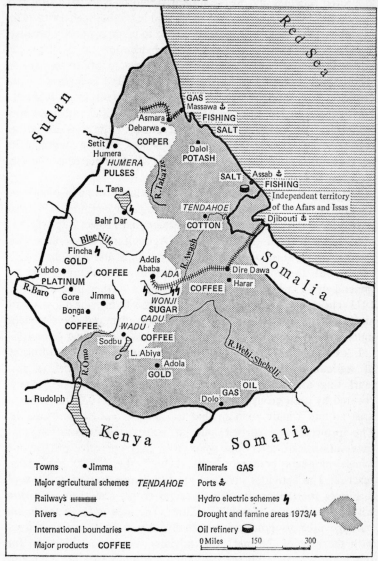

Towns ● Jimma	Minerals **GAS**
Major agricultural schemes *TENDAHOE*	Ports ⚓
Railways ▨▨▨▨▨	Hydro electric schemes ⚡
Rivers 〜〜〜	Drought and famine areas 1973/4
International boundaries ➤➤➤	Oil refinery 🛢
Major products **COFFEE**	0 Miles 150 300

or landlords. It has been confined largely to the Government-sponsored schemes and to the largest landlords who have seen the profits that mechanization can bring and have the finances to take advantage of it. As usual figures are hard to come by, partly because there is a considerable amount of mechanization taking place on private lands, and the average tenant is extremely loth to talk about his landlord; indeed any conversation about land is regarded with suspicion and thought to presage increased taxation or eviction. The majority of law cases in Ethiopia are connected with land and boundaries. However it is clear that most of the mechanization that has occurred is in the southern provinces, where a minimum 50 per cent of the farmers are tenants and at least 90 per cent of them farm less than three hectares.

The major Government scheme that is aimed, even in theory, at the poorer farmers is the Minimum Package Programme. This was started in 1971 and is run by the Extension and Project Implementation Department of the Ministry of Agriculture. It operates with Swedish and Danish aid. AID, the World Bank and FAO have also helped with funding. It was begun with nine programmes and by the end of 1972 there were eighteen, with a further nine added in 1973. The aim of each of these programmes is to provide a lower cost alternative to the large scale and more advanced development units that have been set up at Chilalo and Wollamo (see below).

For each area designated as a minimum package area the Ministry of Agriculture provides five agricultural extension workers, five marketing assistants and a supervisor. The number of farmers covered by each group is ultimately meant to be 10,000 in a given area around a main road so that transport facilities are available. The projects are carried out in stages. Demonstration and observation lead, after four years, to a fully operative programme whose numbers gradually increase until the 10,000 have been reached. The activities involved are the demonstration and use of fertilizers for the production of cereal crops, and their provision with the assistance of credit facilities. The idea is for a minimum package area to graduate eventually into a co-operative society with the help of the marketing advisers. The time laid down for this is three years, and the individual credit schemes are supposed to come to an end at that point.

The most important element of this is the credit scheme, and in an attempt to appeal to the poorer farmers and tenants, facilities are limited to those who farm on twenty hectares or less. However the terms are rather hard—each borrower has to supply two guarantors and, if he is a tenant, a written lease from his landlord as well as a written permission for him to partake in the programme. The credits for seeds, fertilizers and farm implements are in kind, but repayments are in cash over a year plus two months. The interest rate works out at 12 per cent. Furthermore the down-payments required are 25 per cent for fertilizer and 50 per cent in the case of seeds. These terms are necessary because the funds come through the Agricultural and Industrial Development Bank which is required to lend at a competitive rate. The Bank has also enforced a provision that if 25 per cent of the creditors default in any area the funds will be called in and the programme must come to an end in that district.

By definition these conditions actually prevent most tenants and peasant farmers from participating in the scheme, as they lack the necessary finance. While there are no figures on specific incomes at the village level, the Ministry of Finance's estimate that most revenue for the Agricultural income tax comes from those in the lowest level of the scale (under Eth.$300) suggests that the vast majority of farmers must have incomes below this figure. An estimate of 75 per cent of farmers at this level does not seem too high; and 50 per cent of those probably earn half of this or even less in cash.

The Minimum Package Programme thus excludes most of those who would be expected to benefit most from it. A further point is that many of those who do participate are actually landowners with considerably more than the limit of twenty hectares. Some of these inconsistencies are explained by both the innaccuracy of official estimates of land area and by the fact that many landowners do not know the extent of their own lands with any degree of precision. A common method of getting on to a programme is, however, to supply tenants with a written lease and agreement, send them to make the down-payments for seed and fertilizer, and on their return take the lease back from them as well as the seeds and fertilizer, which are then used by the landlord. The fact that the tenant may then default on the credit facility does not really affect the landlord who has acquired free gifts as another "service" from the tenant. In one Minimum Package area, around Sheshamane, the defaulters numbered 23 per cent of those who had taken loans in 1972. In the same year in the nearby area of Neghele the percentage was even higher—31 per cent. In both cases it appears that the high figures are substantially due to chicanery by larger landlowners.[34]

The use and availability of fertilizer has also encouraged the spread of mechanization in these areas. The Sheshamane district had around eighty-five mechanized farms by the end of 1972, all of which have been started since 1968. Most of these farms are on contracted Government or imperial lands—the late Prince Sahle Selassie was a very substantial landowner around Neghele (in Shoa province), and, to the east of Sheshamane, Princess Tegnagna-work is also a sizeable landowner, with a 200 hectare farm and a large forest concession which is being turned over to coffee. The increase in mechanized farms, which covered at least 20,000 hectares in 1971, has led to many evictions. The number has been calculated at around 750 families between 1968 and 1971, and there is every reason to suppose that they are continuing at a rate of about 200 families a year. The town of Neghele became a garrison point for units of the regular army in 1971, mainly as a result of the growth of disorder in the area consequent upon the evictions. Evicted tenants have few alternatives. Some have managed to remain in the area to become seasonal labourers; or to work in sawmills in the nearby forest concessions. Sheshamane, the nearest sizeable town, has absorbed some. A substantial number have turned to banditry, and there have been a considerable number of incidents in the district in the years 1970–72.

Obviously a percentage of the dispossessed tenants do drift to Addis Ababa, which is the most likely place to find work if it is available at all. There are two other alternatives that are relatively common. One is to stay in the area to try to out-bid another tenant at the tenancy renewal, which is not infrequently a yearly ordeal for the tenants. With the increased availability of tenants landlords are becoming prone to encourage this for obvious reasons. Another possibility is to move away in an attempt to acquire poor, unused lands in more remote areas. This depends upon the province to some extent. Shoa and Sidamo are not very good possibilities, whereas Kaffa and Gomu-Goffa are. The problems of such uprooting are, however, considerable and most peasants hesitate before taking a step that involves considerable travel. It is after all easier to squat on unused lands in Shoa or Sidamo of which there are large areas, both Government and private. This of course can lead to trouble when the landlord tries to activate his rights. It is, however, a quite common if temporary solution to the problem of dispossession.

Eviction has also been a marked feature in the much bigger and more comprehensive agricultural development scheme in Chilalo *awraja* in Arussi province. This is the largest of the Government projects—other development schemes like the Awash Valley Authority and the Setit Humera development are essentially Government-organized private developments. The Chilalo Agricultural Development Unit (CADU) was started in 1968 to provide for "economic and social development throughout the project area". It might be mentioned that the original 1966 report put it differently and claimed that the aims were to "develop the ability of the local people to deal with their own problems and to competently lead the progress of their society". The actual practical details of the project are similar to the Minimum Package Programmes which were developed from the CADU experience. Innovations included new inputs of seeds, fertilizers, crops, improved livestock, tools and equipment. New techniques for planting and animal husbandry are taught. Trained personnel were brought in at an intensive level— the project is run under the auspices of Swedish assistance (SIDA). Credit facilities were at first available to any farmers, but in 1970 a limit of up to twenty-five hectares for landowners and forty-five hectares for tenants was imposed. Finally marketing facilities were organized, especially storage and selling arrangements.

The first extension areas were set up in 1967 and they now cover most of the *awraja*. The figures illustrate some of the impressive advances that have been made in production. In 1967–68 480 quintals of grain were brought from the farmers; by 1970–71 the amount had risen to 10,000 quintals. In 1967–68 production of milk was 4,450 litres; by 1969–70 this had risen to 311,126 litres. In 1968 there were 189 farmers in the credit programme and by the end of 1971 there were a total of 14,146. There has also been a growing involvement of tenants using the credit facilities. Only 17 tenants were participating in 1968; by 1971 the number had risen to 4,426.[35]

The adverse effects of CADU'S operations have however already become clear; clear enough for SIDA to threaten to withdraw its aid unless changes in tenancy relations are made. As one report said: "It is difficult to see how the changes that arise from the project can be anything but beneficial to landowners". Landowners in the *awraja* have increasingly become large-scale commercial farmers either taking advantage of the facilities available or learning by example. Mechanization increases have been dramatic, and in the northern areas of the *awraja* 25 per cent was under mechanical farming by 1970—the fastest growth being on the lands of those with more than twenty hectares. Of this area of 10,000 hectares some 44 per cent is worked by modern farmers who have taken up contracts to work the land. This is a further development that has occurred since CADU began operation and there has been a growth of contract farming as outsiders have become aware of the investment potential of relatively large-scale farms.

The increased involvement of tenants in the credit scheme has provided a double gain for the landowners. Increases in rents can be acquired out of the improved harvests, since the tenancies are largely share-cropping. The improved returns have also led to an increased demand for rental of the land, and this has of course driven rents up. On top of the rising rents the tenants have also been at the receiving end of a considerable increase in evictions. One area of northern Chilalo provided figures of some 500 evictions in 1969–70; and a projection based on this suggests that by 1975 around 68 per cent of the tenants will have been ousted. Furthermore a substantial number of the smaller landowners are finding themselves in the same situation.[36]

CADU's administrators are aware of the problems and as a start some 200 tenants have been resettled in an unoccupied southern area of the *awraja*. This is only a token answer, however, as the project has no facilities to do it on a larger scale. In any case resettlement has inevitably to take place on inferior or unfarmed land. As a result most evicted tenants have apparently left the *awraja*, though a minority have stayed to provide seasonal contract labour. The effects have not been limited to evictions, but have also created widespread social disruption in the general area. Markets have had to be changed or abandoned as mechanization has cut across and closed some of the traditional routes; and the traditional stock breeding of the area has begun to decline.

The other large-scale Government project of this type is the Wollamo Agricultural Development Unit (WADU). This started later than CADU, becoming effective only in 1970 and it is largely financed through the World Bank. It is similar in scope to the Chilalo project, but there are differences partly due to the geographical nature of the area. WADU includes a settlement project in the lowland area of the *awraja*. Another major distinction is that the Wollamo administration has started from a position that credit is only to be given to a limited number of farmers. WADU also intends to start intensive dairy farms. The implications of the project however show that little has been learnt from CADU's experiences over land tenure and tenancy. The benefits are already largely falling to the landlords, particularly in the highland part of the scheme where the area is densely populated and competition for tenancies is already acute.[37]

WADU does have some alternative in its settlements in the lowland areas around Lake Abiya. The programme here is first to organize the 700 families that have been settled for some time and then to provide the land and organization for another 1,050. The idea of settlement in this area long predates the existence of WADU. The *awraja* governor in the late 1950s—Germame Neway—began the settlement on unused Government land. After the attempted coup of 1960 this settlement was deliberately disbanded. It was re-started in 1965, and when WADU was begun the area was incorporated into it. The increased number of settlers that WADU is going to put into the area have only just begun to be sent there. Not all are from the highland area of the *awraja*. Some 25 per cent of the settlers are to come from elsewhere. All potential settlers will have to be landless. The farms they receive will be five or six hectares in size and the project has estimated that this will allow for a net income of around Eth. $430 per annum. The farming area is thought suitable for cotton and peppers, both of which will provide seasonal labour as well as a cash crop. The settlers will also have full access to all WADU facilities; and all will be able to acquire credit up to the limit of Eth. $500. In addition to the repayment of credit, settlers will also be liable, four years after taking possession, for an annual sum of Eth. $58 to be paid to the project to cover basic costs, plus an interest rate of 7 per cent. This payment is to continue for twenty years. Although the land situation has not yet been clarified there is a supposition that at the end of this period the land will become freehold to the settlers.[38]

Another type of project that may be loosely classified as Government-organized is the scheme at Setit Humera in the north-west corner of Begemeder province. This actually began in the late 1950s as a private occupation of some lands that were unused except for seasonal grazing. By the end of 1971 it contained some 500 farmers and about 700,000 hectares were occupied; and a further 50,000 were being employed as seasonal workers, largely from the depressed areas of Eritrea and Tigre. The weeding, harvesting and threshing is largely done by hand; however, the area is one of the most highly mechanized in the country. Tractors are used not only for basic cultivation and clearance work, but they are also a necessity for travel especially during the rainy season. Another feature of Humera is that there is now a co-operative society there, with a membership drawn almost entirely from the smaller farmers in the east of the area who were the original users of the area; it has proved to be a considerable success.

Although most of the earlier settlements were on the basis of squatting, the Government now handles land allocation in the district, though in a rather haphazard way. Until recently there were two places to apply for land—the *woreda* district office at Humera, and the provincial office at Gondar, from which an order could be sent to the *woreda* with a request for land to be granted. This latter procedure has now been stopped and the main method is by application at Humera itself, though it is not impossible to obtain a grant from Addis Ababa. Considerable problems have also arisen over land grants, for until the end of 1972 no efforts were made to delineate the size of the grant. It was only done by reference to the surrounding owners.

A considerable number of the holdings are in fact absentee, and although the Government has advertised for landless citizens to take up land there, a large quantity has been taken by absentee landlords of the highest class—one suggestion is that the figure is as high as 55 per cent of all grants.[39] The land remains Government land as no land tax is paid, and it may thus be classified as *maderia* land, though this has not been made clear. Government intervention in the area is now becoming more marked as a whole, however, with the establishment of a World Bank-financed farm project. A bridge has been constructed across the Takazze river and a new road built from Gondar—in an attempt to pull the marketing arrangements of the district away from Asmara (though the road to Asmara has not always been safe due to Eritrean Liberation Front activity.) Water supplies and town development are also under way and an experimental farm is being set up.

Apart from the former claimants to the land, who have received their land in *gebbar* tenure, the general impression of the Humera development is that it is providing lands for the already wealthy through Government grants. Essentially the majority of those who settle there are interested in exploitative farming practices; the more so because of the uncertainties of the land situation. It is also a high cost area, dependent upon mechanization and seasonal labour; capital intensive farming is obviously necessary. While it is true that the Government has called for landless settlers, the paucity of arrangements, credits and other facilities has so far made this an impossibility. The need to claim land at Humera itself is enough of a bar to most landless candidates and it is difficult for any except the elite to apply. This of course may change now that the World Bank has become involved in the area, but there is no doubt that an elite structure has already been established.

An example of another type of Government settlement, one organized by the Ministry of National Community Development,[40] gives an even clearer idea of the attitudes involved in the settlement of landless citizens, and their place in development. At Shemena Kedida in Sidamo, some 103 farms have been established on 15 *gashas*. The conditions for accepted applications were severe, for an Amharic literacy test was included—something that would automatically exclude most of the local people who are Sidama or Oromo. Costs are also high. Repayments for the facilities begin in the third year and a total of Eth. $350 has to be repayed in three annual instalments. It is unlikely that the settlers will be in a position to do this—the main crop is maize and marketing is difficult because of the problem of transport to the nearest town, Awasa, some 33 kms. away on a bad road. The settlement is also constrained by size—only another 10 *gashas* is available. It should be emphasized that until 1968 there were about 200 *gashas* of unused Government land around. Since the settlement started however this has all been given away to others attracted by the opening of a road and the promise of a water supply. Virtually all the owners of these *gashas* are absentees; they do of course block any further expansion by the settlement.[41]

The biggest Government development project is on the Awash River. In 1962 the Awash Valley Authority was set up under a Government agreement with the U.N. for a full survey of the whole river. The Authority is now an autonomous public authority, charted as a perpetual corporate body; its control extends over the planning and administration of the valley and its water rights, and it runs a number of power schemes, irrigation and land utilization developments. It is the only body of its kind in the country and the only one charged to develop all the resources of an entire region.

The A.V.A. had a good start for when it was set up the first hydro-electric power station had already been built at Koka, and the Wonji sugar estate was fully functional. Since then two more hydro-electric stations have been put up and the valley provides 64 per cent of the entire supply for the power authority. A.V.A. also regulates the water levels—though not always successfully as can be seen from the flooding in 1973. Approximately 52,000 hectares have so far been brought under irrigation. The majority of these are in the large foreign-financed Tendaho cotton plantations and Wonji and Metahara sugar plantations. There are also a number of smaller private firms which produce bananas, cotton, maize and other cash crops. It is reckoned that there are a further 123,000 hectares that could be developed for agriculture and livestock in the next ten years—the estimated cost would be Eth.$420 million. When the whole scheme is operative the estimates for gross annual production are Eth.$600 million. In 1971–72 the output was Eth.$120 million. This is Eth.$16 million more than the previous year.

In 1973 there were a total of twenty-seven large and medium size agro-industrial enterprises functioning in the valley. The majority of these are private as the A.V.A. concentrates on providing a range of extension services including credit and the basic infrastructure for settlement projects. Examples are the Melka Sidi farm—52 per cent Italian-financed; three farms at Ambash, Algeta and Sulele—owned by ex-Agricultural College graduates; and Abadir farm which has Israeli finance. The A.V.A. controls some of the other projects—the settlement farms at Amibara and Dubti, though these are still small. Amibara is due to be enlarged soon with the settlement of 800 nomadic Afar families—in 1973 only 240 families were settled. Most of the land will however go to concessionaires from the highlands who will be given small farms. Altogether some 10,000 hectares has been earmarked for this with a further 14,000 undergoing a feasibility study. These areas will take up most of the area expected to be irrigated by 1978.[42]

While the valley, especially in its lower reaches, is not heavily populated the least successful element of the whole development has been the resettlement of the nomadic population. There has been a considerable amount of trouble as the river has been blocked off, and violent clashes have taken place between nomads and police, in particular around the Awash Game Park. As noted above some families have been settled and there are plans to settle more. Nevertheless more and more of the area is going to people from the highlands. In the eyes of the Government the whole valley is Government land because the nomads only pay cattle tax and not the land tax which would be considered to provide a title to ownership. Too many of the nomads are therefore being forced into low-paid seasonal jobs on the bigger plantations as their grazing areas and water supplies are denied to them. This tendency has been violently reinforced by the catastrophic effects of the 1973 drought on the nomads; indeed the drought threatens the continued existence of these people and their way of life.

Foreign capital is not confined to the Awash Valley developments; it is a common feature in many of the more recently mechanized private farms, and agro-industrial enterprises. Its use has led to considerable resentment in some places. A good example of the kind of complaints that occur can be seen in a look at the Elaberet estate in Eritrea, between Asmara and Keren. The farm, which was started in 1908, was worth Eth.$1 million when the present owners, an Italian group, bought it in 1958. They raised its value to Eth.$16 million by 1973. It now occupies 1,250 hectares, and employs 1,820 people regularly and another 1,000 in season. Produce is mixed, with peppers and tomatoes for export, citrus fruit, grapes and wine as well as dairy and beef herds of 1,100 and 500 pigs. The farm has been awarded a Haile Selassie Prize Trust award for its achievements.

Despite these achievements there has, however, been some criticism of the transport and health facilities for the working-force, of educational opportunities for their children, and of the wages rates.[43] Such comments have been levelled at a number of foreign companies operating in Ethiopia. In certain cases the rate of Ethiopianization, or rather lack of it, has also been criticized. As in all developing countries employment of nationals is a subject of concern to the government. But as the students, the most articulate domestic commentators, and even *The Ethiopia Herald* have pointed out on several occasions, a substantial part of the fault lies with the government's own educational policies.

The projects mentioned above are part of a range of other centralized changes that have either been passed, for example the agricultural income tax law, or that are supposedly in the process of being put through. The Ministry of Land Reform has a draft law for a tax on unoccupied lands; more immediate perhaps has been the draft proclamation for agricultural tenancy.[44] It has already been made clear that the interests of the ruling class are very much in opposition to any radical land reform—nevertheless there have been Government-sponsored schemes for improving the situation of the tenants to some degree. The tenancy proclamation went before the new Parliament in 1973, as it has done every year since 1968. Even before the 1974 crisis it was likely to pass for the pressures arising out of the famine had underlined the urgency of the tenants' plight. Now the new Government has promised more significant reform in land though it has not clarified its proposals or developed the practical details of implementation. The proposals include restriction of Government land grants to those who will actually work on the land; restriction of ownership to an amount that can actually be developed by the owner, with the excess taken by the government under compensatory payments; tenants and those who wish to work the land will be given the opportunity to acquire it and large sections of illegally acquired forest lands are to be returned to the public domain.

It is however instructive to look at the 1973 draft of the tenancy Bill for it illustrates the prevailing attitude of the elite's approach to the problem. An analysis immediately raises a number of doubts concerning its value. The proclamation allows for leases to be written or oral; though it specifies that they must be written at the request of either party, or at the demand of the Ministry of Land Reform. The rents which may be paid either in cash or kind are to be limited to one-third of the yield in the case of share-cropping; though if the landlord contributes seed, oxen and the like he may obtain more, providing that the total does not exceed one half of the production. There is also provision for converting the rent to a fixed amount or to cash based on the calculation that the amount of produce equal to one-third of the yield is considered as the fixed rent. Conversion is to be carried out at the market price. The Ministry also has the right to order rent reductions if and when it may be necessary. Tenancies are to be terminated at the agreement of both parties or by the initiative of either. The landlord has to prove default—failure to pay the rent, abandonment, sub-letting or damage caused, providing that it is serious, are all considered to be default. Most insidious perhaps is the fact that the initiation of mechanized farming is considered to be a valid cause for the termination as well—though the tenant has to be given two years' notice, and be paid compensation of not less than two years' rent (and not more than five years'). The tenant may give notice for any reason at one year's notice, or without notice if default can be proved against the landlord. Compensation is required for improvements whatever the reason for terminating the tenancy, and the amount is to be equal to the un-exhausted value of the improvement. The tenant is also to have the first refusal after the immediate family if the landlord decides to sell.

Implementation of these measures is to be in the hands of a tenancy official in the first instance—an employee of the Ministry of Land Reform. There will also be tenancy committees at the district level who will hear appeals from the tenancy officer's decisions and arbitrate on disputes if requested. These committees will have an equal number of tenants and landowners (three of each) and be under the chairmanship of an owner-farmer. Appeal from this body will be to a tenancy tribunal held under a judge appointed directly by the Emperor. Finally, appeal is allowed to the High Court of the province whose decision is final.

These provisions show clearly that the administration has not been prepared to go far in improving the position of tenants. As it is, the majority of members of Parliament did consider it to be too radical and it is hardly acceptable to the landowning class. Incidentally it should be noted that this measure is often called a "land reform bill". This is not the case—it is only concerned with one aspect of the land question and that is tenancy.

As with any similar legislative proposals in Ethiopia the fact that those responsible for adjudicating disputes come from the landowning class inhibits the value of any provisions that do offer a protection to the tenant. In any case it could also be assumed, as has happened on other occasions, that the provisions would be largely ignored by the landowners. It should also be made clear that in the years since the draft proclamation was first put forward the landlords have had ample time to prepare for it by evicting any tenants that they want out and arranging the terms of tenancies to suit themselves, before any of their customary rights in this direction have been eroded. There is considerable evidence to suggest that in the last few years evictions for this reason have been steadily increasing. The expansion of spontaneous settlement into the lowland areas and the marginal lands apparently comes as much from this as it does from the population pressures.[45]

There are more serious errors in it as well. Share-cropping is not excluded—and there is no suggestion of trying to establish monetary payments as a norm. There is an allowance for landlords to obtain up to 50 per cent of the crop; it would seem on previous experience that this is therefore likely to become the normal level of rent. There is no reiteration of the illegality of services, except by implication. The whole arbitration and appeal procedure is geared to the landlord with his superior influence. The process will undoubtedly be a time-consuming one and few tenants will be able to go as far as the provincial high court. What is even worse is the fact that the implementation of sanctions against an offender can only be carried out through the ordinary courts; this means that the lengthy procedure would have to be repeated. All these factors make it clear that the landowners would gain most from the measure if it was passed.

Another draft proclamation that has originated with the Ministry of Land Reform has similar implications. This is the draft proclamation for a tax on unutilized land. This provides for a tax on land that is not currently being used as arable land. Provision is made for the owner to give the necessary returns of size and fertility. In anticipation of the certain inaccuracy of such returns the proclamation also provides for the Ministry to conduct its own assessments if it thinks that it will be useful. As in the land tenure proclamation, provision is also made for an appeal system to be practiced with the co-operation of the local administration and the Ministry of Finance.

It would appear that only two things have actually happened in the last few years that significantly affect the land tenure and tenant situation. The agricultural income tax law poses a long term threat to the continued existence of the *rist* system of ownership, and the growth of mechanized farming is clearly having an adverse effect on the position of tenants. The first however is certainly only very long term, and opposition is strong enough at the moment to prevent it having much influence in the northern highlands. The growth of mechanized farming as it is currently organized counterbalances any threat that there may be to the landowning position in the draft proclamation on tenancy relations. The effect of mechanization has not yet been to encourage the appearance of a large, unemployed urban population (though that already exists in Addis Ababa) as the majority of evicted tenants still look for other lands. What mechanization has done is to improve the position of the landowning elite. The progression might be called one of movement away from a purely feudal landowning system, not to capitalist farming but, rather, to mechanized feudalism. For the future the new Government is committed in general to much more serious changes. As has been shown there will be substantial opposition among certain classes and in the provinces, and real land reform is going to be very difficult to achieve. However it does seem that it is the single most necessary factor for breaking down the feudal elements in the country.

CHAPTER V

Industry and Imperialism

Both a money economy and manufacturing industry are relatively new to Ethiopia. Both are essentially post-war developments and both still affect only a small minority. The basic determinant of the economy is agriculture and this will remain so for a long time to come. Although certain parts of the agricultural sector may have received some Government attention, as noted in the previous chapter, development has generally been minimal and spasmodic. The actual rate of agricultural growth achieved over the last twenty years has barely kept up with the population growth of 2·5 per cent per annum. It is significant that the average calorific intake is only 1,622 calories per capita a day. It must be stressed that this is 328 calories less than the average intake for India.[1] In 1972 there was one of the best harvests in recent years, in 1973–74 a disastrous famine affected seven provinces and over three million people. The fact that Government emphasis on agriculture is limited is shown by the failure to achieve even one-half of the Second Five Year Plan's projected capital investment. Such agricultural development as there is has been essentially turned towards import substitution, at high cost to the consumer, or to cash crops for exports, using mechanization procedures that tend to benefit the larger landowners alone.

It is true that the Third Five Year Plan laid more emphasis on agriculture than the previous plans; and when it was reviewed in 1971 the focus was concentrated on rural agricultural development through schemes like the Minimum Package Programmes. The Chilalo agricultural development project and others like it have also had as their stated aim increased incomes for small farmers. The failures of these have already been noted. They are underlined by the inadequate attempts to organize marketing systems or to fix prices. Equally the tenure system, affecting well over half the farmers, inhibits production. The Government's failure to develop in any direction that might conflict with vested interests is highlighted by the lack of any serious attempt to remedy the situation.

Ethiopia, of course, suffers from the fact that it has no sizeable mineral deposits—extraction is limited and economically insignificant. Some copper production has recently been started and there are other deposits known. The most hopeful area is perhaps oil. In 1972 oil finds were announced in the south of Bale, but there is still doubt about their size and commercial viability. So far, only gas has been found in commercial quantities. Even if oil exists there in sizeable amounts, the problems of utilization will be immense, as the obvious route for a pipeline would be via Somalia. This is politically impossible as large oil deposits will encourage Somalia's already existing claims to the area. The only Ethiopian refinery at Assab cannot take any more crude and the alternative would have to be a new refinery somewhere else. Djibouti is a possibility, and the French have offered to build a refinery and pipeline. But it is also politically dubious as both Somalia and Ethiopia would lay claim to the territory if the French withdrew.

There is also a little platinum and a certain amount of gold, but there is so far only one significant area of exploitation for gold— Adola in Sidamo. This was discovered in 1942 and its production has fluctuated over the years from 1964–65—23,905 ounces, to 1968–69—42,805 ounces. The contribution to the economy has been fairly small therefore; in 1968–69 the output was worth Eth. $3,340,000.

This may not, however, reflect the true output. In the period May 1942–October 1945 the output was officially stated as averaging 3,500 ounces per month. That is, during a period of 42 months about 149,000 ounces were produced. During half of this period, February 1944–October 1945 (21 months), the British records show that a total of 187,196 ounces was exported under exchange agreements; and at least another 19,964 ounces without such agreement. In other words it must be assumed that at times the output of the Adola mine has been at least 40 per cent or more greater than officially admitted. Some of this discrepancy can be accounted for by production from other gold areas—Yubdo, or the Asossa area; but such additions would probably only amount to 10 per cent at the most. It is not surprising that there have been strong suspicions regarding the official figures on the Adola output.[2]

In spite of the concentration on manufacturing industry over the last fifteen years in the Five Year Plans, industry is still very underdeveloped. The growth rate has been about 16 per cent per annum for the last ten years, yet it still only provided 5 per cent of the Gross Domestic Product in 1969. One of the reasons has been that emphasis has been placed on a few areas only—textiles, sugar, drinks and construction materials. Another major reason is the failure to provide increased purchasing power, and thus markets. As a U.N. adviser put it: "Industry will come automatically and at high speed when agriculture changes and farmers begin to get high incomes".[3]

The failure to provide for an internal finance base has meant a considerable reliance on foreign capital—both private and public. The former has been somewhat uncertain, varying from a net outflow of Eth.$5 million in 1969, up to an inflow of Eth.$45 million in 1971. This is in spite of what has been called the most generous investment policy in Africa. One result of this is that the Fourth Five Year Plan now on the drawing-board is going to be geared largely to export potential industries, rather than import substitutes. This is also due to the fact that from the late 1950s there has been a trade deficit. In fact the commodity price boom had such an effect that in 1973 a surplus of Eth.$50 million was recorded but over the previous six years the average deficit has been Eth.$115 million. This deficit has been compounded by the increasing gap between revenue and expenditure. Revenue has inevitably stagnated with the failure to develop local markets and production. The growing costs of the bureaucracy and the armed forces have been the essential elements in the rising expenditures. The gap has had to be filled largely by foreign loans—to a great degree from America (35 per cent)—and from multilateral sources (40 per cent). The speed with which the debt has grown is striking. In June 1968 it was Eth.$324 million; by June 1973 it was Eth.$592 million, a rise of approximately Eth.$53 million per year.

The area that has shown particular growth, and to which a considerable amount of World Bank money has gone, has been the infrastructure. Both roads and communications have been continuously supported. Highway development is now in its fifth project, which is for asphalting and providing feeder roads; it is jointly financed by U.S.A.I.D. and I.D.A. and will also receive a section of the massive Eth.$100 million Chinese loan granted in 1972. I.D.A. finance has also been supplied to start the establishment of microwave connections throughout the empire. Another World Bank interest is tourism which has attractive potential and the recent plan calls for Eth.$150 million over the next ten years. This has been accepted by the Government and a start has been made with an agreement for four new hotels to be managed by the Hilton Corporation.

None of this however provides the answer to the strains that the economy has undergone, and is undergoing. The effects of the upsurge of 1972–74 due to the high world commodity prices for oil seeds and coffee has already been eroded by the need to import grain for the disasters of 1973 and the spiralling cost of oil. Although the Fourth Five Year Plan is not yet published and is now being revised by the new Government the emphasis will still apparently be in areas that will not increase local purchasing power, and will not improve the agricultural production. The previous government remained obstinately committed to foreign capital. In 1967, 75 per cent of the paid-up private capital was foreign and the percentage has not fallen since.[4] It is unlikely that the new Government's needs will allow it to break away from this commitment.

The Government's approach to economic development cannot be seen in isolation from the social factors. The mode of agricultural production is still mostly feudal, and it is this that produces most of the export revenues. The manufacturing and service sectors, although they have been growing relatively fast, have not led to the creation of an Ethiopian national bourgeoisie of any significance due to the dependence on foreign capital. These factors underlie the whole economic structure and must be emphasized in any discussion of the economy.

The predominantly agricultural nature of Ethiopia reflects itself most clearly in the export trade (see Table 17). Of the elements that go to make up the food sector the most important is coffee, and although the dependence upon it has been reduced from 66 per cent of the value of exports in 1965 to under 50 per cent in 1973 it obviously remains critical. The table illustrates the fluctuations that this can give rise to, and also shows the effect of the price rise on other exports.

TABLE 17.

Value of Exports in millions of Ethiopian dollars

	1965	1966	1967	1968	1969	1970	1971	1972	1973
Coffee	188	156	139	153	174	181	175	182	181
All others	95	111	111	105	119	114	135	175	268

Source: Adapted from National Bank of Ethiopia, Quarterly Bulletins *December 1972 and 1973.*

Coffee has until recently been on a quota system that has helped
to iron out some of the price fluctuations, but not with complete
success as can be seen from the figures for 1967. A marked change
appeared in 1972–73 when the export values showed an increase,
especially in the other exports—due almost entirely to the sudden
and high rise in world commodity prices. In the first half of 1974
these began to decline again while the effects of higher import
prices, especially of oil, continued to be felt. Coffee remained
relatively firm in fact, but it can hardly be considered to be a major
growth sector for the future because of the quota agreements, and
it is further handicapped at the moment by its ties to one market—
the U.S.A.—which takes 70 per cent or more of the coffee exported.

The industry is regulated by the National Coffee Board set up by
decree in 1957 and proclamation in 1962. It is worth noting that the
members have been appointed by the Emperor and hold office at
his discretion; this has been the case in most of the State boards.
The Coffee Board has been active in seeking improvements in
quality and processing, as in the setting up of a Coffee Processing
Centre to provide a higher grade of washed coffee; but it has not
production or marketing functions, and like several of the State
Boards it was accused of corruption in 1974.

The coffee comes from a variety of areas. In Hararge and Sidamo
it is mostly grown on plantations; in Kaffa, Illubabor and Wollega
it tends to come from the wild forest coffee—there are in total about
90,000 hectares of cultivated coffee. The yields from the forest
production are low, though as progress is made in opening up the
areas with modern transport, storage facilities and improved organization, higher yields are occurring. These improvements are viable
only for the larger producers. The small farmers are normally
forced to sell their crop at harvest time when the prices are at their
lowest; equally they do not benefit from subsidies on inputs or from
price supports, as the larger producers do. A few steps have been
taken in the direction of improved marketing arrangements with
the setting up of some co-operatives. There were altogether seventeen
of these in 1972 with a total membership of 4,029. Their capital was
only Eth.$271,000 and their efficiency in management, financial
and technical skills, small. This is mainly because the Government
failed to assist with finance or training. It should also be noted that
co-operatives of this type do nothing for the poorest farmers and
peasants because they cannot find the necessary outlay, small
though that may be.[5] While Ethiopia has not progressed far in

co-operative ventures the evidence suggests that a situation parallel
to that found in other areas of Africa is already emerging—the
domination of these ventures by a "kulak" class who do have greater
resources and entrepreneurial skills.

One other point about the coffee industry that should be noted is
the lack of foreign investment. It is almost exclusively confined to
private Ethiopian money. One exception is the Ethiopian-American
Coffee Company which started production in 1961. This has a
two million tree estate and it is 70 per cent financed by American
money. Most producers do in fact use the Agricultural Investment
and Development Bank (A.I.D.B.) of Ethiopia which finds coffee
lands a very satisfactory form of security on loans.

Of the other main productive areas the one with the most potential
is livestock and hides and skins. There are currently five schemes
under consideration. The Southern Rangelands, the Dermatu
Range development, the Second Livestock Development Project,
the North-east Rangelands Development and the Jigjiga Livestock
Development. Little has been done, though drilling for water has
begun on the Jigjiga Project. The estimates for Ethiopian livestock
are thirty million cattle and as many sheep and goats—though this
was before the recent drought, which has caused considerable losses.
As yet only a minute proportion of this wealth is utilized in terms of
exports of meat products, and there is virtually no export of live
animals.[6] For the future however it is clear that, once the *rinderpest*
eradication schemes are finished and the cattle are considered to be
up to international standards, there is great potential. It should be
emphasized that the rangeland projects are essentially for the wealthy,
while the prospects in hides and skins are of more interest to the
average peasant farmer, from whom these commodities come. This
is largely reflected in the quality which is fairly low, and little has
been done to upgrade it.

In general the export situation has remained virtually unchanged
over the last ten years. The effect of the increased commodity prices
of 1972–74 has improved the value and the relative importance but
not the pattern. The quantity and value of the exports has climbed
steadily but only one item has been added to the list in recent years
and this is sugar.

Imports have seen more marked changes over this period. The
percentage of textiles imported has gone down by nearly two-thirds,
and a considerable number of items have increased—machinery
and equipment, chemicals, rubber, iron and steel. Not only has the

whole import bill risen enormously from Eth.$166 million in 1957 to Eth.$469 million in 1971; over a third of it now goes to machinery and equipment and nearly another third is devoted to manufactured articles or consumer goods. To a considerable extent this does reflect the importation of inflation from the developed world, but the switch from consumer to industrial items does play an equal part. Once again 1972–73 provides a change as import controls were established in the wake of the deficit of Eth.$155 million recorded in 1971, and the import bill for 1973 was down to under Eth.$400 million.

Ethiopian trade has also changed direction considerably during the last few years. Most notably, imports from the U.S.A. have been declining steadily, although the U.S.A. remains the largest trading partner since most of the coffee goes there. Exports to the Far East and to Europe have been rising steadily in value but the imbalance remains as imports are rising faster. The largest change has been the growth in trade with Africa, although this is entirely on the import side. In a normal year such as 1970 the deficits were: with Japan, Eth.$47 million; Israel, Eth.$2.6 million; Western Europe, Eth.$129 million; Africa, Eth.$19 million.[7]

TABLE 18

Export Values by Commodity Groups 1964–72

	1964	1965	1966	1967	1968	1969	1970	1971	1972
Live animals	2·3	3·1	2·3	3·3	2·7	3·4	2·3	2·5	4·2
Meat (canned and frozen)	5·8	7·4	7·3	5·9	5·4	4·3	6·0	8·9	15·1
Cereals	0·3	0·7	0·03	1·0	0·4	1·0	0·8	1·1	1·2
Pulses	13·7	14·5	21·2	19·7	21·4	22·0	15·8	22·2	26·2
Fresh fruit	4·7	4·5	5·2	6·1	4·9	4·8	3·4	3·2	5·2
Vegetables (canned and frozen)	1·8	1·8	2·5	2·4	2·3	2·0	2·1	3·0	4·0
Sugar	4·5	0·08	—	—	1·0	1·3	3·3	4·1	9·1
Coffee	158·9	188·3	156·0	139·5	153·3	174·0	181·3	175·2	182·5
Spices	2·1	0·8	0·8	2·9	2·5	2·3	2·2	1·3	3·2
Oilseed cakes	3·5	3·4	4·8	4·4	3·7	4·1	3·4	5·6	6·0
Hides and skins	21·9	23·5	35·6	29·8	24·9	29·2	24·5	25·7	47·6
Oilseeds	26·6	24·9	21·8	22·7	21·4	23·2	28·4	32·1	48·7
Chat	5·1	1·8	2·2	2·9	3·0	5·0	1·7	3·7	3·2
Beeswax	1·1	1·4	1·3	1·4	2·2	2·1	1·5	1·4	1·2
Others	6·8	6·7	7·5	7·9	9·0	14·0	17·9	20·7	19·6
	259·1	283·1	269·1	250·0	258·0	292·6	294·8	309·6	377·1

Figures rounded to Ethiopian dollars (millions)
Source: Adapted from National Bank of Ethiopia, Quarterly Bulletins, *December 1972 and 1973.*

TABLE 19

Import Values by Commodity Groups 1964-72

	1964	1965	1966	1967	1968	1969	1970	1971	1972
Food and live animals	14·0	19·9	30·9	23·0	19·1	19·7	31·5	28·6	20·0
Beverages and tobacco	3·8	4·9	5·1	5·0	5·7	5·5	5·2	5·8	8·4
Raw cotton	9·8	4·5	6·5	5·3	6·7	7·6	3·8	5·8	4·7
Petroleum products	24·1	23·3	126·3	31·1	26·7	27·6	33·4	43·5	35·7
Chemicals	10·8	13·7	17·3	20·1	24·2	27·8	31·5	36·8	33·4
Medical, etc.	7·0	8·1	8·7	9·4	10·1	11·1	13·5	13·8	11·6
Soap and polishes	4·3	5·3	5·9	5·0	6·7	4·7	5·3	5·2	5·9
Rubber products	9·1	10·7	13·3	13·5	13·1	12·7	18·2	21·0	19·2
Paper and paper manufactures	8·8	10·9	9·4	9·5	9·2	7·6	9·0	8·0	8·3
Textiles	37·2	43·0	31·6	27·9	21·6	22·9	25·1	28·4	25·5
Clothing	15·4	17·3	15·0	14·4	14·4	12·9	12·2	7·9	7·4
Metal and metal manufactures	26·4	28·2	35·9	34·6	42·4	36·5	48·9	49·1	35·3
Machinery, including aircraft	54·9	81·5	92·6	59·9	118·8	74·8	82·4	87·3	81·8
Electrical materials	17·0	25·5	21·0	24·7	22·4	25·5	27·3	30·4	34·5
Motor vehicles	36·0	39·4	42·6	42·0	42·0	40·4	46·9	54·2	62·8
Others	38·9	39·4	41·7	32·1	49·5	51·1	36·0	43·7	41·2
	307·7	375·7	404·3	357·4	432·5	388·3	429·1	469·5	435·6

Figures rounded to Ethiopian dollars (millions)
Source: Adapted from National Bank of Ethiopia, Quarterly Bulletins, *December 1972 and 1973.*

TABLE 20

Import and Export Totals 1946-73

	Imports	Exports†	Trade Balance
1946	59,562,000	53,230,000	−6,332,000
1953*	137,850,000	169,403,000	+31,553,000
1964	307,687,000	262,530,000	−45,157,000
1965	375,671,000	289,833,000	−85,838,000
1966	404,250,000	277,522,000	−126,728,000
1967	357,369,000	252,737,000	−104,632,000
1968	432,522,000	266,031,000	−166,491,000
1969	388,302,000	298,123,000	−90,179,000
1970	429,078,000	305,793,000	−123,285,000
1971	469,525,000	314,061,000	−155,464,000
1972	435,582,000	384,245,000	−51,336,000
1973 estimates	399,500,000	449,500,000	+50,000,000

In Ethiopian dollars
* First full year of federation with Eritrea.
† Includes re-exports.
Source: Adapted from Ethiopian Observer, *Vol. I, No. 5, June 1957, and* National Bank of Ethiopia, Quarterly Bulletins, *December 1972 and 1973,* African Development, *May 1974.*

It is this imbalance that has been particularly responsible for the concentration on import substitution, and it has been fairly successful. It is also clear that the economy is emerging out of the depressed state of the last few years, even allowing for the probably temporary effect of the commodity price rises. The Third Five Year Plan's expectations were badly dented by the closure of the Suez Canal and by the sudden drop in private investment after 1965. It did in fact only recover in 1969. Coffee, too, was suffering from low prices in the late 1960s and the whole economy was under a considerable strain. In this sense the present prospects are much brighter though it is, to say the least, unfortunate that at a time when there seems to be an awareness that the highest priority should be agriculture, there should be a catastrophic drought. Paradoxically this may turn out to be something of a blessing in disguise, as it has focused the attention of the Government even more strongly on the agricultural sector and already plans have been made to begin a number of long and short term projects.

Although in 1972 it was still estimated that 91 per cent of the population were to be classified as rural and that 88 per cent were employed in an agricultural capacity, there is no doubt that manufacturing has increased greatly over the years. Its contribution to the export sector was still only about 5 per cent in that year and it employed less than 1 per cent of the population. Nevertheless the change in the last two decades can be described as considerable. In 1958 there were only ten small industries in Ethiopia of which one, the Wonji sugar mill, was major; the others were flour, soap, cotton, cement, tobacco, brewing and soft drinks, meat and shoes. Nearly all operated in Addis Ababa and to a considerable extent were started by the Emperor immediately after the war.[8] This growth has been sizeable both in number and type of establishments, especially in the later 1960s as can be seen from the tables below.

TABLE 21.

Industrial Growth

	1964/5	1966/7	1968/9	1969/70	1972/3*
Establishments	272	395	442	479	
Employees	47,700	44,349	47,432	48,903	
Wages plus Salaries†	33·0	48·9	57·9	61·8	
Gross output†	219·7	357·1	467·0	542·6	700·0

* Estimate.
† Ethiopian million dollars.

Source: E.C.A. Summaries of Economic Data (January 1973).

TABLE 22.

Growth of Industrial Sectors 1964–70

	1964–65	1969–70
Meat (tons)	10,543	9,142
Sugar (tons)	61,698	96,967
Salt (tons)	205,310	218,150
Flour (tons)	40,358	40,019
Beer (hectolitres)	157,395	280,239
Soft drinks (hectolitres)	252,235	334,184
Cigarettes (millions)	441·0	870·4
Cotton fabrics (000 sq. metres)	33,956	69,706
Blankets (000s)	276	833
Shoes (leather pairs in 000s)	628	822
Shoes (plastic pairs in 000s)	—	1,287
Shoes (canvas/rubber 000s)	9	671
Timber/plywood (cu. metres)	14,752	31,212
Cement (tons)	72,899	175,405
Glass bottles (000s)	15,721	7,850
Iron bars (tons)	—	9,610
Corrugated iron sheets (tons)	—	22,281
Matches (million boxes)	—	22·8
Soap (tons)	—	6,700

Source: E.C.A. Summaries of Economic Data (January 1973).

TABLE 23.

Regional Distribution of Industry

Province	No. of estab.	Total employees
Shoa	223	37,426
Eritrea	165	13,901
Hararge	42	4,991
Wollo	10	47
Begemeder	9	70
Gojjam	2	2,096
Kaffa	4	255
Sidamo	8	182
Tigre	2	21
Arussi	1	15

Bale, Gomu-Goffa, Illubabor and Wollega—none.

Source: Commercial Bank of Ethiopia—The Ethiopian Economy 1970.

However, the fact remains that the percentage of the population employed is still very small. Furthermore the lack of regional distribution of industry is striking. Addis Ababa and Asmara accounted for 70 per cent of the industries in 1969, and on a provincial basis Shoa and Eritrea have the majority of establishments with Hararge a poor third.

These figures do not take account of the cottage industry production which is much more widespread. Local artisans and those involved in weaving, carpentry and so on are to be found all over the country, but their production is geared to local needs. It is also, in many cases, being undercut today by the appearance of industrially produced goods at the local markets. Little Government effort has been put into trying to solve their problems although the Third Five Year Plan laid stress on the need to do so. This is surprising in view of the estimated gross value of cottage industry output, which was Eth. $212 million in 1967, from a labour force of approximately 335,000. The rate of growth that this sector showed during the period 1960–65 was about 6 per cent per annum.[9]

There has in fact been only one attempt at an industrial development programme at the regional level; and this has been at best only a qualified success. Indeed the attempt exposes some of the problems as well as the possibilities of such an approach. In 1961 *Ras* Mengesha Seyoum became Governor-General of Tigre in succession to his father. One of the first things he wanted to do was to try to revitalize the incense industry. He also had plans to set up a series of other plants to process linseed oil for soap and paint production, to build a jute factory, and to start the production of oil cans and aluminium utensils. After a certain amount of political lobbying he obtained Government support for this unheard-of idea, or rather more important, he got imperial backing. The Ministry of Finance agreed to back the issue of shares and the Emperor granted an incense monopoly. Further he allowed *Ras* Mengesha to collect the previous year's taxes that had been remitted because of the disastrous famine of 1958–59. This incidentally aroused considerable ill-feeling in the province which was not assuaged by Mengesha's arguments that the money was going to go into developments that would profit the entire province.

The early stages of the whole project were a disaster. After two years there was nothing to show except a considerable amount of obsolete and unsuitable machinery from India and from the U.S.A., and no money. It was at this time that the first actual investigation

into the various possibilities was actually made.[10] This was extremely
pessimistic about nearly all the possibilities that *Ras* Mengesha had
had in mind with the exception of the collection of incense. This in
fact has been the main source of revenue for T.A.I.D.L. and T.D.O.,
the two companies that had been set up.

TABLE 24

Incense Exports

Year	1964	1965	1966	1967	1968	1969	1970	1971	1972
Tons	1,863	2,343	1,754	1,849	1,258	2,186	2,883	1,968	3,304

In metric tons.

Source: National Bank Quarterly Bulletin, *December 1972 and
1973.*

However, as can be seen from these figures the quantity for export
has continued to fluctuate, although the improved collection methods
have made a difference and have provided the basis for further
projects. One less ambitious project has been a considerable success.
This is the weaving plant employing 250 people and producing
locally inspired designs and cloths. Another venture has again been
over-ambitious. This is the suede leather factory set up to produce
suede garments for the luxury North American market. However
no feasibility study was carried out and the suede had to be bought
in Addis Ababa from the Dhamar Tannery and transported to
Makalle. There were further problems in acquiring machinery and
training operators; and although the project was functional in
1973 its output was negligible.

At the moment, therefore, the whole prospect for regional industrial development in Makalle seems to be extremely limited. In fact
the failures have been used by people in Addis Ababa to point up
the impossibility of trying to do anything of the kind without foreign
money and know-how. Within limits there is a certain amount of
truth in this, as the failures have been those of planning and finance.
Planning was by and large non-existent and the finances ineptly
handled. Of the six general managers that T.A.I.D.L. has had, three
have been accused of some form of embezzlement. The situation
has been complicated by the total lack of proper accounting procedures, and *Ras* Mengesha's energy in providing and handing out
money has proved no real substitute for this. It might be added that

the main losers have been the local people who put money into the original shares; there has also been a considerable amount of disappointment locally over the failure to provide more jobs.

In the industrial sector the policy of the Government has been to try and attract foreign capital, partly by the provision of monopolistic enterprises. This has been coupled with a policy of encouraging import substitution and providing high tariff protection. These have partly been necessary in response to the very low purchasing power of the domestic market, which would not otherwise provide incentives for foreign investment. It also obviates the need to concentrate directly on raising domestic consumption. The primary case of this is sugar where a monopoly position has provided very high profits at a high cost to the local consumer. It can be paralleled in other sectors and altogether between 1950 and 1967 Eth. $262·8 million was invested in Ethiopia by foreign firms. The declared profits in this period were calculated at Eth. $216·1 million—in 1967 alone the profits were Eth. $21·6 million.[11]

The Government's first step in the encouragement of foreign capital was the announcement by the Minister of Finance in 1950:

"The Imperial Ethiopian Government has decided upon a general working policy for the encouragement of foreign capital investment in Ethiopia of enterprises deemed to be beneficial to the country. For the achievement of this policy, the Government is prepared to grant special facilities to new enterprises started with foreign capital . . . New enterprises will be free from payment of profit tax for five years from the date production is started . . . The necessary machinery . . . will be free of customs duties."[12]

Remittance was also to be allowed for a fixed percentage of the profit earned though the amount was not specified.

This was followed up by a clause in the Income Tax Decree of 1956 which allowed tax exemption on industrial, transport and mining enterprises investing not less than Eth. $200,000 for a period of not more than five years from the beginning of their activities. In 1961 the Income Tax Proclamation clarified this to show that the enterprise had to be a new one and that the tax exemptions began when operations started. It also allowed for investments to existing facilities to be exempt, providing that another Eth. $0·5 million was added to the capital. Two years later further modifications were made in detail. Exemptions were extended to agricultural and tourist investments; and for expansion eligibility was reduced to Eth. $0·4 million and the period to three years. An Investment Committee was set up to study and recommend tax exemptions and other possible benefits for foreign companies.[13] Finally further changes were made in 1966 when the Investment Committee was given the power to decide on, and not just recommend, the exemptions to be made; and the amount qualifying for relief for expanded investment was reduced to Eth. $0·2 million.[14]

It can be seen from this that the investment climate in Ethiopia has become steadily more favourable to foreign capital over the years. Exemptions may now be granted to almost any type of company—the exception is commercial companies—and no distinctions are made as to the form of the company, nor as to its nationality. No requirement is made that the company should be new or even necessary to the economy. A great deal of authority is in the hands of the Investment Committee which not only decides on eligibility but determines the actual exemptions that may be offered, and these vary from case to case. It may also be noted that the legislation does not actually define the categories of company, so such definition is also the prerogative of the committee.

It is not easy to establish whether income tax exemption has positively attracted private foreign capital into the country, for business taxes are low in any case. The basic rate is 20 per cent with two surtax charges of 10 per cent over Eth. $30,000 and Eth. $150,000.[15] It seems likely that potential investors have been equally attracted by these rates and by the other inducements that have been offered through the various agreements that have been made with the specific companies. Such special agreements have been the normal method used with companies that want to invest. The field has been largely that of agricultural processing and import substitution, especially sugar and textiles.

The sugar industry is one of the oldest-established industries and illustrates most clearly the type of inducement offered to foreign investment and the possibilities available. It was set up in 1951 when H.V.A.—a Dutch company—needed somewhere to move to after expulsion from Indonesia after its independence. Arrangements were made for the company to move to Ethiopia under a special agreement, which was revised in 1954. It has not been published but the major provisions are known.[16] Two thousand and seven hundred hectares of land were granted at a nominal rent (of Eth. $1·0 per *gasha*; that is a total of Eth. $67·5) for sixty years with automatic renewal for a further thirty. From the date that sugar production started income tax was exempted for five years; a remittance of 10 per cent of capital and 15 per cent of profit was also allowed annually. Under the revision H.V.A. agreed to employ Ethiopians where possible.

In 1958 it was decided that the plantation should be expanded, and at the same time the government made it clear that it wanted a stake in the company. So a new company was set up—H.V.A. Ethiopia—with a share capital of Eth. $28 million; this was almost immediately expanded to Eth. $50 million to cope with the setting up of a new factory. Twenty per cent of the share holding in 1969 was held by Ethiopians—5 per cent by the Government, 15 per cent by private individuals. At the same time a new agreement was negotiated which included a guarantee that the government would take protective measures against imports if the purchase price of sugar was less than the market price. A further expansion was carried out in 1966 when another estate was started at Metahara, lower down the Awash valley. This was actually a separate company— H.V.A. Metahara—financed by an International Finance Corporation loan, H.V.A. Holland, H.V.A. Ethiopia, Government (with a 30 per cent holding in 1969) and private shareholdings.[17]

H.V.A. Ethiopia has been a conspicuous success in terms of output and profitability, and has provided total import substitution—though at a considerable cost to the consumer. In the first year of operation— 1954—production was 15,850 tons; by 1964 it was 62,747 tons; and in 1972 the production from both companies was 135,000 tons of which 16,000 were exported. Cost of production is low for a number of reasons—one being the tax exemptions on income tax, export and import taxes, and the low land rental. More important, however, appears to be the cost of labour. The unskilled daily wage was Eth. $1·00 and the total wage bill in 1969 was between Eth. $6·0 and Eth. $7·0 million, which is extremely low considering the high salaries among the foreign management staff who have a near monopoly of the senior posts.[18]

Profitability also depends upon the local sales. Here the company has a monopoly and imposes its own price structure. The landed cost of sugar at Djibouti had been averaging about a third of the market price in Addis Ababa until the upsurge in sugar prices in 1973—the wholesale price of 100 kgs. in the market went up Eth. $68·34 in 1971. It is not surprising that in spite of increasing tax payments—excise and turnover taxes paid were Eth. $18 million

in 1968 (Eth.$6 million in 1958)—profitability has been high
enough to lead to accusations of exploitation. While it is not easy
to calculate it appears that profit as a percentage of turnover has
been high, as can be seen in the table.

TABLE 25

H.V.A. Ethiopia—Profit as percentage of Turnover[19]

1960	1961	1962	1963	1964	1965	1966	1967	Average
38%	19%	18%	24%	26%	22%	24%	23%	24%

The net profit in these eight years amounted to Eth.$58 million,
which provides an average rate of return on capital of 16·7 per cent
per year. It might be noted that over 50 per cent of the profit was
repatriated. Since then net profits have risen rather than fallen with
H.V.A. Metahara now showing a profit and with sugar exports
averaging 19,000 tons (1970–73). In addition, a molasses contract
was signed in 1973 that will be worth another Eth.$1·6 million a
year—export started in mid-1974.

Sugar is the only field where such domination is exercised by a
single foreign company, but private foreign investment is large in
other areas particularly textiles. Textile production in fact shows a
rather different pattern because it was in general demand and in
production before the advent of modern techniques. Before 1957
there were only three modern spinning and weaving mills and most
textiles were either produced at home, or imported through Dire
Dawa and Harar whose wealth derived mainly from them.

The importance of the trade has been such that the Government
has always taken a considerable interest in it right from the restoration. In June 1943 a company called the Ethiopian National Corporation (E.N.C.) was set up by the then Minister of Agriculture, Ato
Makonnen Habtewold. The principal shareholders were the Emperor,
the Empress, Makonnen himself and Ato Yilma Deressa, the Vice-
Minister of Finance. The original object was to control the export
of cereals and the company was given a monopoly, which produced
a "gross income in commissions of over 300 per cent on its initial
capital".[20] The initial capital being 250,000 MT (equal to £25,000),
later raised to 500,000 MT. In August 1943 Ato Makonnen was
moved to the Ministry of Commerce and immediately afterwards the
E.N.C. was given a monopoly on the distribution of sugar which
guaranteed the company another 400,000 East African shs. (£36,600)

of gross income. In October of the same year it also obtained for itself and its shareholders a substantial portion of the cotton-goods quota. This amounted to a quantity worth £600,000 for the year 1943–44 on which the legal profit rate would have been £60,000. In fact in early 1944,

> The Minister of Commerce obliged merchants to bind themselves to give him an option to buy at control price 20 per cent of their cotton imports ... When the goods actually arrived, they were held up in the Customs on the order of the Minister until the merchants agreed to cede 50 per cent of their goods against delivery orders issued by the Ministry of Commerce. For the third quarter of 1944 onwards the percentage taken from importers was raised to 100 per cent of all sheetings and yarns, and there has latterly been a tendency to include any other cotton goods of a profitable nature.[21]

Most of the goods thus taken were delivered to another company, the Ethiopian Society for Commerce and Transport (E.S.C.T.), also set up by the Minister of Commerce and having some of the same personnel as the E.N.C. According to the British adviser to the Ministry the E.N.C.'s monopoly was such that it created a severe shortage; to relieve the shortage the E.S.C.T. released the goods through the black market. The profits taken this way were alleged to be £37,800 on yarn and £212,200 on sheeting *per month*. "I called the attention of the Minister of Commerce to these facts in December last. His only comment was that if one Ethiopian robbed another by profiteering, at least the money remained in the country".[22]

The calculation for the total profits of the E.N.C. alone suggested that for the year 1945 they would reach between £1,200,000 and £1,800,000. By way of comparison it may be noted that the total revenues for the whole country were estimated at £3,170,256 for 1943–44.[23] It should also be mentioned that the situation was such that a commission of enquiry was set up to investigate the E.N.C. The members of the commission, were Ato Yilma Deressa, Vice-Minister of Finance; the Vice-Minister of Interior; and a Director-General in the Ministry of Commerce and Industry. The company was exonerated from any accusation of malpractice.

The situation gradually changed as supplies became more widely available after the war-time shortages. The steady growth in demand and the industrial emphasis that the Five Year Plans induced gave rise to the establishment of modern mills under a high protective

tariff. By 1969 there were fifty textile concerns with a gross production value of Eth.$157,282,000, though this still made it necessary
to import to the value of over Eth. $48 million. Government interest
in the textile sector turned towards import substitution as the trade
with India and Japan became more and more unbalanced. The
encouragement was expressed partly through investments—as of
1969 there were Government holdings of 18 per cent in Indo-
Ethiopian textiles, 38 per cent in Ethio-Japanese textiles, and 100 per
cent in the Debre Berhane Wool factory and the Bahr Dar mills.
It also appeared in the usual tax concessions for private investors,
in the steady growth of the tariff against imported fabrics and in the
tax exemptions for customs duties on raw materials. To offset the
revenue losses that might be incurred excise taxes were imposed
which have been, to some extent, reflected in higher prices for the
consumer.

Under these circumstances the textile industry has received a lot
of foreign capital. The largest firm is Indo-Ethiopian Textile S.C. at
Akaki near Addis Ababa. The equity of this company is Eth.$6·75
million of which 41 per cent comes from the Birla Bros. of India
who managed the company under a fifteen year agreement signed
in 1956; under this they got a fee of Eth.$30,000 per annum and
10 per cent of the net profits. The rest of the equity is divided between
the Government 18 per cent, private Ethiopians 7 per cent, Indian
residents 13 per cent and other companies 21 per cent. Among the
shareholders at one time was the Emperor, who apparently acquired
1,000 shares in 1959. The letter quoted here is of some interest as
showing the methodology of imperial involvement. It is supposedly
from the Ministry of Commerce to the State Bank directors.

Dear Sirs,

   At the request of the President of the Board of Directors of Indo-
Ethiopian Textiles S.A. as per their letter dated 26 September
1959, please transfer to the name of H.I.M. Haile Selassie I
Emperor of Ethiopia one thousand shares at par of the above
company from the shares held by the State Bank of Ethiopia.
The equivalent of these shares amounting to Eth.$100,000 will
be paid in cash to the State Bank.

It may be noted that the company was exempt from income tax
for its first five years, and from customs duties for machinery,
stores and spare parts for the first eight years. It has also been under
fire at various times for the low wages paid—the average for an

unskilled worker, which most of the nearly 4,000 employees are, was Eth. $1·5 a day, before the inflation and crisis of 1974.[24]

During the last ten years Japanese finance has begun to enter the textile scene. Three ventures were inaugurated in 1964, largely it seems because of the Sabean Utility Corporation's difficulties. This corporation, which had a 50 per cent Government participation, had incurred Eth. $8·25 million of bad debts and an overdraft of Eth. $8·0 million in 1963. Its subsidiary, the Cotton Company of Dire Dawa (now the second largest textile establishment) made a loss that year of Eth. $750,000. This was due to a prolonged labour dispute lasting for six months. An associated company—Fibre Co. of Ethiopia—also made a half million dollar loss in 1963 as well.[25]

In the consequent reorganization the Cotton Co. became fully independent, though Sabean retained 16 per cent of the shareholding. An agreement was made with Fuji Spinning of Japan to take a 30 per cent holding (the capital of Eth. $12·5 million was 50 per cent Government). Fuji were also to provide management skills under an agreement giving them 7½ per cent of net profits. Another Japanese company was brought in to set up the Sabean Metal Products Co. under a similar arrangement, though with 50 per cent Sabean and 50 per cent Japanese holdings. The third Japanese venture started in 1964 was the Ethio-Japanese Synthetic Textiles. This was originally 50 per cent Government owned, though by 1969 Government participation had fallen to 38 per cent of the Eth. $3·5 million equity. In this case there was a management fee of Eth. $30,000 for the first three years and then 5 per cent of the net profits.

Japanese capital is not confined to the textile sector, and it is still growing. In early 1973 two companies took a 35 per cent stake in the Addis Tyre S.C., under a management agreement. More significant has been the move into the mineral sector. Nippon Mining is one of the two major equity holders in the Ethio-Nippon Mining Co. set up to exploit the copper discovered in Eritrea. The first mine at Debarwa became operative in late 1973 and production by April 1975 will be 17,000 tons of copper concentrates per year, providing that there is no repeat performance of the raid in early 1974 by guerillas which stopped production for several months. There are three other potentially exploitable sites in the province, and although none of the deposits are thought to be enormous they are all commercially viable.[26]

Copper is one of the very few success stories in the mining sector—which has swallowed a great deal of capital for little return. A lot of this has gone into oil exploration, especially by U.S. companies. Sinclair, Mobil, and Gulf, as well as Shell have all prospected widely; Tenneco currently has large concessions in the south. Of these the Mobil concession off the coast of Massawa has produced gas and there have been rumours of substantial oil finds but nothing has been officially announced. The Tenneco concession has also produced gas in three out of the four wells. Oil has certainly been found but not apparently in sizeable quantities, though the French are impressed enough to have offered to build a pipeline to and a refinery at Djibouti. Their partner would be Total which already has a distribution network in Ethiopia.[27]

Another area that has used up a lot of capital has been the potash concession in the Danakil Depression. Attempts to exploit this started in 1949, and they were taken over by a U.S. firm—Parsons—in 1957. The firm put in a substantial investment and by agreement with the Government they were to build a 600,000 ton refinery as well as actually exploiting the deposits. The agreement also apparently involved "certain rights of a semi-political nature".[28] Under the Third Five Year Plan an investment of Eth.$110 million had been expected to lead to production worth Eth.$45 million by 1972–73. In fact the difficulties of the area—the Danakil Depression is the hottest place on earth—and changes in the international potash markets has made the exploitation unviable for the time being. Parsons have therefore pulled out and the future of the entire project is uncertain, with nothing being done to develop the concession at the moment.

A whole variety of other companies have also been set up with private foreign capital. The largest is the British stake in the Tendaho Cotton plantations which had a share capital of Eth.$21 million in 1973. This is partly Government owned—49 per cent in 1965, 37 per cent in 1969. The other main cotton producer—Cottonificio Baratolo of Eritrea—is locally financed with the money from Italian settlers. The cotton industry has been one of the successes of import substitution and now produces 20,000 tons out of the 26,000 tons necessary in 1972 for local textile needs. Their methods do not, however, always meet with the textile manufacturers' approval, since the producers have the option of exporting when world prices are favourable and the monopolistic control operated by a very few companies makes it possible for prices to be raised suddenly.

This happened in 1971 when the producers jumped prices by 20 per cent; in September 1972 the producers held back sales because the world prices were low and waited until the prices rose again at the beginning of 1973.

Other areas where foreign capital has been important are the insurance, hotel and banking sectors which have received British, American and Italian funds. The number of externally-owned insurance companies is now virtually zero though there were some thirty of them in 1967. In 1970 the Insurance Proclamation limited the percentage of foreign capital to 49 per cent; as a result most of the companies are now Ethiopian-owned although there is still a lot of overseas money in them.

One of the most interesting foreign companies is the drug firm Epharm which is Israeli-financed. Epharm has had a checkered history starting in 1963 with a 50 per cent British holding. The British company pulled out in 1966 and after an unsuccessful Hungarian interlude the Israeli company, Teva, took a 49 per cent share, leaving 51 per cent to the Ethiopian Government. Under the agreement signed in 1970 the company received the usual tax exemptions which in 1973 were the 41 per cent import taxes and duties on the sales to the private sector and the 16 per cent tax on sales to the Government. Over and above this Epharm also got a 15 per cent price preference over the goods of competitors which gave its profit margins on sales to the Government a considerable boost. These exemptions were calculated to be worth Eth.$1·3 million in 1973, and in that year the company announced an Eth.$0·8 million loss. It is not surprising that in the freer climate of expression after the 1974 crisis that the firm was vigorously criticized in the press.[29]

The areas of private investment listed above are by no means complete but they give an idea of its spread. Certainly the concessions have been substantial with the tax exemptions, tariff protection, duty free imports, free repatriation of profits and dividends and price control assistance. For Americans there has also been the added guarantee signed in 1962. This provides the investor with a U.S. government assurance that he will be protected against expropriation, loss through war or the unconvertibility of funds.[30] The Ethiopian Government agreed to allow the free transfer of any currency credit or investment without hindrance. The amounts that all these inducements have brought in has however not met with the Government's requirements. It does not appear that the

Third Five Year Plan target of Eth.$340 million over the period 1968–73 was realized—a major reason was the failure of the potash mining.

In fact the influx of aid has been of more significance to the economy than private capital. This has of course been vital as the rate of saving and the availability of local capital has been far too low to provide self-sufficient development. With the amount of investment more than doubling for each of the Five Year Plans the need for aid has increased proportionately.

TABLE 26

Planned Investment

	Total Investment*	Foreign Capital*	%
1st F.Y.P.	673·6	198·0	29·4
2nd F.Y.P.	1,696·0	638·5	37·6
3rd F.Y.P.	3,415·0	1,051·1	30·8

* In millions of Ethiopian dollars.

Source: Five Year Plans.

TABLE 27

External Debts as of December 1970

Source	Cumulative credits/loans†	Cumulative disbursements	%
Multilateral	332,000 (341,800)	222,867 (219,445)	67·1 (64·2)
I.B.R.D.	244,500 (244,500)	166,040 (152,117)	67·9 (62·2)
I.D.A.	87,500 (79,750)	56,827 (49,779)	64·9 (62·2)
I.F.C.	— (17,550)	— (17,550)	— (100)
Bilateral	810,480 (769,029)	432,958 (402,001)	53·4 (52·3)
U.S.A.	280,712 (287,504)	217,628 (231,098)	77·5 (80·4)
W. Germany	58,512 (53,798)	19,774 (16,797)	33·8 (31·2)
U.K.	14,555 (15,171)	2,555 (3,171)	17·6 (20·9)
U.S.S.R.	251,369 (251,259)	44,459 (44,459)	17·7 (17·6)
Czech	29,115 (29,087)	12,929 (7,054)	44·4 (24·3)
Yugoslavia	34,882 (35,391)	27,124 (27,098)	77·8 (76·6)
Italy	75,926 (29,725)	62,382 (27,247)	82·2 (91·7)
Sweden	28,165 (28,165)	8,863 (6,289)	31·5 (22·3)
Others	37,244 (38,929)	37,244 (38,929)	100 (100)
Totals*	1,142,480 (1,110,829)	655,825 (621,446)	

Figures expressed in thousands of Ethiopian dollars.
* Totals rounded. † Figures in brackets are for 1969.

Source: Ministry of Finance; in C.B.E. Monthly Report October/November 1972, Addis Ababa.

The total aid that has been offered up to December 1970 (shown in Table 27), amounted to Eth. $1,142 million, though only 57·4 per cent was taken up. Table 28 shows the sectoral distribution. Neither table includes the military aid, most of which has come from the U.S.A. It is not clear whether the figures are entirely accurate. According to U.S. sources Ethiopia has received over Eth. $600 million in civilian aid, only half of which appears in these figures from the Ministry of Finance. It is of course true that substantial aid has been given since 1970—an Eth. $100 million loan from China, and six other World Bank loans bringing the totals for I.B.R.D. loans (up to September 1972) to Eth. $269·5 million and for the I.D.A. to Eth. $201·0 million. Nevertheless the Ministry's own calculations do not seem to agree from year to year; for comparison the figures published in 1969 are included in brackets.

TABLE 28.

Sectoral Disbursement of Credits

Sector	Cumulative credits	%	Cumulative Disbursements	%	% Disbursed
Agriculture	35,692	3·9	7,375	1·1	20·7
Mining	2,927	0·3	2,927	0·4	100·0
Manufacturing	87,181	9·6	73,749	11·2	84·6
Electricity and Water	153,888	16·9	102,852	15·7	66·8
Construction	6,356	0·7	1,223	0·2	19·2
Trade, Hotels, Tourism	9,250	1·0	9,004	1·4	97·3
Transp./Communications	448,971	49·4	321,534	49·0	71·6
Financial Agencies	93,044	10·3	75,764	11·6	81·4
Community/Social Services	52,635	5·8	42,348	6·5	80·5
Miscellaneous	19,049	2·1	19,049	2·9	100·0
Total	908,993		655,825		

Figures in thousands of Ethiopian dollars.

Source: Ministry of Finance; in C.B.E. Monthly Report October/November 1972, Addis Ababa.

These figures point up the priorities that the Government has shown in practice, whatever the attitudes and ideas visualized in the Five Year Plans may have been. Agriculture has not only received a small amount of aid; but little of that has been distributed and used. As the Commercial Bank has noted: "Aid has often been given for projects, the function of which in the general development strategy of the country was difficult to assess".[31]

160 *The Dying Lion*

These massive amounts of aid have also provided the country with a sizeable debt-servicing problem. As of December 1972 the outstanding debt was Eth. $569 million, with repayments and interest charges running at well over Eth. $50 million a year, and taking up an increasing amount of export earnings.

TABLE 29

Loan Repayments

Year	Loan repayments in million Eth. $	As % of total export earnings	1970 C.B.E. (figures)
1964	21·6	5·6	21·6— 6·1
1965	24·5	5·4	24·6— 5·9
1966	32·0	6·9	32·0— 7·8
1967	39·0	9·1	39·0—10·2
1968	42·1	8·5	46·1—10·8
1969	48·9	9·5	53·6—11·8
1970	55·5	10·7	
1971	56·0	10·1	

Sources: C.B.E. Market Report October/November, 1970; C.B.E. The Ethiopian Economy, 1972.

It is clear from these figures, although they do not entirely agree, that the servicing has been steadily increasing. It may be assumed that the percentages will have fallen for 1973, the export earnings for that year being considerably higher than for some time previously, due to the world commodity price-rises. The upsurge has, however, been tempered and will almost certainly be reversed in 1974 by the severe drought and the oil crisis of 1973.

In spite of the massive amounts of foreign capital, a considerable quantity of the funds for development is still expected to come from internal sources—both Government and private. The Government industrial and development projects are carried out through a variety of financial institutions and wholly owned subsidiaries. The main one, as from 1970, has been the Agricultural and Industrial Development Bank (A.I.D.B.). This was set up by merging the Development Bank of Ethiopia and the Investment Corporation to act as the major Government instrument "to mobilise and channel investment funds for the accelerated development of Ethiopia's agriculture and industry".[32]

The A.I.D.B. was capitalized at Eth. $100 million, of which Eth. $45 million had been disbursed by the middle of 1972—56 per cent to the agricultural sector, 28 per cent to industry and 16 per cent to services. This is at first sight impressive but a breakdown of the elements reveals some shortcomings. In 1971–72 the loans to the agricultural sector totalled Eth. $19 million. Of this Eth. $6 million went to three large farms, Eth. $9 million went to 107 individual farmers, and only Eth. $4 million went to what could be described as small farmers through loans to co-operative societies. Therefore, while the A.I.D.B. does lend more to the agricultural sector than has been the case in the past or with other institutions, its loans are still aimed very much at the larger farmers. Only 7 per cent of the loans granted in this period can be classified as being directed towards those who most need them. The insistence that the A.I.D.B. must lend at commercial rates obviously has a serious effect on the numbers of small farmers who can afford loans. Even the Government organized Minimum Package Programme (see Chapter 4) suffers from this situation.

The commercial banks as a whole have an even worse record in making loans to the agricultural field, as this table of the Commercial Bank of Ethiopia lending for the years 1968–71 shows.

Table 30

C.B.E. Loans, Advances and Bills Discounted, 1968–71 in percentages

Sector	1968	1969	1970	1971	Average
Industrial	19·8	17·7	16·2	17·4	17·8
Local Trade	18·8	18·9	21·7	20·7	20·0
Export	17·1	18·9	17·7	16·4	17·5
Import	17·1	17·0	18·3	20·5	18·2
Construction	16·3	16·1	16·4	15·7	16·1
Agriculture	9·3	9·2	8·2	8·0	8·7
Miscellaneous	1·6	2·2	1·5	1·3	1·7

Source: C.B.E. Market Report October/November 1972, Addis Ababa.

The essential problem is that, in the commercial sector in particular, security is demanded. By and large for the banks this means land, which is the most acceptable form of security. For over half the peasants this is impossible as they are tenants; for the majority of others the commercial interest rates are too high because so many are not in any position to market their crops to obtain the necessary cash. Credit-worthiness is thus largely confined to those who are sizeable landowners or those who are on a salaried basis. This is underlined by the pattern of the branches of the Commercial Bank in 1972. Out of 108 branches there were 40 in Shoa, 26 in Eritrea and the next provinces—Hararge and Sidamo—had only 6 apiece, and Arussi, Bale and Gomu-Goffa had only 1 each.

It is in fact clear that for all the Government talk of regional development, which has been considerable since the start of the Third Five Year Plan in 1968, actual development has been largely confined to two provinces—Shoa and Hararge. In this context Eritrea's situation is mainly the result of the Italian colonial period. Regional development is to be seen in some of the agricultural schemes, as at Chilalo, Wollamo and Humera and in the Awash valley. The latter in particular is an example of a multi-level project incorporating hydro-electricity, agro-industries and irrigated farming, and it is by far and away the most considerable effort in the country. It is also in Shoa, and as has been noted in Chapter 4 there are certain problems connected with this as with all the regional schemes. The only attempt at a regional industrial approach in Tigre has been more or less a failure.

The approach of the Government to development is underlined by the whole system of public finance. A glance at the budgetary figures makes it clear that the Government priorities have never been particularly geared to development. Table 31 shows that the sector that provides the greatest resources, and the livelihood of nearly the entire population, is almost totally neglected. By contrast with agriculture the various elements of security and administration are most generously catered for. This is still the practice and the latest budgets show no signs of change. Over 30 per cent is earmarked for defence and internal security for 1972–73. In the previous year it was 31 per cent with only 2 per cent going to agriculture. The only social sector that is relatively generously treated is education (17 per cent in 1972–73).

Investments shows the same situation. The estimates for investment during the three Five Year Plans are in Table 32. It should be emphasized that these figures are the estimates and not the achievements. Once again the lack of interest in the agricultural sector is, by comparison, very marked.

TABLE 31.

Ordinary Expenditure: Comparative figures from four budgets

Ministries	1944/5	1957/8	1965/6	1970/1	****
Civil List*	2,716,707	3,968,055	5,755,628	9,669,102	(5,986,721)
War/Defence	11,498,724 (inc. B-Guard)	39,000,000	102,548,275	87,380,158	(89,059,896)
Interior	8,660,897	23,270,511	78,994,548	74,111,984	(75,181,321)
Justice	1,245,427	4,140,161	7,131,147	7,153,147	(7,965,680)
Information	**	1,256,519	6,050,268	7,171,383	(5,959,240)
Education	1,697,240	14,554,736	63,882,386	76,978,983	(75,909,256)
Health	**	4,605,797	25,355,342	23,399,615	(23,606,548)
Agriculture	583,458	1,656,803	10,251,589	11,545,676***	(13,406,994)
Community Development	**	2,856,593	3,327,170	4,373,267	(4,767,285)
Commerce and Industry	205,201	634,805	1,374,890	2,332,399	(2,374,362)
Ordinary expenditure total	41,099,235	158,535,978	403,213,234	507,097,969	(516,234,666)
Capital expenditure	—	67,706,350	104,372,349	124,278,718	(131,901,120)

Figures in Ethiopian dollars.

* Includes the Imperial Court, the Ministry of the Pen and Haile Selassie's Private Cabinet (and for 1944/5 the expenses of the Senate and Deputies).
** These were not separate ministries at this time.
*** Includes the Ministry of Land Reform, the Awash Valley Authority and the Wild Life Conservation Department.
**** The figures in brackets are the original estimates for 1970/1.

Source: Adapted from M. Perham, Government of Ethiopia, 2nd Edition, London 1969, p. 204; Ethiopian Observer: Vol. III, no. 2, 1959, pp. 58–61, Vol. X, no. 3, 1966, pp. 192–98; Ministry of Finance, Budget F.Y., 1964 (1970–71).

TABLE 32.

Provision for Investment 1957–73

Sector	1st F.Y.P.	2nd F.Y.P.	3rd F.Y.P.	Percentage of total 1957–73
Agriculture	92·1	363·0	312·1	15
Mining/Power/ Manufacturing	138·0	455·3	864·4	29
Transport/Building Communications	240·0	325·4	624·4	24
Social/Services Government	57·0	120·8	173·1	7
Housing	122·5	250·0	524·6	16
Others	24·0	66·5	366·8	9
Total	673·6	1,581·0	2,865·4	

Figures in Ethiopian dollars (millions).
Source: The Five Year Plans.

The Government method of taxation provides an example of a similar approach. Taxes on agriculture are negligible compared to the importance of the sector in the national economy. Obviously this is partly because agriculture to a great extent lies outside the cash economy, and the incomes from it are still mainly subsistence. This status of a very low or non-existent income for the majority is compounded by the very high degree of evasion, both legal and illegal, in the higher income brackets; further there is a considerable lack of efficiency in the collection of taxes. In fact the Government policy has been orientated to avoidance of direct taxation as a whole, and concentration on indirect taxes. The position in 1950–51 when direct taxes were only 23 per cent of the tax revenue has only marginally improved to 27 per cent today (see Chapter 3).

There are of course obvious criticisms that can be made of this approach which emphasizes the social divisions and penalises the less well-off. It also contributes to the threat of inflation; and most important, it is tied to revenue production as the major factor, and does not have much to do with development. There is little sign that Government policy uses the tariff possibilities to do more than raise its revenues and to provide monopoly positions for certain industrial projects. All manufactured items are subject to a high indirect tax—the one exception is textiles. The following was written in 1964: "The further increase of the tax burden borne by lower income groups would seriously obstruct the extension of the home market and, consequently, of economic development. On the contrary, the heavier and more efficient taxation of big landowners will prevent the actual waste of resources and lead to the better use of resources".[33] Since this was written the position of the lower income groups has deteriorated with the new income tax. Although the intention may have been to implement the schedules for the higher levels as well, the fact remains that there has been little evidence of this and the tax certainly does press almost exclusively on those who can least afford to pay it.

It is true that the new Government of *Lij* Endalkatchew announced its intention of changing the tax structure and of committing itself to greater social equality; but until 1974 the Government's commitment was clearly to inequality. So until March 1974 when the demands of the workers for the tripling of the basic wages was accepted by the Government in the face of the massive inflation of late 1973 and early 1974, the wage position of the average worker had improved little. The basic daily wage for an unskilled worker had remained static for the previous decade.

It might be expected that this would lead to the growth of a substantial labour movement. However the small size of the industrial sector has limited both its appearance and its effectiveness. Equally important has been the jaundiced view that the Government has had of any type of labour organization. The origins of the movement lie in the workers' associations and syndicates in the period before the Labour Relations Decree of 1962. (This was proclaimed in 1963 and approved by Parliament in 1964). Until that decree, although the revised constitution specifically promulgated the right "to engage in any occupation and, to that end, to form or join associations, in accordance with the law", there was no law allowing unions and so none could be formed. In 1962, however, the Government accepted the fact of organized labour bodies and therefore regulated their activities.

Some of the rights granted were rather specific—as for example the right to strike. This was allowed only to a union and then only providing the Labour Relations Board had been called in to arbitrate at least sixty days before the strike could begin. Large categories of workers were also exempted from the right to strike—public servants, including virtually all Government employees, and employees in public service enterprises such as electricity, water and transport. For example, in 1964 a strike on the domestic flights of Ethiopian Airlines was declared illegal on the grounds that the grievances had not been submitted to the Board sixty days in advance; that the airline was a public transport service; that a strike injured the public and that they were specifically forbidden to strike by the Labour Decree. A year later a two-day strike by the employees of the General Transport Co., that operates the Addis Ababa buses, was declared illegal because the company was a transport company. Incidentally, employees in these sectors were allowed to form unions but they could be used only for collective bargaining or other innocuous activities.

Prior to 1962 the labour movement consisted of a number of autonomous organizations set up on a factory basis for welfare purposes. They may be compared with such social groupings as the *ekub* and the *mehaber* (see Chapter 9). The Railroad Workers Syndicate of Dire Dawa, formed in 1947, was such a case; and although it was involved in a fierce strike that was put down by troops in 1949, this was exceptional. Its main purpose was welfare and, by and large, the leadership co-operated with the Government. Much more significant use of workers' power was to be seen in Eritrea where there was a larger working-class even after the running down of the Eritrean economy during the period of the British mandate. The Syndicate of the Union of Free Workers was set up in 1952 under the leadership of Woldeab Wolde Mariam. From the beginning it was very much used as a political instrument to protest against the steady takeover of Eritrea by Amharas. Woldeab himself went into exile and joined the E.L.F. Under these circumstances the unions were regarded as political dissidents when the Federation ended in 1962. Nevertheless unionism, which had been fostered by the British, was too powerful to be removed. The alternative was to try and control it, and it was largely because of the Eritrean situation that the Labour Decree was passed in that year.

Once the Labour Decree made it legal to form unions they sprang up quickly, and there were forty-two within a year. These formed themselves into the Confederation of Ethiopian Labour Unions which claimed a membership of 70,000. If this figure is accurate expansion has been very slow as there were 80,000 members in 167 affiliates in 1973. Part of the reason for this has been the exclusion of public servants from the right to form a union at all; equally, a number of unions have disappeared for various reasons, especially in Eritrea. In fact C.E.L.U. has not been a great success, although it has had some substantial wage victories and has done good work in the field of education. Nevertheless it has been severely criticized especially for its subservient attitude towards the Labour Relations Board.

This board is under the auspices of the Ministry of National Community Development and has been the government's main instrument for controlling the labour movement. It has the right to adjudicate and arbitrate in a dispute, as well as powers to enforce the Labour Proclamation and to enforce agreements between employers and unions. Through it the Government also has a vital say in the staffing of the administration of the C.E.L.U. In fact although the growth and militancy of the unions seemed to take the Government by surprise immediately after 1962, these controls have been essentially successful. Before 1974 there was very little activity that might be called political, apart from an attempt to lobby Parliament in 1965–66.

There were signs that this situation was changing however even before 1974. For example, C.E.L.U. has long had contacts with the students, at first through graduates who were involved in its administration and who ran the "Voice of Labour". It was largely their influence that encouraged the movement to operate literacy campaigns, organise Thrift and Credit co-operatives and hold seminars for them around the country. The more radical students have also had strike contacts. On two occasions one of the most militant unions in the country—the sugar workers on the H.V.A. Ethiopia plantations—has appealed for student support, in 1967 and 1969. Although in neither case were the students prepared to turn out in support, they did collect money. In return the unions supported striking students with funds, especially in 1969.

Symptomatic of the dissatisfaction with the C.E.L.U. is the dispute that broke out in 1973. The confederation, against the wishes of its own staff, divided itself into three zones for practical purposes—Asmara, Addis Ababa and Dire Dawa. In mid-1973, after elections for officers of the Asmara zone were held, the confederation declared the results null and void, and appointed new officers without any election or consultation. Not surprisingly this led to considerable anger and over forty unions stopped paying their dues and decided to set up their own confederation. In July, the Ministry of National

Community Development took a hand and forced both sides to sign an agreement to suspend the dispute until March 1974 when a general assembly was due to be held.

The problem was not just one of administration and jurisdiction. Accusations by the disaffected unions were wide-ranging and comprehensive. The C.E.L.U. was accused of being corrupt and its leadership of being composed of members without unions, as well as employers who were co-opted without consultation with the membership. It was claimed that the constitution and the whole organization needed to be completely restructured. Most serious, C.E.L.U. was accused of co-operating with the Government in helping to dissolve twenty-five unions in Asmara alone. There were two elements to this. It was thought of as being anti-Eritrean by the remaining Asmara unions; it was also thought to be part of a long term strategy by the Government threatening the viability of the labour movement as a whole. The growing number of strikes and their significance, as well as the actual and potential links with student dissidence, were believed to have frightened the Government into believing that its control was slipping.

Workers' militancy came to the fore in early 1974 and in fact it was the strike of taxi-drivers in February that played a considerable part in precipitating the political crisis. More important was the general strike called by the C.E.L.U. on 7 March because of the previous Government's inattention to demands put to them. The strike, which was a successful exhibition of solidarity, lasted four days and produced a Government response to most of the seventeen demands. These were concerned with the legal position of striking and of dismissals, salary increases and the regulation of a minimum wage; with price control, labour pension schemes, conflicts of interests when civil servants sit upon company boards, job opportunities and Ethiopianization and with the activities of the Labour Board. Over and above this demands were concerned with the cancelling of the Education Sector Review, the necessity for free education for all and for a free press.

In the months after the strike, labour militancy continued in a series of smaller strikes by various groups. These were largely concerned with pay, with attempts to get unions and agreements where there were none before and to remove certain officials. These later strikes emphasize that the militancy of March should not be considered as an isolated event. For the future it will clearly be a feature of political life, and the signs are that the workers, along with the students, will provide a radical element in Addis Ababa at least. The C.E.L.U. has already made it clear that it hopes to be able to form a political party under the expected constitutional revisions, and its platform would include radical land reform.

The major factor that has been behind this steady growth of industrial unrest over the last fifteen years has been inflation. Up to 1973 industrial wages increased by 20 per cent over a twenty-year period for the average worker. The retail price index for Addis Ababa in particular has shown a much faster rise, especially in the decade 1963–73.

TABLE 33

Retail Price Index—Addis Ababa 1963-73
1963 = 100

	1969	1970	1971	1972	1973
Cereals	136	180		129	143
Meat	145	147		144	159
Dairy products	141	159		156	174
Fruit/Vegetables	143	133		125	188
Spices	163	163		160	238
Total food	135	156	155	137	154

Source: C.B.E. Market Reports 1973. Addis Ababa.

In the first three months of 1974 prices were rising uncontrollably at the rate of 80 per cent per quarter. The situation began to ease after the improved rains of 1974. The new Government also made vigorous, though not entirely successful, efforts to impose controls especially on the basic foods. Conversely, however, the pay rises granted to the armed forces and the wage increases that were sanctioned were inflationary so the position remained precarious.

Such a radicalization of the industrial proletariat is of considerable importance considering the class divisions of the Ethiopian state and introduce a new dimension into the political possibilities. The alliance that exists both explicitly and implicitly between imperialism—especially that of the U.S. in Ethiopia—and the ruling classes of Ethiopia, both at Government and private levels, has been highly successful in its own terms. The growth of a national bour-geoisie has been stifled at birth and the feudal landowners have acquired two other groups to strengthen their position—the *comprador* and bureaucratic bourgeoisie.[34] Both have been infiltrated thoroughly by feudal elements. They have assisted the landowning class to invest in capitalist development through mechanization on the land, and thus provided for a mechanized feudalism, rather than any true development of capitalist modes of production. This policy has introduced tensions among various elements of the feudal landowning class, which, of course, is not really homogeneous—there are various levels identified within Ethiopian society by the terms *mekwanint* and *balabat*. It must also be emphasized that the peasantry is not homogeneous either. A "kulak" class may be identified particularly among the *rist* owners of the Amhara/Tigre highlands. Nevertheless the basic contradiction within most of the Ethiopian empire has been between the landless tenants, small peasant landowners and a growing rural proletariat, and the land-owning aristocracy as a whole.[35]

Since 1941 there has also been the growth of new classes within the state. Various elements of a bourgeoisie have appeared, in particular the bureaucratic element, which is identified with the landowning interests by its administration of the state on their behalf. Another rapidly-growing element has been the petty bourgeoisie—small traders, craftsmen, professional groups and students. These can be clearly delineated into "left" and "right", with most professional groups finding substantial advantages in an alliance with the bureaucracy. It should be noted that both the bureaucratic bourgeoisie and its allies among the petty bourgeoisie can be classified as reformist. It is this group which sees advantages in improved administration and in political activities on the western parliamentary model.

The "left" elements within the petty bourgeoisie are to be found in alliance with the other classes that have appeared since the war. The proletariat in Ethiopia is still very small in spite of the steady growth of the industrial sector in relative terms; its politicization has still a long way to go. Its major potential ally is the lumpen-proletariat of unemployed which is the fastest growing socio-economic category in the country—due to evictions consequent upon mechanization in rural areas, and to the increasing shortage of job opportunities in urban areas.

While it is true that the most vocal revolutionary element today is to be found among the student sector of the petty bourgeoisie, the most practical revolutionary elements are currently concentrated in the national movements now operating in Eritrea and Bale. Since

1970 both of these have become revolutionary socialist movements
—they cannot be so described before this date—and they spearhead
revolutionary, as opposed to reformist, attitudes at the moment.
Since 1970 there has been an attempt to bring together the national
movements and the student radicals, especially those overseas. The
process however has not gone very far nor has it included an alliance
with the proletariat in any meaningful way. Peasant unrest is still
the most valid, if undirected, revolutionary force in Ethiopia; it
seems likely to remain so for a considerable time.

PART THREE: NATIONAL MOVEMENTS AND OPPOSITION

CHAPTER VI

Militant Opposition I—Amhara, Tigre and Eritrea

Haile Selassie's efforts throughout his long reign have been directed primarily at the maintenance of his own imperial power. It is to this end that such changes as have occurred have been carried out. The pattern is set firmly in the history of Ethiopia. What the Emperor has done is to adjust to circumstances, to perform the minimum requirements to keep the throne strong. There have been reforms, but the Emperor's motives for reform have remained rooted in his need to preserve the imperial position. All the imperial reforms fit the centralization schemata of the strong Emperors of the past: removal of one set of provincial rulers, replacement by another group drawn from those that could be trusted, but all from the same limited class; a centralized bureaucracy to carry out the administration much more efficiently than before; education kept to the minimum extent necessary to adapt to world situations and to modern technology.

The Emperor has never been able to centralize as far as he might perhaps have desired, and he has always been prepared to compromise and negotiate when necessary. Centralization has therefore never been carried to extremes. Certain provinces, strong in their own regional or national feelings, have been allowed considerable autonomy; Tigre is the major example, but Wag and Gojjam have received or enforced some consideration as well. In a number of other cases, provincial nobility have been allowed to hold posts as high as the *awraja* governor level and even, though much more rarely, at the level of *Enderassie—Dejazmatch* Kassa in Wollega, Major-General Jagama in Bale. At the lower levels of the provincial hierarchy the lesser nobility have been almost exclusively used in the Amhara/Tigre Christian provinces. In the southern and western provinces the local indigenous nobility have been used to some extent at the *woreda* level, and more rarely at the *awraja* level, but to a great degree these posts have been filled with Amharas, usually from Shoa—though many of these are settlers who have been in the area for over seventy years, and have therefore identified with the people of the province, in so far as landowners in their position can be expected to do so.

Regional autonomy has therefore been allowed to a limited extent when expediency dictated. This has been paralleled by a lessening of imperial power that has taken place as the Emperor has aged and as the Government has become too complex for any individual to control. The Emperor's actions can perhaps be explained by the argument, as they usually are by his apologists, that he has modernized as fast and far as he was able in the face of traditional opposition. The facts more accurately seem to fit the interpretation offered here; that he has "modernized" as little as is compatible with the maintenance of imperial sovereignty, and that with his advancing age and weakening control there has been some assertion of power by others—an explanation that fits into the normal Ethiopian historical pattern. There is, however, one distinction, vital to the future. The devolution has had a regional base to some degree; power has also fallen into the hands of office holders and institutions originally created for the maintenance of the imperial position.

This of course begs the question as to how far the process of centralization has actually worked; whether Haile Selassie will leave behind him institutions (or individuals) which are really capable of efficiently governing such a disparate empire. Indeed at this point it is worth considering how far Haile Selassie has succeeded in this during his own reign. Superficially he certainly has. Nothing has been lost and the empire is, on the whole (though with some reservations about the recent growth in Somalia's strength) reasonably prepared against external aggression. There is a well-trained and adequately large army available; and even if this force has within it the seeds of serious divisiveness it is still a powerful force. However, as mentioned before, the Emperor elected to control the army by balancing out its factions as far as possible. These divisions are not going to disappear when the Emperor goes.

The technique used has been a largely personalized approach to Government—individuals of significance from the landowning class are the ones that matter. There has thus been little or no emphasis on the people, either as a whole, or even in groups at the provincial, social or religious levels. This insistence on governing expediently through over-emphasis on individuals and on one class has been a

fundamental weakness of imperial theory. Rebellions may collapse
if the leaders are removed; equally they may not if they are widely
based. They may after all have no real individual leader. Haile
Selassie has always been more competent in breaking a conspiracy
than a provincial movement. Wider expressions of dissatisfaction on
the level of a province or of student demonstrations on a national
level have tended to reduce him to sorrow and bewilderment, to
judge by his public utterances on these subjects.

Certain efforts at a more generalized emphasis have at times been
apparent. In 1935–36 foreign aggression provided the opportunity
for national consciousness. This occurred, but it was above all
an anti-Italian, an anti-foreign attitude, rather than a pro-Ethiopian
one. Ethiopia may be a concept to the educated elite—though not
to all of them by any means—it certainly is not to the average peasant.
"It would be an oversimplification to call *Leul-Ras* Hailu (of Gojjam,
who collaborated with the Italians) a traitor, as Ethiopians often
do, for he may well not have accepted the premises on which the
judgement is based, i.e. that Ethiopia was a nation state and that
as such it demanded his first loyalty".[1] This view of *Ras* Hailu is
supported by his activities, both before the war and during the
Italian conquest. His main aim was the preservation of his dynasty,
in acquiring the title of *Negus* and in the preservation of a particular
status for Gojjam. He had little love for either the Emperor or the
Shoan Amharas and none for the Italians except in so far as they
were useful to him. It is simplistic to say that the first loyalty is to
the region and the historic province, yet in the Christian highland
areas this is true. In the non-Amhara and non-Christian provinces
the first loyalty is to the region and to the people. There is often an
implicitly anti-Amhara feeling that now runs very deep in some areas.
Spasmodic attempts have been made to eradicate this and to provide
alternative points of loyalty that might prove more agreeable; the
emphasis has however been laid, not on Ethiopia, but upon Haile
Selassie himself, upon the Emperor. Loyalty is personalized like the
style of Government, not institutionalized.

Given the degree to which attempts at assimilation have been
confined to the educated elite and to the nobility through marriage
and office; and given the systematic exploitation of the tenants
and the lowest levels of the peasant farmers, it is hardly surprising
that there have been many challenges to imperial rule—or to the
Amhara control, for the two are usually seen as synonymous. Some
of these challenges are those that might be expected in any

Byzantine-like court based largely upon personal relationships, and thus intrigues, with individuals constantly jockeying for favourable positions. Throughout Haile Selassie's reign, plots by disappointed individuals have been common. Many of these have been personal, similar to the semi-coup of 1928 when *Ras* Tafari, as the Emperor then was, obtained the title of *Negus*. Such plots have been directly aimed at the person of the Emperor. In most cases there has been little evidence that the perpetrators have been thinking in anything but individual terms. Some of the plots have indeed been aimed at other members of the Government. This is inevitable when personality is carried to the extremes that it has been under Haile Selassie.

Some of these challenges have been more significant because they have provided an ideological threat to the regime. The attempted coup of 1960 falls into this category because of the revolutionary ideals of its main leader, even though the feelings of most of those involved appear to have been more restrained. Some of the plots of *Blatta* Tekle Wolde Hawariat had overtones of republicanism or a constitutional monarchy. The most obvious example has been the student unrest of the last few years. This has become, with the aid of students educated overseas, more and more socialist-orientated. Similar elements may also be discerned, although faintly, among the small labour force in the main cities. Some sections of both these latter groups also have the same reformist ideas as can be found in the army and the bureaucracy: the desire for reform attached to constitutional change.

Another phase of the opposition has become firmly based on national lines which have provided a much wider base of support. As might be expected this has surfaced most strongly among the Eritreans and the Oromo, the two largest non-Amhara groups; in both cases it has been inflamed by religious feelings. Another example that is more questionable is the Tigrinya-speaking Christian community of Eritrea and Tigre. There have been some incipient national feelings, notably in 1943, but they have been weakened by the far longer attachment of the areas to the empire, the common religion, and the fact that the tradition of the empire is a joint Amhara/Tigre one—indeed the origin of the empire, Axum, lies in Tigre. Regional dissatisfaction has positively surfaced in Gojjam, an Amhara province. Here the factors have been a strong traditional desire to look after their own affairs, coupled with a dislike of Shoan Amharas.

In all these cases a very significant factor has been the general situation of the peasantry. In Gojjam and Tigre this applies not only to the landless, but to the smaller landowners as well; elsewhere the discontent has tended to come from the tenants. In either case they are both heavily over-taxed. It has of course been normal in Ethiopia, given the importance of deference as a social factor, for a relatively important individual to lead such movements and revolts. This must however not obscure the fact that, whatever such a leader's motivations, for most of those involved much more radical changes are desired than the promotion of an individual. The crucial lever that brings about such revolts is the generally depressed state of the peasantry. The spark may be a charismatic leader or it may be a spell of exceptionally bad government. The people need a leader but their acceptance of one comes out of their own situation.

None of these categories is meant to be exclusive. The Eritrean revolt for example has, or has had, at various times as significant factors, Eritrean nationalism, Moslem separatism, anti-Amhara feeling, individual dissatisfactions, peasant unrest and socialist theories. All of these except the first can be seen in the Bale revolt, which had overtones of Oromo and Somali nationalism. It is not always easy to disentangle the threads. It might be noted here that the Government and security forces have shown considerable skill in playing on the divisions that inevitably appear. They have encouraged and used Eritrean separatist feelings to try and divide the students at various times—sometimes quite successfully. The one thing that has not been done to any great extent is to try and reform the situations that have given rise to the revolts. In the case of the provincial revolts the answer has been forceful and vigorous suppression, followed by changes of local administrative personnel and usually an amnesty over unpaid taxes, palliatives rather than any attempt to remove the causes. It must however be made clear that on the whole these efforts have been successful in the short run at any rate. The one exception to this has been the aftermath of the attempted coup in 1960, because this was far more directly threatening than anything else that has occurred in that the only real force in the state was involved—the Armed Forces. The coup brought to light a number of deep-rooted dissatisfactions and made it quite possible that other sections of the army might take it into their heads to try similar actions. It was therefore deemed necessary to carry out some reforms, though the most radical efforts, such as the local government reforms, were soon neglected or shelved. Nevertheless the process was successful in that it was not until February

THE WOYANE REBELLION. TIGRE 1943

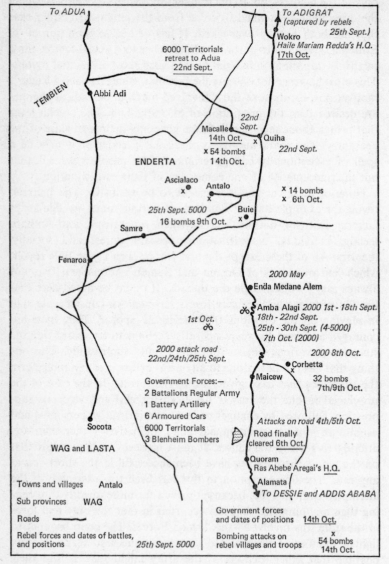

To ADUA

To ADIGRAT
(captured by rebels
25th Sept.)
Wokro
Haile Mariam Redda's H.Q.
17th Oct.

6000 Territorials
retreat to Adua
22nd Sept.

TEMBIEN

Abbi Adi

*22nd
Sept.*
Macalle
14th Oct.   x   Quiha
x 54 bombs   *22nd Sept.*
14th Oct.

ENDERTA

Ascialaco   x 14 bombs
x   Antalo   x 6th Oct.
x
25th Sept. 5000   Buie
16 bombs 9th Oct.   x

Samre

Fenaroa
2000 May
Enda Medane Alem

1st Oct.   Amba Alagi *2000 1st - 18th Sept.*
✂   *18th - 22nd Sept.*
25th - 30th Sept. (4-5000)
7th Oct. (2000)

2000 attack road   *2000 8th Oct.*
22nd/24th/25th Sept.   Corbetta
x
Government Forces:—   Maicew   *32 bombs*
2 Battalions Regular Army   *7th/9th Oct.*
1 Battery Artillery
6 Armoured Cars   *Attacks on road 4th/5th Oct.*
6000 Territorials   Road finally
3 Blenheim Bombers   cleared 6th Oct.

Socota   Quoram
Ras Abebe Aregai's H.Q.
WAG and LASTA   Alamata
To DESSIE and ADDIS ABABA

Towns and villages   Antalo

Sub provinces   WAG   Government forces
and dates of positions   *14th Oct.*
Roads   ———
Bombing attacks on   x
Rebel forces and dates of battles,   rebel villages and troops   54 bombs
and positions   *25th Sept. 5000*   14th Oct.

1974 that there were any open manifestation of a similar kind from the Armed Forces.

Almost the first example of these problems that the Emperor faced after the war was an outbreak of regionalism in the province of Gojjam. The causes of this were several—taxation was one, and there were an extended series of incidents beginning in 1942 and lasting several years. The most dangerous trouble revolved around the family of *Ras* Hailu Tekle Haimanot, who was taken to Addis Ababa in 1941 and remained there until his death in 1951; and around the patriot leaders especially Belai Zelleke, who was perhaps the most famous patriot in Gojjam.

Belai, who was the son of a *shifta*, had been rewarded at the return of the Emperor by being made a *Dejazmatch* and Governor of Bichena. However he was disgruntled by the fact that the three other major patriot leaders of Gojjam had received greater positions —*Dejazmatch* Hailu Belew was made a *Ras* and Governor-General of Gojjam, Mengesha Jambere was made *Bitwoded* and Deputy-Governor-General of the province, Negash Bezabeh was made *Bitwoded* and President of the Senate. It should be noted that all of these leaders were related either directly or by marriage to *Ras* Hailu Tekle Haimanot, the former ruler of Gojjam.

Coupled with substantial discontent in both Bichena and in Motta (where his father-in-law *Fitawari* Admassu, a nephew of *Ras* Hailu, was Governor) Belai felt strong enough to disobey orders both from the Governor-General and from Addis Ababa in 1942. However when *Bitwoded* Mengesha moved against him with over 3,000 men, Belai found himself deserted and was forced to surrender. He was brought to Addis Ababa, and imprisoned along with two grandsons of Hailu—*Dejazmatch* Mamo and *Dejazmatch* Kebede Haile Mikael. One of these, *Dejazmatch* Mamo, escaped briefly early in 1944 but was caught when he got to Gojjam.

Trouble over tax still continued in Gojjam and the Emperor found it necessary to visit Debra Marcos in mid-1944. His visit, accompanied by the distribution of large sums and the gift of 100,000$ M.T. (approximately £9,000) for distribution to the poor, had some effect, as did the announcement that the land tax proclamation of 1942 was amended for Gojjam (as well as for Begemeder and Tigre where there had also been trouble). For the future the land tax was to be collected on the traditional basis of a tribute for the whole province, and at the pre-Italian levels. This cut out the reason for most of the disturbances.

Nevertheless the situation was fragile enough for the Emperor to take severe fright when both *Dejazmatch* Mamo Haile Mikael, with his brother and half-brother, as well as *Dejazmatch* Belai with his brother, broke out of prison, killing a guard in the process. They were captured after only three days, on their way to Gojjam. After a trial by a commission that included *Ras* Birru Woldegabriel, Major-General Abebe Damtau, and *Dejazmatch* (later *Ras*) Mesfin Sileshi, all five were sentenced to death and were hung in the *mercato*, the bodies being left up for three days. Public reaction to this was marked and the execution of *Dejazmatch* Belai was much criticized because of his war record. The hanging of a grandson of *Ras* Hailu also came in for some criticism and it is probably that it could only have been done because of *Dejazmatch* Mamo's collaboration with the Italians. The severity of the sentence clearly stressed the anxiety that Gojjam feelings caused the Emperor. *Ras* Hailu was still a potent force, and although there was no sign that the escapees had even intended to try and free the *Ras*, the possibility was there. Even without *Ras* Hailu the group could have commanded significant and dangerous support in Gojjam. Coming at a time when a major threat had only just been put down in Tigre, there was clearly need for an example.[2]

Another Gojjami ex-patriot leader was involved in a serious plot to assassinate the Emperor in 1951. This was *Bitwoded* Negash Bezabeh. However, his involvement does not seem to have been directly related to the province in any way, though there had again been trouble in Gojjam the previous year. There had been an attempt to classify and assess the *rist* lands of the province in accordance with the system in use elsewhere. Opposition was apparently based on the idea that this was a first step to the replacement of *rist* holding by *gebbar* holding. It also involved an attempt to increase the actual rate of taxation in the province.

Gojjami reaction was considerable and there was armed resistance as well as a deputation to the Emperor. Once again the Government backed down and an amnesty was granted to the rebels. Early in 1951 the Governor, *Dejazmatch* Kebede Tessema, was replaced by one of the royal house of Gojjam, *Ras* Hailu Belew (nephew of *Ras* Hailu Tekle Haimanot who died that year). It is more than possible that *Bitwoded* Negash's involvement in his conspiracy came from his failure to be given the position. The Governors of Debra Markos and Metekel were also replaced—the latter by a Gojjami. The question of the tax was more or less shelved, though later it was

Connections of the Gojjami Patriot Leaders with the Royal House of Gojjam

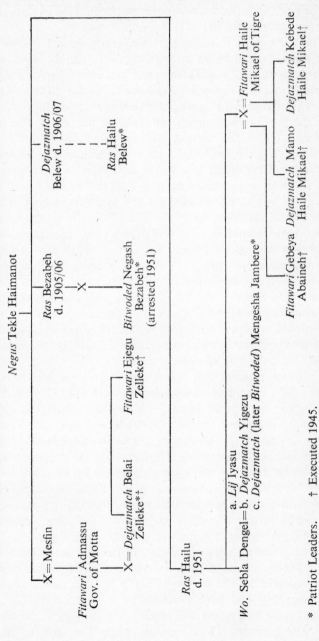

Negus Tekle Haimanot

X = Mesfin

Fitawari Admassu
Gov. of Motta

X = *Dejazmatch* Belai
Zelleke*†

Ras Bezabeh
d. 1905/06

X

Fitawari Ejegu   *Bitwoded* Negash
Zelleke†   Bezabeh*
(arrested 1951)

Dejazmatch
Belew d. 1906/07

Ras Hailu
Belew*

Ras Hailu
d. 1951

Wo. Sebla Dengel = a. *Lij* Iyasu
b. *Dejazmatch* Yigezu
c. *Dejazmatch* (later *Bitwoded*) Mengesha Jambere*

= X = *Fitawari* Haile
Mikael of Tigre

Fitawari Gebeya   *Dejazmatch* Mamo
Abaineh†   Haile Mikael†

Dejazmatch Kebede
Haile Mikael†

* Patriot Leaders.   † Executed 1945.

insisted on, at least formally. However the evidence suggests that in the mid-1960s the tax rating was still being paid at the previous rate, so the effectiveness of this formality may be doubted.

The third major disturbance in Gojjam broke out in 1967—and was again sparked by an attempt to change the tax laws, coupled with accusations of bad Government with especial reference to the Shoan Governor-General, *Dejazmatch* Tsehai Enko Selassie. During the trouble it also became clear that many in Gojjam believed that the province was under-represented at the centre. The trouble centred around the income tax proclamation of 1967 which abolished the tithe and levied a tax on production. For the majority of Gojjam farmers the rate would have been at the lowest level, Eth. $1·50 on an income of up to Eth. $300. The assessment was to be carried out by two local elders and by a Government official in each district, and Ministry of Finance officials. From the beginning there were accusations of unfairness and corruption—hardly surprising as such assessment was almost impossible to do accurately. Much more important was the very strong fear that the policy would involve much-increased taxes ultimately, and was the first stage in the measurement of *rist* lands. This last would not only interfere in the traditional system, but would certainly involve individuals in higher tax payments for there had been substantial land tax avoidance in the province, helped by the peculiarities of the system, and the lack of measurements.[3]

From the moment that orders went out to organize assessment teams, there was trouble. Meetings took place and general agreement not to pay soon spread. In early 1968 violence broke out when the Governor attempted to use the Police and then the Territorial Army to escort the assessment teams. Non-cooperation rapidly turned into active opposition. The farmers in the *awrajas* of Bichena and Motta began to organize themselves. In February in Dega Damot a leadership was elected by the rebels—consisting of their own district governor, sub-district governors and replacements for the *atbia danyas*. "The main qualifications for office seem to have been the possession of a gun and the will to oppose the tax".[4] This leadership was to remain in control of the area until December.

During the middle of 1968, several attempts were made to enforce submission in the affected areas—partly by force, partly by negotiation. In May and June a delegation was sent to Addis Ababa demanding a halt to tax assessments, and changes in the governor and sub-governors. There were also threats to blow up the Blue

Nile bridges and so isolate the province's road communications. By this time the rebels were in control of most of the Gojjam highlands and were threatening Debra Marcos.

In August a Government commission reported and the Emperor backed down. New governors were appointed to the province, and to the *awrajas* of Motta, Bichena and Debra Marcos. In the case of Motta the new governor had been governor early in the 1960s and the new appointment to Bichena was also a former governor of the area—both were popular choices and both were from Gojjam.The assessments were however to remain. This proved insufficient and renewed attempts to enforce the new tax were strongly resisted. There were violent clashes with the police commando units that had been ordered into the province (as had a battalion of the regular army, partly to guard the bridges). Several jet strikes were also made against rebel concentrations and a number of villages had houses burnt.

The increased use of force had the desired effects. The Emperor published a second amnesty in December and this time it was accepted. Tax assessment teams were withdrawn, though the income tax was not. However the rebels essentially agreed to pay the new tax, partly in return perhaps for the cancellation of unpaid taxes over the previous seventeen years (that is since the last provincial trouble of 1950). No reprisals were taken against individuals and the province once more became quiet.

There is no doubt that, although a prime cause was taxation, this movement must be seen as partly regional in inspiration. As is normal in such circumstances the elected leaders were often men of position or title, but it was equally a spontaneous peasant revolt. Those that suffered most were those who tried to enforce the Government orders—*chika shums* and *atbia danyas*, a number of whom were killed, as were elders who tried to act on the assessment teams. A certain number of deaths were also attributable to the paying off of old grudges and in order to make some out-of-court settlements of land claims. Defence of the *rist* system of land ownership was also a common factor involving those who resisted; and the movement had little appeal outside the *rist* areas.

The experience of 1967–68 was very much in line with the previous resistance of the province in 1950 and in 1942–44; and essentially for the same reasons. Gojjam has shown strong objections to being too closely involved in Shoan rule, and this has been recognized on a number of occasions by the Emperor—the necessity of appointing a member of the ruling family as Governor in 1941 and again in 1951; and of appointing important Gojjam nobles to lower positions as well. Attempts to tax it more heavily or to try and alter the traditional land arrangements have been an immediate signal for resistance. For all the close cultural connections between Gojjam and Shoa, the Gojjamis do not want Shoan imperial interference or rule.

This emphasis on Gojjam may suggest that regional movements against Shoan aristocratic control has been confined to this area. However, this is far from being the case. The nobilities of other Amhara areas have proved equally regionalistic, and have made several attempts to overthrow the control of the royal house of Shoa. There is a distinction, of course, to be drawn between individual conspiracies at the imperial centre and regional Amhara protests, though the two might be combined. The other Amhara areas of Begemeder and Wollo have also had regional movements and these have had to be acknowledged at times by the central authority. As an example, the position of the *Wagshums* of Wag and Lasta may be cited, where semi-autonomy, based on the 13th century legend of the transfer of power from the Zagwe rulers to the Shoan emperors of the house of Yekuno Amlak, still survives.

The ruling family of Semien and Yejju (part Oromo) have also been prominent in such efforts—the Empress Taitu in particular made a strong attempt to seize control in the last years of Menilek. Her nephew *Ras* Gugsa Walie made an attempt to overthrow *Negus* Tafari (as Haile Selassie was then) in 1930. After the war there was trouble in Begemeder in 1944, partly at the imposition of Amhara control. It is possible that an outbreak of disturbances in 1970–71, which involved an assassination attempt on the Governor, should also be seen in this light, though resentment of taxation also played its part.

These regional problems are, however, different from movements in both Tigre and Eritrea, which have more claim to be considered as actual or potential (in the case of Tigre) national movements. The case of Tigre is perhaps more arguable, although the Italian emphasis on a Tigrinya-speaking administrative area, as well as the rule of a Tigre Emperor in the nineteenth century, have given rise to some attitudes that can only be considered as national. It is true that the Tigrean nobility is relatively well-integrated through intermarriage and they share with the Amhara a common tradition (by and large); nevertheless this has not affected the continued use of their own language and the growth of a separate subsidiary history based on the period of the Emperor Yohannis, and the virtual autonomy of the area for 150 years previous to this.

Into this pattern the *Woyane* revolt in Tigre fits. It arose essentially out of dissatisfaction with the imposition of imperial rule over the area after the war. In the first instance, due to British pressure, the ruler with the best hereditary claims—*Ras* Seyoun—was returned to the area. However the Emperor more or less enforced his residence in Addis Ababa fearing that Seyoum might have come to some agreement with the British to shift Tigre into an Eritrean orbit. This failure to allow the return of their own ruler, plus accusations of corrupt and bad government by the Shoan officials, was a major reason for the revolt. Independence from Shoan rule was raised as a rallying cry and proved popular.

Discontent appeared in Tigre very soon after the restoration of Haile Selassie. When the British forces moved into Tigre in 1941, they found *Ras* Seyoun and "*Ras*" Haile Selassie Gugsa, who had been used by the Italian administration. Both of these sent messages of loyalty to the Emperor and were kept on by the British. But the British found Haile Selassie Gugsa completely ineffectual and removed him to Asmara,[5] appointing *Ras* Seyoun as governor of the whole province. This appointment was confirmed by the Emperor, who in mid-1941 called *Ras* Seyoun to Addis Ababa to submit to him. Once in Addis Ababa the *Ras* was detained there; while his loyalty was not too highly suspect, he *had* collaborated with the Italians. Furthermore, the Emperor complained that he was refusing to accept the new administration that the Emperor wanted to impose. Seyoun was to keep the governorship, but all the sub-governors and provincial staff were to be appointed by the Palace. This lessening of his power was unacceptable to *Ras* Seyoun and so Haile Selassie kept him in Addis Ababa.

However, under direct threat from the British that they would be forced to send a British official to take control, *Ras* Seyoun was allowed north to help in a campaign in South Tigre to deal with the *shifta*. These were Oromo who had been threatening the British lines of communication on the road south of Quiha towards Dessie, and along the Dessie to Assab route. Before they surrendered, the Italians had armed the Azebo and Raya Oromo, hoping to use them for harassment. The arms remained after the Italian defeat, and were rapidly used for raids on the road and on the Danakil. At the same time, large concentrations of men were also observed in Southern Tigre, especially around Alamata and Amba Alage.

The first campaign, in early 1942, which was against the Oromo was a relative success and the region seemed superficially quieter later in the year, apart from an isolated pocket of trouble in Agame, on the Eritrean border. This was illusory. The discontent over Seyoum's continued residence in Addis Ababa was not assuaged by the presence of his 16 year-old son, Mengesha, in Makelle. The governorship was put in the hands of a Shoan of the Moja family, *Fitawari* Kifle Dadi, the director of the province; and there were considerable complaints against him. Certain leaders began to emerge—notably *Blatta* Haile Mariam Redda, Yekuno Amlak Tesfaye, (a nephew of Haile Selassie Gugsa), and *Dejazmatch* Araya Degala of Raya. While there is evidence to suggest that Yekuno Amlak's ideas were more concerned with his own advancement, *Blatta* Haile Mariam was most interested in the province of Tigre.

Haile Mariam appealed to the past glories of Tigre under Yohannis IV and publicly suggested that the British would support joint Tigre-Eritrean independence. He also played on some of the ideas that Haile Selassie Gugsa had propagated in 1935–36 to justify his desertion of Emperor Haile Selassie. These included the argument that the Emperor had deliberately played off the Tigrean nobility against each other, and sown discord among them so that in the resultant disorder it would be possible to impose Shoan governors, and that the Emperor had also deliberately kept the Tigrean governors in Addis Ababa in an attempt to encourage a lack of Government and turn the people against their rulers. The populace could have no hope from an Emperor whose only aim was to procure the wealth of the province for himself and his friends.[6] It was necessary to have governors who belonged to the province, not outsiders. Haile Mariam also emphasized that if this could not happen within Ethiopia then it would be necessary to withdraw. All of these factors played their part in encouraging a wide response in the sub-provinces of Enderta, Azebo-Raya and Tembien.[7] *Ras* Seyoun's son, *Dejazmatch* Mengesha, took an interest in the movement and, although he did not fight, he was with some of the dissidents in Tembien.

Haile Mariam turned out to be an organizer of considerable skill. The movement gathered strength in 1942 and early 1943; and then began activities by blocking the road near Quiha.[8] By August 1943 the rebel movements were causing considerable alarm, and units of the new regular Ethiopian army accompanied by their British advisers were sent to reinforce the territorial troops in the area. They were under the Minister of War, *Ras* Abebe Aregai, who was under orders to settle matters. By this time Haile Mariam, whose headquarters were at Wukro, north of Makelle, controlled most of Tigre. There was a regular army battalion at Adua, which did not dare move outside its base until things were all over, and 6,000 territorials at Makelle and Quiha. The latter also showed no activity and decided to retire in mid-September when rebels advanced and Haile Mariam captured the towns without a fight.

By then heavy fighting was going on to the south as *Ras* Abebe's forces began advancing up from Dessie where they had concentrated. The key point was the natural fortress of Amba Alagi where the Italians had surrendered in 1941. This is actually the last of a series of mountain barriers that start just north of Alamata, all of which are eminently defensible; but it was Amba Alagi which saw the main fighting. The government forces reached Amba Alagi in strength on 18 September and after four days of hard fighting they cleared the area. They were not however able to advance. For the last five days of September and again on 7 October they were vigorously attacked by rebel forces of up to 5,000 men. At the same time the road south to Maicew and between Maicew and Quoram was subjected to a series of attacks rendering the line of communications unsafe.

The situation was serious enough for the British advisers, and *Ras* Abebe to ask for bomber support for the 2,000 regular troops, 6,000 territorials, six armoured cars and an artillery battery. In fact the ammunition situation was so critical at one stage that the Government forces nearly had to retreat. The British Foreign Office believed that this would probably cause the fall of the Emperor and had judged it necessary therefore to agree to the request for bombers. In addition the military argued that the north road was vital to their communications. In the first instance only pamphlets were dropped as the British originally refused to allow bombs to be used. The first leaflets were dropped on 15 September, the fifth and last of the series on 6 October when the bombing began. It is interesting to see from the "address" how the revolt was spreading— Number 1 is addressed to "the people of Makelle, Enderta, Wajirat, Azebo and Raia"; Numbers 2 and 3 added Enda Mahone to the list; Number 4 is addressed to Makelle, Tigrai, Adua, Axum and Warae, Tembien, Agame, Haramat, Aulala and Shire. Number 5 is to "the Chiefs, *Balabats*—people of Tigre Province". The tone also changes from a plea, for the rebels to be handed over, to threats: "From now onward, if you do not hand over the malefactors, if your houses are burnt by aeroplane, and if the country is destroyed and the blood of old men, women and children is shed in vain, before God and man the responsibility will be on your own heads". The last pamphlet is from the *Ichege* (the others were sealed by Haile Selassie) and the final sanction of excommunication for "Those that do not give up evil" is employed.

Three Blenheim bombers were brought over from Aden and flew a number of missions from 6 October, culminating in the raid on Makelle where seventy people were killed and 200 wounded. Unfortunately most of those killed were in the market place, and were actually at market; they were not combatants any more than were most of those killed when Corbetta was bombed twice. These raids which hit at villages and rebel concentrations north of Amba Alagi, and to the east of Maicew had the desired effects. The Government troops were in any case able to advance after the last attack on Amba Alagi on 7 October. On the 14th they recaptured Makelle and three days later were in Wokro. The opposition, including the leaders, melted away; *Dejazmatch* Mengesha came back to Makelle under grave suspicion and was in fact condemned to death, although later pardoned; all that remained was the mopping-up operation, which was carried out on a wide scale and has left some bitter memories. It might be added that not all the territorials had their hearts in crushing the rebellion, and on several occasions they voiced their unhappiness to the British advisers, pointing out that the fighting was caused by Shoan misgovernment, and that Tigre could be happier united with Eritrea.

There is no doubt that *Blatta* Haile Mariam tapped a deep source of discontent in Tigre and among the Raya Oromo. It stemmed from peasant dissatisfaction—it was primarily a peasant revolt—coupled with overtones of Tigrean desires to be independent of Shoa. This analysis is not contradicted by the fact that the leaders were from the local nobility, and were disappointed members of their class. Their influence was considerable but it was not sufficient to obtain the support of all those who followed them. *Blatta* Haile Mariam was a member of the *Mekwanint*, of the extended family of Woldu, a nineteenth century *Shum* of Agame; but his *mekwanint* status was relatively inoperative outside Agame; and he was not of the same status as a nephew of Haile Selassie Gugsa, yet he was clearly the leader of the movement, which had many followers largely from outside Agame. Men who fought with him describe how inspiring his speeches were, and how he made them see that the taxes they paid were excessive; and appeals to an independent Tigre also moved his listeners greatly.

It is noteworthy that the Emperor took this movement so seriously. This was largely due to the danger that a rising of this type might have, indeed probably would have, received British support if it had been successful. There were other provinces that could then have followed this pattern, Gojjam being a very possible addition at the time. Although it was certainly not a direct threat to the throne, it was also more than possible that it could have sparked off another round of plots and conspiracies. It was therefore very sensible to back-pedal fairly quickly over Shoans in the administration of Tigre. Although *Ras* Abebe Aregai was left as governor in Tigre, the troops were soon withdrawn and Tigreans were widely used as sub-governors. *Ras* Seyoun was allowed to return to the province only in 1947. From then on Tigre was given an extremely free hand. It has paid land tax according to the tribute system which means that the Tigreans themselves decide who pays what. The great majority of the *awraja* governors and those in lesser positions were appointed on the recommendations of *Ras* Seyoun, or after 1960, of his son *Ras* Mengesha, and have been Tigreans from the extended ruling family.[9]

The violent phase of the *Woyane* revolt was shortlived and its repercussions small. Far more serious, indeed in terms of Government policies it may be classified as insoluble, has been the revolt in Eritrea. This had similar gestation in anti-Government and anti-Amhara feelings; but the Eritrean Liberation Front which has grown from these protests over exploitative government is now a fully-fledged national and revolutionary socialist movement with considerable outside support.

Trouble in Eritrea broke out immediately after the area was totally re-incorporated into the Ethiopian empire in 1962. The roots, however, go back much further. Historically the province of Eritrea had been subject to the Emperors to a greater or lesser degree up to 1890s. The highland part of the province was largely Christian while the people of the coastal area and the northern and western areas were Moslem, over whom the Emperors had a somewhat fluctuating authority. In the 1880s the appearance of the Italians led to a takeover of Eritrea which was accepted by the Emperor Menilek II in 1896. In spite of his great victory over an Italian army at Adua, he felt it impossible to attempt the reconquest of the province and so it became an Italian colony. It remained so until 1941 when the British troops expelled the Italian forces as part of the effort to free Ethiopia from Italian control.

By and large Italian development in Eritrea was not great; although there were some grandiose settlement plans they were never really implemented. Nevertheless the economic development of the area was considerable, especially in the period immediately proceeding the 1935 invasion of Ethiopia. The enormous influx of men and materials in preparation for the war had a great, if temporary, effect. One of the common accusations against the present regime in Ethiopia is that it has allowed the Eritrean economy to run down. By comparison with the brief period of prosperity, 1932–38, this is true; but it is an invalid comparison and for most of the colonial period development in Eritrea was minimal.

What the Italians did leave in Eritrea were some good communications, the nucleus of some agricultural and industrial developments, and about 60,000 Italians. (The number has gradually fallen to under 5,000 in 1970.) They also, during their period of rule, reinforced certain attitudes and ideas. As part of a re-organization of the whole of Ethiopia in 1936–41, they had re-drawn the administrative areas on an essentially ethnic basis. The Christian Eritreans were largely Tigrinya speaking, so the Tigreans of Tigre and Eritrea were administered together in a greater Tigre Province. Immediately after 1941 the British also had ideas about trying to continue a similar sort of arrangement under their control, and as late as 1943 they were threatening Haile Selassie with it.

The Italian administration also interfered very little in the traditional structure at the local level. The same important landowning families remained paramount throughout the period of colonization —and indeed remain so today in the Christian part of the province. *Ras* Baraki of Hamasien received his title from the Italians and during the British period over half of the sub-province was ruled by his sons and other relatives. Around Adi Ugri the family of *Ras* Kidane Mariam Gebre Meskal remained significant. *Ras* Kidane Mariam was governor of the area before the Italian colony started and remained governor until his death. His sons followed him. First *Fitawari* Laynie (who became Governor of Akale Guzay *awraja* in December 1964), and ended up as a Senator; then *Kegnazmatch* Yohannis, another relative who became Parliamentary deputy for the area also succeeded to the governorship. One change that did occur was in the removal of substantial lands from the great monasteries. To some extent they were returned when Eritrea became part of the Empire again, but by no means in every case. The great Tigrean monastery of Debra Damo lost substantially and one of its grievances today is that the Emperor never restored its former Eritrean lands, nor even the lands taken from them by the Italians in Tigre between 1936–41.[10]

The political question of who should control Eritrea after 1941 proved to be extremely complex. At the various wartime conferences the question was shelved. The British wanted to hang on after the war; the Russians thought they should administer Eritrea; the Italians (after 1943) demanded its return; and the U.S. got involved when it was granted a military communications facility in Asmara in 1942. Haile Selassie, of course, claimed Eritrea as part of the Ethiopian empire (as he did Italian Somaliland); and Egypt and other Moslem states were interested by virtue of Eritrea's Moslem community. The British estimated in 1952 that the province was almost exactly divided between Moslem and Christian. It should be noted that there are numerous Moslem communities within the predominantly Christian areas of Eritrea, and Moslems are not confined to the coastal and western lowlands.

All these interests failed to produce a settlement for the future of Eritrea, and the British continued to administer the territory. There were continued discussions, inquiries, U.N. Resolutions and the like until a compromise solution was adopted in 1950 and implemented in 1952. This was a federation under the sovereignty of the Emperor. This compromise came out of the four main proposals put forward, none of which could gain mass support either in the U.N. or in the province. These were: outright annexation by Ethiopia; complete independence of Eritrea; partition between Ethiopia and the Sudan; and a U.N. trust territory under Italy or Britain. The U.N. resolution recommended that Eritrea should be an autonomous unit of Ethiopia. The federal Government was to have control of foreign affairs, defence, finance, commerce and ports (this was important as Massawa and Assab were to be Ethiopia's only two direct outlets to the sea). The Eritrean Government and assembly were to have full internal powers over all functions not vested in the federal Government; and an Eritrean administration was to be set up and an assembly elected before the federation took effect.[11]

The assembly was to be elected on the basis of the political parties which the British had allowed, and indeed encouraged, during their period of control. These parties coalesced around the various options that appeared to be possible. The Christian Tigrinya-speaking highlanders tended to join the Unionist Party, which was for full union with Ethiopia. This was heavily supported and partly directed by the Ethiopian Government and the Orthodox Church, and during the pre-1952 period a variety of important Ethiopians visited Eritrea on various missions. The Unionist Party was headed by the future Chief Executive of Eritrea, Tedla Bairu, who had been an administrative officer under the British. But by no means all Christians joined the Unionist Party, for many remembered the Tigre/Amhara rivalries of the late nineteenth century and had no desire to be under Shoan control. Such people turned to a Christian separatist party, the Liberal Progressive Party, which wanted an independent Eritrea, preferably with Tigre as an adjunct. There is some reason to believe that this party received support from the British, just as the Italians tended to support a pro-Italian party.

The Moslem response to these Christian-orientated groupings was to set up the Moslem League in 1946, based on a number of Moslem parties. This too was in favour of full independence, and for a time it united with the Liberal Progressive Party in a short-lived Independence Bloc. After the failure of this united effort the western Moslems formed the Moslem League of the Western Province. This left the Liberal Progressives isolated and forced them into the arms of the Unionist Party. This rather implies that the basic political attitudes split sharply on religious grounds. This was not, however, entirely the case. Many Moslems were also to be found in the Unionist Party, and in the unionist-orientated labour unions; just as many Christians preferred separatism—Woldeab Wolde Mariam, active in the Liberal Progressive Party and later an important exile, being one.

The political campaigning was fierce and sometimes bloody. One Moslem leader, Abd el-Kadir Kebire, was assassinated in 1949, and other separatist leaders survived or failed to survive a number of attempts on their lives. The election for the assembly of 1952 was held under British control and resulted in a roughly equal Moslem/ Christian division but with a Unionist Party majority. This accepted the constitutional proposals of the U.N. as did Haile Selassie in Ethiopia, and the British departed in September 1952, leaving Tedla Bairu, the Unionist leader, as chief executive.

It was unlikely from the beginning that federation would work successfully. Eritrea was endowed in 1952 with a variety of attitudes and institutions that were in total contradiction to those of Ethiopia. Unions, political parties, elections and a free press were all non-

existent in Ethiopia where power emanated from the Emperor, not
the people. The British had done very little in their time in Eritrea
but they did feel that they had left a "people who were learning to
think and act for themselves".[12] All this was anathema to the
Ethiopian Government and the Imperial Representative in Asmara
was soon using his powers to interfere in the political process.

From the beginning there is no doubt that Haile Selassie was
determined to remove the federation and attach Eritrea as another
province of Ethiopia. There was a steady pressure on the Eritrean
newspapers, arrests of politicians and above all use of the unlimited
patronage available to the imperial Government. Several politicians
fled abroad—Woldeab Wolde Mariam among them—and *Dejazmatch* Tedla Bairu was forced out of his position as Chief Executive
in 1955. More amenable members of the Unionist Party were
appointed to top positions. In the elections of 1956 no political
parties were allowed. In 1958 the assembly voted to discard the
Eritrean flag, in 1959 the Ethiopian law code was extended over
Eritrea, in 1960 the Eritrean Government became the Eritrean
administration, and finally in 1962 the Eritrean assembly was persuaded to vote itself out of existence.

The reasons for the takeover occurring specifically in 1962 were
probably international as much as internal. Sudan was independent
by then, Somalia had become so in 1960, and in 1961–62 Egypt was
becoming embroiled in the Yemen. A Moslem revolt in Western
Eritrea in 1961 looked as though it might provide the excuse for
Arab interference. Finally there were enough incidents taking place
within the country to suggest the need to establish a much firmer
control.

These changes were not accomplished without considerable opposition and the last years of the federation saw a considerable number
of disturbances and strikes. Opposition was not only internal. Some
of the prominent separatist leaders in exile (including Ibrahim
Sultan Ali, ex-leader of the Moslem League and Woldeab Wolde
Mariam, ex-L.P.P. leader) set up an Eritrean Democratic Front in
Cairo. This was active on the diplomatic front and tried to alert
the U.N. to the Ethiopian pressures. It also tried to influence the
African Heads of State conference at Addis Ababa in 1963 by sending
a letter to draw attention to "the calamity of the people of Eritrea
who are giving their last breath under the feet of the barbaric
conquerors, the Ethiopians". In view of the fact that a majority
probably favoured full union in 1952, it is striking that by 1962 a

very considerable majority most certainly did not. For this the tactics of the Ethiopian federal institutions must take a large part of the blame, and there is no doubt that the closing down of newspapers, the removal of political parties and unexplained arrests contributed largely. There were also other factors of course. The Eritrean economy continued at its relatively low ebb—the Ethiopian Government was unable to return it to the 1930s level—and this brought accusations of exploitation and considerable disappointment. In fact Eritrea was better treated than any other province except Shoa, in terms of economic development, but it was not sufficient to prevent the continued run-down of such towns as Decamare; and the building of grandiose churches did not compensate for lack of work.

At the time that the Federation ended, opposition, although apparent, was relatively small-scale. The Eritrean Liberation Front (E.L.F.), founded in Cairo in 1958 when it became apparent that the federation would not last much longer, announced its conversion to direct action in September 1961. For a number of years, however, its activities were relatively small-scale and did not impinge widely. They were in fact quite active but at this stage their efforts were essentially geared to Moslem separatism and were centred in the Moslem areas of western Eritrea. Little effort was made to get the support of Christians and the few Christians who did join it at this time found life difficult in the predominantly Moslem environment. Nevertheless there were a number of reasons why such a situation could not last. The E.L.F. could build upon a substantial ground-swell of dissatisfaction. The most obvious element was the control from Addis Ababa. There might not have been much in the way of action in the immediate aftermath but there was a lot of feeling. It was easy to couple this to specific Moslem dissatisfaction. As in other parts of the empire, despite the vaunted religious equality, Moslems felt that they suffered from discriminatory actions in the fields of education and administration; and above all that the Christian Government of the province, and of the empire, actively encouraged all facets of Christianity at the expense of Islam.

In this sense the wider political scene has been very relevant to the growth of the E.L.F. Since Ethiopia was receiving aid, both military and civil, from the U.S.A., and in return allowing America a large communications base at Kagnew in Asmara, where a force of some 2,000 troops were stationed at one time, and since it was one of Israel's footholds in Africa (and allowing Israel to push aid

through to the rebels in the Southern Sudan), it was not surprising
that the E.L.F. was able to call on Moslem support for an anti-
American, anti-Zionist struggle. Sudan allowed itself to be freely
used as a base and as a refuge. In 1965 the quantity of arms coming
through Sudan became so obvious that the Sudan Government
announced in June that it had discovered eighteen tons of Czech
arms at Khartoum airport intended for the E.L.F. Syria and Iraq
also supplied funds, arms and training.

By 1967 the E.L.F. had become an extremely active force with
widespread support particularly north and west of Massawa; and
in the western and northern parts of the province.[13] It was also
gaining recruits from other sections of the population by the mid-
1960s. An imperial visit in January 1967 did little to solve the problem
in spite of Haile Selassie's considerable distribution of money, titles
and offices. Numbers by this stage were probably up to two or three
thousand and groups of near-battalion strength were hitting the
Ethiopian forces in sizeable battles. It has been very difficult to
assess the validity of the E.L.F. Damascus radio communiques about
its successes, from the start of the broadcasts in the mid-1960s. From
the Ethiopian side the Front's activities have been consistently
played down. Nevertheless it is clear that prior to the 1967 Israeli-
Arab war the E.L.F. had succeeded in laying a substantive network
of connections within Eritrea, and were operating at a dangerous
level, in Christian as well as Moslem areas. More than one governor
in the Christian parts was removed for supposed or actual contact
with the E.L.F. In March 1967 the former Chief Executive, *Dejazmatch* Tedla Bairu, also defected to the Front, though his defection
appears to have been substantially personal in origin.

The E.L.F. attitudes at this time were, however, still essentially
Moslem separatism and anti-America and Israel. As they told the
British Consul in Asmara when he was kidnapped for three days in
1967, "Of course, we had no intention of harming you, you are
British. Had you been an American or an Israeli, we would have
shot you on the spot!"[14] The Ethiopian army retaliation was, by
1967, also on a considerable scale. Figures from Sudan suggested
that in March that year 7,000 refugees had crossed into the Sudan
and 1,000 were arriving daily. They were fleeing from attacks on
villages in the western parts of the province.

After the Israeli-Arab war of 1967, however, the movement
appeared to be losing ground, as a number of members surrendered
under an amnesty—which guaranteed their freedom, although it

had to be earned by a period of corrective training which was, according to several amnestees, extremely brutal.[15] Official statements reflected considerable optimism. The back of the rebellion was broken, claimed Government spokesmen in Asmara. Figures released in mid-1968 by the E.L.F. said that their casualties in the previous four years had been 1,068 killed and that the Ethiopian forces had also killed nearly 1,000 civilians and destroyed 300 villages. Arab aid also fell off for the time being and Sudan in July 1967 agreed to pull back the refugee camps at least fifty miles from the Sudan border.

The Sudanese did not, however, agree to closing the border and the number of refugees continued to rise as the army continued to push hard at the guerillas—for example five villages were burnt in September 1968, and there were various bombing attacks on supposed E.L.F. centres in reprisal for a number of attacks spaced throughout 1968. The most serious was the guerilla assault on the 500-man territorial camp at Hal Hal near Keren, when rockets and mortars were used. The guerillas claimed 200 to 300 killed—certainly they were not driven off until units of the 2nd Division fought their way through ambushes on the road to relieve the camp. This was almost certainly a defeat for the Front and most of the casualties appear to have been theirs.[16] The amount of activity forced the Eritrean provincial Government into setting up chains of fortified villages, arming their loyal supporters and bringing in people from outlying villages to try and cut down the Front's freedom of movement. Reprisals such as public hangings in Keren and Agordat were also carried out. These measures did not have a great deal of effect in gaining local support, rather the reverse.

What did influence the position of the Front was a severe internal split which came to the fore in 1968–69 and was related to a shift of emphasis and ideology in the campaign. The links with the Palestinian freedom movements going back to the mid-1960s bore fruit in an attempt to capture some world publicity by moving into the field of highjacking and aircraft destruction.[17] On 11 March, 1969, a bomb damaged an Ethiopian Airlines Boeing 707 jet at Frankfurt, injuring several people. Damascus radio carried the E.L.F. claim to have been responsible. On 18 June another Boeing 707 was attacked at Karachi and the plane badly damaged. The three men responsible were captured and got one-year sentences after claiming they had done it to draw attention to the tyranny of Ethiopian rule in Eritrea. Also in June an Eritrean blew himself

up in Rome. Police believed the bomb was to be used in an attack
on the Embassy. On 9 August and 13 September two internal
flights were highjacked. The first was taken to the Sudan by six
University students—not all Eritreans—and a government official;
they agreed it was done for E.L.F. propaganda reasons. The other
flight was taken to Aden and on landing, police captured two of the
three men; the other was shot by a security guard on the aircraft.
The last in this series was the attempt by two men to highjack another
707 over Madrid. They were both shot by security guards though
there were some questions over exactly how this was done. Passengers spoke of one of the highjackers being deliberately killed after
he had been forced to surrender. The E.L.F. claimed that the two
men had merely been trying to distribute pamphlets to the passengers
and crew, but this version was denied by police and the air crew.
Another would-be highjacker was also arrested two days earlier
at Madrid airport with explosives—apparently he was also connected
with the attempt.

These actions were linked to a lessening of activity within Eritrea
although the Asmara water supply was disrupted and convoys
ambushed on several occasions. The split was in fact partly over
tactics. It did, however, go further than this; and in October 1969
one communique said that "we sharply condemn support for our
struggle on sectarian grounds. The struggle led by our front is a
national struggle with humanitarian aspects. Moslems and Christians
alike are participating in the struggle". This followed a meeting at
Adobha in August 1969, when the Revolutionary and Supreme
Councils were dismissed and a General Command was substituted,
though the news was not made public until April the next year, from
Baghdad.

The Baghdad statement was made by Tesfai Tekla, a member of
Eritrean Liberation Army high command. It also said the various
willayas—areas under E.L.F. military control—would lose their
separate status and that the army was to be united. A central General
Command was going to be elected to direct the military activities;
and it would set a date for a conference to draw up a clear programme
for action. The E.L.F. offices in the Arab countries (ten) and in
Stockholm, Italy and Pakistan would also be taken over.

The aftermath of this soul-searching was greatly increased activity
within Eritrea—and since 1969 there have been only two highjack
attempts, both internal—one in January 1971 by students successfully and a failure in December 1972 when six of the would-be

highjackers were killed and the seventh critically injured. In April 1970 two retired High Court judges who had sentenced E.L.F. members to death, and four others, were assassinated in Asmara. In May there was a sizeable battle along the Red Sea coast in which the E.L.F. claimed 3,000 troops were involved against them. There were renewed army reprisals in the *awraja* of Akele Guzai where several villages were destroyed and thirty-two suspected collaborators shot. Eighty-eight members of one tribe were also supposed to have been killed resisting resettlement in the coastal area near Massawa.[18] E.L.F. activities reached a crescendo in November —three sizeable road bridges were broken, and a train highjacked and driven off the rails. On 21 November, the General in command of the 2nd Division, the main Ethiopian unit operating in Eritrea, was killed in an ambush.

The result was a very strong reaction by the army. The E.L.F. claimed that 1,000 civilians were killed in the next two weeks and detailed some other specific massacres: 112 shot in a mosque at Bascadara 27 November; 600 killed in one village near Keren 1 December; and sixty killed in a mosque at Elaberet. None of these claims has actually been denied by Addis Ababa, and the Keren evidence has been reliably attested by foreign sources. The number of refugees in the Sudan greatly increased. Martial law was declared for most of the province and in January the Governor, *Ras* Asrate Kassa, who had stood for a relatively moderate policy, was replaced by the tough Commander of the Ground Forces, General Debebe Haile Mariam. More troops were sent up to the province; and since then there have been the 2nd Division, several brigades of the Imperial Bodyguard and police commando and militia units. The Air Force also keeps some of its F.5 jets and F.86 Sabre jets and a squadron of T.39 bombers at Asmara.

The Army and Police also instituted a much wider programme of fortified villages, accompanied by resettlement, into places that can be defended "for the safety of the people". Stringent checks were instituted on all lightweight food stuffs suitable for guerillas. All supplies of coffee, tea, sugar, rice, etc., had to be checked in and out of all towns. This applied to private cars as well as lorries. This at first seemed to have little effect on the guerillas' capacity for carrying on activities as usual. Two battles between battalion-size forces were reported by the E.L.F. in June 1972; and in February 1972 when the Emperor was actually visiting Asmara the Front blew up the finance office there. As a demonstration of their elusiveness it was a notable gesture, considering the massive security precautions that are taken when the Emperor does visit Eritrea.

Nevertheless, during much of 1972 the Front was fairly quiescent. One reason for this was Ethiopia's improved situation *vis-à-vis* Sudan; particularly after the Emperor's intervention and assistance in bringing the Anya-Nya revolt in Southern Sudan to an end. This was a marked change from a time not four years before when he was allowing weekly supply flights into the Southern Sudan by the Israelis. Sudan tried to close the border; agreements over refugees were made; and many Eritreans were sent back, as were most Southern Sudanese. It also appears that some agreement was made about joint action. In March 1973 there were reports that numbers of E.L.F. fighters had been driven out by Sudanese forces into the waiting arms of Ethiopian troops in Eritrea—costing the guerillas some 400 casualties.[19] Probably more important was the continued split in the E.L.F. itself. The new General Command set up in 1969 was rejected by some elements because of suspect ideology; and the People's Liberation Forces appeared in opposition to them in early 1970. In December 1971 the General Command called a National Congress—to which the People's Liberation Forces did not come—and set up a new Revolutionary Council and the People Liberation Army on a Socialist basis. The Congress denounced "the command of the Popular Liberation Forces represented by the counter-revolutionaries for its role in creating and complicating the problem; and the political and military results of the command's un-natural and un-revolutionary behaviour".[20]

The division between the P.L.F. and the Revolutionary Council broke out into open war in 1972 and there were several months of fighting. It should be noted that the problem of analysing these divisions is complicated by the fact that the propaganda bureau has throughout been in the hands of Osman Saleh Sabbe, former Secretary-General of the Supreme Command; and has reflected only one side of the struggle. Although Osman appears to be relatively isolated now, the communiques put out do not entirely support this.

While it is not exactly clear how the civil war ended and the splits healed, there has been no internecine fighting since mid-1972. The divisions appear to have been healed, at least outwardly, although another conference was called to deal with unity in May 1974. The leadership now rests with the militant military field command, under the title of the People's Liberation Forces, which has support from Syria, Iraq and South Yemen. Most of the former Supreme Council—the leading political figures in exile—have been put on the side-lines and isolated to a substantial extent. Certainly activities during 1973 have increased and suggest that the Front has resolved its difficulties, and been able to concentrate on taking the offensive again. They remained quiescent during the February/March crisis of 1974, probably to avoid distracting the 2nd Division from its mutiny and from the events taking place in Addis Ababa. In April and May, however, they started a renewed offensive, putting the copper mine out of action for six months and capturing several Americans and Canadians working for an oil company.

In the latter part of 1973 there occurred a fundamental shift in Ethiopia's foreign policy. In October the Government announced that the U.S. Kagnew base at Asmara was being run down, and that after July 1974 only a skeleton staff of one hundred technicians would be kept on. More important, relations were broken off with Israel. If, as seems likely, this break in relations hoped to gain some sort of *quid pro quo* over Arab support for the E.L.F., it has not entirely worked out, for in January 1974 Somalia announced its support for creation of a revolutionary government in Eritrea—and this at the time when Haile Selassie was actually conferring with a Palestinian delegation in Addis Ababa.

It is difficult to quantify the effect that the change in relations with Israel will have both on the E.L.F. and on Ethiopia's dealings with the Arab States. Israel's interest in Ethiopia was considerable prior to the break—the Israeli Chief of Staff, General Bar-lev visited Ethiopia on a "purely personal" visit in 1971; and Israeli involvement in counter-guerilla training was extensive. There are obvious common interests between Ethiopia and Israel in the Red Sea; and these will remain. The E.L.F. have consistently claimed that several Ethiopian islands in the Red Sea have been leased to Israel, but there has been no confirmation of these charges. It may be noted also that there is some reason to believe that the break in relations with Israel has not meant the withdrawal of Israeli military advisers.

In the climate of Arab-Israeli negotiations it is possible that the need for Israeli-Ethiopian links will disappear. As regards the U.S.A., if the running-down of the Kagnew base is symptomatic of a general withdrawal of U.S. interest, it will be more significant. It is reasonably certain that Kagnew took an interest in the E.L.F. and there were several reports of involvement. The Front claimed to have

killed six American advisers in one series of battles in April/May
1969; and U.S. personnel have been captured on a number of
occasions.[21] The prime area of U.S. involvement, however, was in
providing training and supplies through the Military Mission to the
army as a whole. Haile Selassie's requests to President Nixon for
extra and more modern arms were reportedly turned down in 1973
and it is likely that his visit to Moscow in late 1973 related to this
point as Russia has bolstered the Somalia army to a position where
it could possibly defeat Ethiopia. This does not directly relate to
Eritrea, but it could mean a greater need to station more troops in
the south, thus relieving some of the pressure in Eritrea.

None of these foreign policy problems looks like bringing the
Eritrean crisis to an end, though they may affect supplies of arms to
both sides. Feelings now run very deep and nothing short of a
fundamental reversal of Government policy is likely to produce a
solution. Only one of the major criticisms of Ethiopian policy has
been seriously tackled—Christian/Moslem dissension, Tigre resentment of Shoan Amhara domination, and resistance by the nomadic
western tribes to central government remain untouched—only the
question of foreign assistance has been affected by the events of 1973.
The Army clearly can contain the situation, though it equally clearly
cannot stop E.L.F. activities. The E.L.F. is not at the moment capable of defeating the army but it can maintain itself. This potential
stalemate may explain why stories of E.L.F. contacts with other
dissident groups are now becoming more frequent. Given the
revolutionary socialist ideals now professed by the E.L.F. such
contacts could presage a much broader spectrum of joint opposition
to the regime, especially since there is no sign of the new Government or the Army coming up with anything that will satisfy the
E.L.F.

It is true that both the Government and the Army have recently
allowed public comment on the situation; there are also rumours
that both sides have agreed in principle to accept negotiations.
The E.L.F., however, seems most likely to continue to insist on
the basic premise of independence. This will almost certainly be
unacceptable to any Government, which is unlikely to offer any
more than something on the model of the settlement in the southern
Sudan. This basic split might heal if a real attempt to change the
structure of the regime comes out of the 1974 crisis.

CHAPTER VII

Militant Opposition II—Oromo and Somali

The largest single ethnic group in the empire are the Oromo. Population estimates are dubious but it seems that out of approximately 27,000,000 people about 40 per cent are Oromo and about 30 per cent are Amhara. It must be emphasized that the Oromo are not homogeneous, but are scattered across southern and western Ethiopia in a number of diverse groups, with others to the north as well. Diversity is reflected in religion, culture and agriculture, the latter ranging from semi-nomadic cattle-raising to intensive cash agriculture. They have by and large remained distinct from the Amhara in language and culture in spite of being closely associated for over 200 years in some areas.

The degree of assimilation to Amhara culture is perhaps the most important point in the relationship between the two groups. It is impossible to be dogmatic. At various times the imperial Government has practised a definite policy of cultural assimilation; equally it has usually confined the relationship to one of exploitation, though this depends upon the area. In the eighteenth and nineteenth centuries there was a great deal of intermarriage between the imperial house of Gondar and the Yejju Oromo who settled in Wollo and Begemeder. This policy was also practised by the imperial Shoan house. The Emperor Menilek's marriage to the Empress Taitu allied him to the leading Yejju family and his daughter Shoareged married the head of the leading Wollo Oromo family, *Ras* Mikael of Wollo. Their son, who became the Emperor *Lij* Iyasu, was more than half Oromo. His cousin *Ras* Tafari Makonnen, who was heavily involved in *Lij* Iyasu's overthrow in 1916, also joined the same family when he married Menen, a grand-daughter of *Negus* Mikael. This policy, although it was typically feudal, involving personal marriage relations, was also tied in with forcible conversion. The Yejju were converted to Christianity by the Emperor Yohannis IV (1872–89) as were many of the Wollo Oromo.[1] The results, at any rate superficially, have been to make the members of the great northern Oromo families indistinguishable from the Amhara nobility to whom they are frequently related.

The other main Oromo area where a similar effort has been made to assimilate through intermarriage at the higher level is in the province of Wollega; though there the policy is essentially post-1941—Wollega was not, of course, brought into the Empire until the late nineteenth century and even then remained virtually independent until 1941. The governor in the early 1970s was *Dejazmatch* Kassa Woldemariam, a member of one of the leading Oromo families; he is married to Princess Sibla, a grand-daughter of the Emperor. The governor appointed in May 1974 was another member of the same family. Another Oromo of the province, though not of important family, *Ato* Amanuel Abraham, who has served in a number of important diplomatic and ministerial posts since the war, had his daughter married to Eskunder, the Emperor's oldest grandson. Representatives of other important families have also held prominent positions, most notably *Ato* Yilma Deressa, former Minister of Finance, and then a member of the Crown Council. His wife, Elizabeth, is descended from *Negus* Sahle Selassie of Shoa, the founder of the present dynasty. As among the Yejju, the degree of assimilation has been such that at the highest levels there is little or no distinction to be drawn between Oromo and Amhara. It is noticeable, however, that a number of the Wollega Oromo are Protestant, for missionaries were allowed to operate in the province.[2]

These marriages emphasize the landowning class identification that pervades the Empire. Certainly the highest members of the Oromo aristocracy in most areas have been incorporated into the Shoan aristocracy; though not always successfully as the episode of *Lij* Iyasu's reign has shown. At other levels of society, policy has been essentially different. For the majority of the Oromo peoples in the southern provinces especially, the conquest at the end of the nineteenth century brought extensive slave trading, loss of land, the status of serfs for themselves, onerous burdens of taxation and corrupt and inefficient Government. Although the Orthodox Church was established in these areas it was for the Amhara settlers and little attempt to convert was made, and then only on the superficial level of mass baptisms.

The most serious effort at assimilating a greater number of the Oromo people of the south has come in the post-war years with the

establishment of an educational system. This has imposed Amharic
as a national language; before the war large numbers obviously
learnt some Amharic, but this was only of necessity. Naturally
this has had considerable effect as had the realization that Amharic
was a necessity for advancement. Nonetheless, in the last few years
coincident with the successes of the largely Oromo movement in
Bale, (see below) Oromo students have begun to display a consciousness of their own culture. The Oromo magazine *Do you know?* has
also done something to encourage this. *Do you know?* has been
appearing irregularly since 1968. It was of course clandestine, and
attempts to provide Oromo speakers with a genuine Oromo paper.
It is partly educational—giving lists of Oromo words and proverbs,
folk tales and geographical accounts of the Oromo areas. Stories
and poetry, sometimes allegorical, are also included. It is intended
to appeal to all ages, and all Oromos. It is difficult to judge how
much it is read; though it obviously does have appeal outside the
student body, its circulation is limited.

This stirring of Oromo attitudes has a long history, although the
present elements are far more sophisticated. During Haile Selassie's
reign there have been several major incidents which have presaged
it to some degree: the Azebo-Raya revolt of 1928–30; the Wollega
independence movement of 1936 and the outbreak of Oromo revolt
in Bale in 1964. This does not include the numerous other peasant
revolts that have occurred in all the Oromo areas. By and large, the
Oromo land owners have kept aloof from the troubles, being identified with Shoan aristocratic interests. There have, however, been a
few cases, most notably Wollega, where class interests have been
subordinated to national ones.

It should be emphasized again that the Oromo areas have been
very diverse over the last 200 years. The only common feature
has been language—though even here the various branches have
diverged to some extent. There is only one potentially pan-Oromo
movement today—the Ethiopian National Liberation Front—and
historically the Oromo have been as quick to fight each other as to
act together. The various rebellions described below are certainly
not to be seen as facets of positive pan-Oromo nationalism—only
perhaps as early stirrings.

The first significant outbreak of revolt belongs to the period
when Haile Selassie was still Crown Prince and Regent, although the
effects lasted well into the 1930s. This was the Azebo/Raya revolt
of 1928 which became involved with the rebellion of *Ras* Gugsa

THE PROVINCE OF BALE

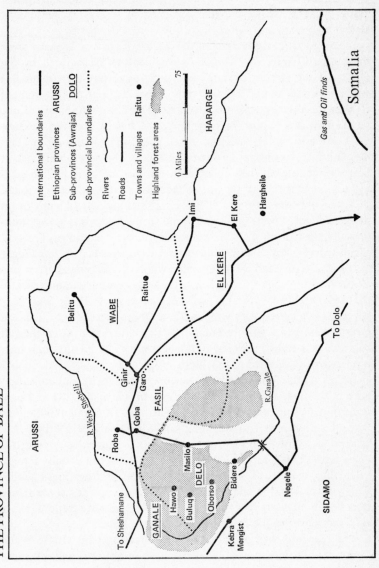

Walie in 1930. Information about this is scanty and early in the 1970s people were reluctant to talk as it involved a movement against Haile Selassie. However, the sequence of events is reasonably clear.[3]

In early 1928 the governor of the Azebo, Raya and Wojerat areas in southern Tigre, *Ras* Gugsa Araya, became exasperated by the failure of the Oromo peasants and nomads to pay their taxes. He was also under considerable pressure from the central Government to stop the raids against the lowlands. The first attempt to enforce payment was a failure for the number of troops involved was not sufficient and merely had the effect of pushing many of the tax-dodgers into co-ordinating their resistance. The rebels were not at first well-armed but they occupied a position of considerable strategic importance across the line of the main north-south trade route. By early 1929 the road was effectively closed and the Italian Consul at Dessie was reporting that all trade from Wollo was going south and the road north was too dangerous to use. The central Government ordered *Ras* Gugsa Araya to get the assistance of *Ras* Gugsa Walie (the Governor of Begemeder who was descended from one of the leading Yejju families and who had hereditary importance in the area) to deal with the problem. However, neither was very successful or indeed very willing. Their troops were loth to fight the Oromo who had a fierce reputation, and even when a *Kitet* (the call to arms) was called, very few of the peasantry obeyed although such a refusal was classified as rebellion.

It was at this point that the rebels entered into communication with other dissidents in the neighbouring province of Lasta and also, according to Italian sources, began to acquire arms and ammunition from the French in Tadjura.[4] In a battle in October 1929 the rebels overcame a considerable force of troops, capturing over 2,000 rifles and 12,000 cartridges; and this success came only a week after they themselves had lost 1,000 rifles to *Ras* Gugsa Walie. This victory had the effect of stiffening resistance, for some rebels had begun to surrender both guns and captured cattle after a renewed drive by the forces of *Ras* Gugsa Araya.

The rebellion then acquired a new dimension. *Ras* Gugsa Walie announced his intention of withdrawing from the area and returning to his province in defiance of direct orders from the Empress Zauditu. When he did so he became a rebel as he must have known he would. It is clear in fact that he had decided to move against *Negus* Tafari. In the next two months he collected his forces and baggage animals while Government forces also gathered from the southern provinces. In March 1930 *Dejazmatch* Mulugetta, the Minister of War, met the *Ras* at the battle of Zebit and won after a stiff fight. The victory was gained essentially by the first use of aeroplanes in war in Ethiopia; the *Ras* was killed, and his forces dispersed. The next day a sizeable contingent of Azebo-Raya on the way to help *Ras* Gugsa Walie was also defeated. In the aftermath of this, very large numbers of troops were finally used to crush the Oromo as well as defeat the last remnants of *Ras* Gugsa's troops.

The rest is speculation. It is, however, obvious that at the end of 1929 if not before, *Ras* Gugsa Walie entered into some sort of agreement with the Azebo-Raya rebels. Since he himself was Yejju by descent it is possible to see his revolt partly in terms of another attempt by the Oromo of that area to gain more independence and power. Certainly a number of those involved in the attempt of *Lij* Iyasu in 1916 to crush the Shoan nobility were also involved with him. *Ras* Gugsa Walie also had correspondence with other non-Amhara nobility—for example, *Ras* Seyoum Mengesha, in Tigre and *Ras* Hailu of Gojjam. Not too much must be made of this though, as more personal reasons were paramount. *Ras* Gugsa Walie was the former husband of the Empress Zauditu, and he made it clear that he was not attacking her in his propaganda, but was aiming at *Negus* Tafari. It seems most likely that he was merely utilizing the Azebo Raya rebels for his own ends.   -

The rebellion among the Azebo-Raya was perhaps something more. While it was obviously a peasant revolt protesting against corrupt government there are a number of pointers to suggest a further dimension. The rebels possessed a considerable degree of organization; they acquired a large quantity of arms and were more successful in battle than was usual in this period. There is the possibility that they acquired some arms from abroad and there was collusion between them and *Ras* Gugsa Walie. The failure of the revolt did not mean that the area became quiescent. In 1935–36, already bribed by the Italians to change sides, they attacked the Ethiopian armies both before and after the battle of Maichew. So threatening were they that the Emperor himself did not dare to retreat through that part after the defeat of Maichew in 1936. Even after the expulsion of the Italians, numbers of these Oromo were implicated in the *Woyane* revolt in Tigre in 1943, a revolt which had overtones of Tigre "nationalism". Since that time there has been continuous small-scale trouble, represented by attacks on landlords in the area. All this makes an assumption that there was more to the revolt than mere banditry or tax evasion, even though these were clearly the sparks that set off the trouble.

In the other important Oromo outbreak of the 1930s, in Wollega, there is no doubt that a desire for independence from Amhara rule was involved. Wollega, like Jimma, was rather different from most of the provinces. Since neither area had resisted Menilek, the indigenous rulers had been allowed to remain in power without restriction. All that was required of them was the annual payment of a fixed sum to the treasury in Addis Ababa. The two provinces were, however, different in some respects. Jimma was an Oromo Moslem Sultanate under Aba Jifar who had ruled in semi-independent fashion for many years. In 1932, ostensibly because of his failure to curb the slave trade, general bad government and a refusal to carry out certain directives from Addis Ababa, the Sultan's powers had been severely curtailed.[5] Consequently the Sultan was already in communication with the Italians before the invasion, and he declared his allegiance to them as soon as was practical. The Oromo of Jimma and the surrounding areas showed their dislike of the Amhara control in the aftermath of the Italian military victories by attacks on the remaining Amhara officials in the middle of 1936; and they welcomed the Italians as deliverers when they finally reached Jimma.

The Sultan also showed a mild interest in the far more significant movement in Wollega, which took place in 1936. The most important figure in the province (Wollega) was *Dejazmatch* Habte Mariam descendent of one hereditary ruler (*Dejazmatch* Moroda who had ruled central Wollega). He had married into the other main family, that of *Dejazmatch* Jote who had ruled southern and western Wollega, though he had eventually been removed by Menilek for extortion. In addition to these hereditary claims to rule, Habte Mariam also had official Government sanction. In 1935 when mobilization was ordered against the Italians, Habte Mariam was distinctly backward in his efforts, and almost no troops from Wollega took part in the battle for the northern frontier. It is clear that even at this stage a number of his advisers were thinking in terms of what to do should Ethiopia be defeated. Once the news came of the Italian entry into Addis Ababa and the flight of the Emperor, immediate moves were made. A series of meetings were held between various minor hereditary chieftains of Wollega and *Dejazmatch* Habte Mariam. Thirty-three chiefs then signed a document translated as follows:

We the hereditary chiefs declare herewith that our population is under control by our chiefs(;) our definite decision is that we wish to be placed under British Mandate, and we appoint *Dejazmatch* Habte Mariam as our head chief, and we agree to accept the agreement which he will make and sign with the British Government, that the mandate remain until we achieve self-government.[6]

From this and from despatches of Captain Erskine, British Consul at Gore,[7] it is clear that by the end of May 1936 the very half-hearted support of the Oromo for the war was crystallizing into something different. It is true when the remnants of the imperial Government were first established at Gore in 1936, *Dejazmatch* Habte Mariam agreed to await the results of peace negotiations and accept directions from Gore in the meantime. However, at the same time, the following memorandum was being sent to the British Foreign Secretary through the British Consul:

Excellency,

I have the honour to inform you that His Excellency *Dejazmatch* Habte Mariam (Governor of Wallega, and head of the Western Galla Confederation) has appointed me Chief of the delegation which is now in Gambella to get in touch with His Brittanic Majesty's Government in Great Britain and Northern Ireland.

Consequently I have to inform Your Excellency that His Excellency *Dejazmatch* Habte Mariam has taken note of the communication made to him by His Brittanic Majesty's Consul at Gore to the effect that Italy has defeated the Shoa Army and has occupied Addis Ababa to form a new Government. He has also taken note that a new provisional Government is in the process of getting formed at Gore for the Western Gallas.

As Your Excellency is well aware the people of Western Galla have never completely lost their independence. On the contrary they have always enjoyed a full measure of autonomy within the frame of Ethiopian Empire. This autonomy was fully expressed in the form of complete independence in matters of local government administration. The people of Western Galla have always been ruled by their own hereditary Chiefs of which His Excellency, *Dejazmatch* Habte Mariam's family has been most prominent. The authority exercised by the Shoa Government over the Western provinces has been for the most part a receipt of annual revenue from the chiefs of the province.

Historically the people of Western Gallas have never been subjected to the sway of the Shoa Government by means of military conquest. Nor have they been absorbed by the Shoas so as to become an integral part of Shoa. They have come within the framework of the Empire of their own free will in order to benefit the advantages of free trade as well as the advantages which has to be gained from becoming a member of a larger administrative unit.

Economically the peoples of the Western Gallas live largely by cultivation and cattle-rearing. They have also of late years taken up coffee plantation which today dominate the economic life of the country. They export coffee and other raw materials to the Sudan and buy much manufactured products as they are in need of through the Sudan. Thus for a decade or more their economic life has been connected more with the Sudan and less with the rest of Ethiopia. The advantage which they have had in view when they joined the Ethiopian Empire has been reduced to military protection alone. Today this sole advantage is lost.

At this critical moment of its existence the people of Western Gallas are faced with a problem of pulling itself out of the unfortunate circumstance in which it finds itself and for which it is in no way responsible. With this object in view they have formed a confederation under the leadership of His Excellency *Dejazmatch* Habte Mariam to bring their cause before the bar of world public opinion. And they are confident to obtain justice with the help of your Government.

His Excellency *Dejazmatch* Habte Mariam is now busy in organizing civil administration. He has so far set up Health Office, Financial and Commercial Department, Political and Foreign Relation Department, Army and Police Department, and a Communication Department. To run these Departments he has in his service a good number of young men educated in Europe and elsewhere. By establishing a model army under the direction of young and trained officers and by taking a firm action he has already saved the provinces of Western Gallas from chaos which has infested the rest of Ethiopia as the result of Italian invasion. His Excellency has already started the work of facilitating communication for commerce by constructing roads and bridges under the direction of young engineers educated in England. He also has policed the commercial roads from Kurmuck to Nakamte. Merchants travel along this route unmolested by *shiftas* (brigands).

Sir, I have already communicated to your Excellency that the people of Western Gallas have formed a confederation and have desired to become a League of Nations Mandate the mandatory power of which will be exercised by the Government of Great Britain and Northern Ireland. We are proposing to take this step because we realize Your Excellency's Government has so far taken decision to act through the League of Nations alone as far as the affairs of this country is concerned. If necessary we are ready to defend our rights by force of arms, but we hope that Your Government will use its influence to avert any more blood- shed in this part of the world. We are confident that with the help of your Government the League of Nations will do us justice.

Sir, Confident in the justness of our cause we appeal to your Government the principle of which we realize is inspired with justice.

I avail myself of this opportunity to express to Your Excellency the expression of my high consideration.

The document is signed by all of the six delegates sent by *Dejaz- match* Habte Mariam to the British officials.[8]
The delegation which presented this memo also explained the term "Western Gallas". The Chiefs who came together under *Dejazmatch* Habte Mariam controlled a territory bounded on the north by the river Abbai on the east by the river Gudi and in the south extended to about Maji. They admitted that they had not communicated with those in the far south but they believed that, as many of them were Gallas, they would wish to be associated.
It is quite clear from this that the western Oromo had agreed among themselves that they did not want any further Amhara control. While this may have been precipitated by the collapse of the empire it was a feeling that had deep roots. It cannot be explained by bad Government from the centre, as Wollega had been virtually independent of Shoan control. It is explicable only in terms of Oromo nationalist feeling which, even if it is in 1936 to be attributed essentially to the very small minority of foreign-educated individuals among the western Oromo, was nonetheless real. The attempt at independence was a failure due to the British refusal to support it and the Italian advance. After the war, when the Emperor

reimposed his authority, Wollega hopes for independence came to an end. As we have seen, however, it is noticeable that the Emperor made considerably greater efforts to re-attach Wollega with a series of marriages; and he tended to favour Wollega people in terms of Oromo appointments to high positions. And indeed the policy has been successful—Wollega has been relatively quiet for the last twenty years.[9]

The most complex of the problems with the Oromo provinces was the rebellion in the province of Bale between 1963 and 1970.[10] Bale is not solely an Oromo-inhabited province, and trouble first began among the Ethiopian Somalis living in the El Kere *awraja* in the south of the province. This outbreak was essentially personal in origin, starting with a quarrel over the ownership of the salt works there. The loser started a revolt, gaining support from nomadic Somalis who had complaints about tax collection. This did not, however, last long—within a year one of the leaders was dead and the other had fled to Somalia. The episode was essentially unimportant in itself, but it stimulated more serious trouble in another district of the province—the *awraja* of Wabe, where the people were largely Oromo, though a number of Ethiopian Somalis promptly emulated their fellows in the south and joined the Oromo.

Actual fighting in Wabe broke out in April 1964 when the local governor led a police force into Ratitu to collect taxes; there had been reluctance to pay for as long as ten years. On the way his force was surrounded and defeated. This was a victory for groups who were essentially unorganized and it caused some stir in official circles; the Governor was subsequently relieved of his post and the Colonel of Police was deprived of his rank. In both cases the decision was reversed at a higher level shortly afterwards.

This success encouraged the rebels, who until then were little more than bandits. Shortly afterwards the capture of the town of Belitu, one of the few towns in the *awraja*, led to the rapid spread of resistance throughout Wabe. Within a few months the example was copied in another *awraja*, Delo. By the end of 1965 virtually the whole central area of the province was rebel-controlled except for the towns of Ginir and Garo. One aspect of the spread of the revolt in Delo was the impetus given by an inter-tribal conflict in the neighbouring province of Sidamo. Trouble between the Oromo in Boranna and the Ethiopian Somalis south of the Ganale river, led the Government to order the resettlement of some groups in Delo.

When this was resisted the Oromo forcibly drove them across the river into Delo *awraja*. Their appeals to the local administration for redress or for land in Delo met with no response. They were therefore left with little option but to join the rebellion.

Most of the leaders were minor officials or men of local importance from *balabat* families. Hajji Yisihag of Rayitu who had great influence in the eastern part of the province, though he spent much time in Somalia, was one of the Wabe *balabats* involved. Another leader was Isimi Aba Washah a former lawyer from Ginir. In Delo and Ganale the leaders were Wako Gutu, Wako Lugo, and Ahije Chiri—all men of some importance in their own areas. Although they operated in different areas the contacts between them were close. Under the overall leadership of Wako Gutu they ran their own administration in the areas under their control, which gained some reputation for fairness and efficiency. The emphasis that was apparently laid on individual leaders is significant. At this stage there is no evidence to suggest that the movement was either genuinely nationalist or revolutionary; though the sophistication of tactics suggests some specialized training.

The tactics used were classic guerilla ones: operating out of bases in the heavily-forested highlands, they made raids on Amhara police and Territorial Army posts, cutting roads and making the supply situations too intolerable for units to be left in isolated villages. It was apparently Waku who was responsible for much of this and for co-ordinating the spread of the rebellion over most of Bale and into Boranna, and for holding the Oromo and Somali together. This was the hardest problem, and typified two of the elements in the rebellion—the Somali desire for union with Somalia, and the Oromo element which gradually moved more towards independence. National feeling among the Oromo was at first subordinate to the main cause of the revolt—peasant exploitation. In fact Waku himself never appears to have been particularly nationalistic, or rather, only in a traditional sense. Certainly he accepted a title from the Government when he surrendered in 1970; it may be assumed that this was part of the bribe offered to him. Nevertheless his seal carried the legend "General of Western Somalia" and the fact that the movement accepted the title "Liberation Front for Western Somalia" suggests he was fully alive to the practical necessities of gaining Somali help, if no more.

The Liberation Front for Western Somalia was established in Mogadishu in 1960. Its aim was "the separation of Hararge, Arussi,

Bale and Galla Sidamo from Ethiopia and their annexation to Somalia, believing that the majority of inhabitants belonged to nationalities almost analagous with the Somali nationality and linked together by the religious bond".[11] It is not clear how far the original outbreaks of peasant discontent in Bale among both Oromo and Somalis are to be linked with the Liberation Front for Western Somalia. They appear to have been separate and spontaneous. Indeed the Bale activities do not seem to have been co-ordinated with other activities in the Ogaden (see below).

In any case the Front was highly successful in Bale in 1965 and 1966 particularly in Delo *awraja*. They captured the town of Obarso; and Bidire was saved only by a relief force of regular soldiers from Negele (this was the first real use of the regular Army). However, as soon as the troops withdrew Bidire was taken. The governors of the *woredas* of Ababa and Ganale were both killed; and raids were made up to the outskirts of the provincial capital of Goba; the only all-weather road in the province linking Goba with Shashemane and Addis Ababa was virtually cut in 1966.[12]

By late 1966 the Front was being too successful. The central Government finally accepted that the Police and Territorials could not cope and committed regular Army units on a sizeable scale. A state of emergency was declared in the province and two brigades of the 4th Division were assigned to move on to the offensive, operating out of Neghelli in the south and Roba near Goba in the north.

The main job for the southern brigade was to cut the supply routes from Somalia, and their efforts were co-ordinated with diplomatic moves attempting to settle the border situation. The diplomacy was not a great success but the operations along the border from Dolo eastwards were more successful in closing the gap between the Webe and Ganale rivers. Arms still continued to come in— some coming through the Ogaden—and Somali radio continued its Oromo broadcasts. At this period Ethiopian radio had no Oromo programmes; in any case reception from Mogadishu was considerably better than from Addis Ababa. The Army activities were supported by the use of air power and numbers of villages were destroyed with much loss of life. It was the advantage of the air support that enabled the Army to pacify El Kere *awraja* relatively quickly. By February 1967 fighting was virtually over in the area and at least one major leader had become reconciled with the Government.

The other brigade operating in the northern part of the province, in Wabe, found stiffer resistance and it took six months to clear out most of the opposition. Again, bombing attacks on villages were used to frighten the rebels, with equal success. Once the area had been relatively pacified a push was made against the central positions in Delo and Ganale. In February 1967 a large force from the 7th Brigade accompanied by police and militia advanced towards Hawo and Buluq in Dalo. This advance brought some of the fiercest fighting of the rebellion, for the Front decided to try to hold these towns. There were four days of continuous fighting around Buluq before it fell in March—Hawo was captured three weeks earlier. It appears, however, that the guerilla forces withdrew in reasonable order. Certainly they were able to regroup fairly fast and to carry out harassing tactics.

Before the end of 1967 the Government forces were compelled to withdraw from the area. One reason for this was the friction between the regular Army and the Territorials, many of whom were Oromo. The Army also managed to supply itself with heavily-guarded convoys, but the Territorials were left to fend for themselves. This they were largely prevented from doing by the guerillas; and a significant number deserted. The retreat of the Army left the rebels in control of Delo once again. Officially the area had been declared pacified in March 1967 and so it was maintained that the need for troops had disappeared by November. In fact there is little reason to doubt guerilla claims that the Army was not able to maintain itself in the difficult terrain, with only half-hearted Territorial support. The Army could keep the road open to military-escorted traffic but it could not make them safe, and non-military traffic was not allowed beyond Goba.

The failure of this offensive led to a change of tactics on the part of the Government. There were no more head-on attacks of this kind. The Commander of the 4th Division, Major-General Jagama Kello, a Christian Oromo from Bale, was given a freer hand to deal with the problem. Almost the entire division was put into the area. New roads were made through the heart of the rebel area, from Negelli in the south up to Goba, with a large army base set up at Masilo halfway in between. This was made possible by the building of a bridge over the River Ganale, by British Army Engineers. Strict control over people's movements, a close watch on food supplies and extensive use of air power, helped to bring the situation under some control.

By 1968 the main guerilla forces were boxed into the Delo forest

areas. There they were virtually impregnable. Air attacks were
unsuccessful and the accuracy of the rebel bazookas caused some
concern. It was at this time that American experts were brought in
to improve the fire power on some of the jets. However, the Front's
efforts to break out of the area were equally unsuccessful. For much
of 1968–69 a virtual stalemate resulted.

However, in 1969 the military coup in Somalia brought a significant change. The new Government was at first unprepared to support
the Liberation Front of Western Somalia. Several of the Front's
members in Somalia were arrested; and, more important, arms and
ammunition supplies began to drop off. At the same time Major-
General Jagama met Waku on at least one occasion to try and persuade him to surrender. According to an eye-witness of an encounter in 1969 they were not so much old enemies as old friends.
This report lends credibility to the story that one reason for Wako's
success had been Jagama's sympathy towards the Front's activities.
It was certainly made clear that it would be in Waku's interests if
he surrendered. He finally came in March 1970 with a quantity of
arms and a small number of followers and was promptly given the
title *Grazmatch* and pardoned by the Emperor. Another leader,
Wako Lugo, had also surrendered a month earlier. All together
about a hundred rebels were actually named as having surrendered;
most of the others melted away to their villages.[13]

The surrender of these leaders brought the first publicity within
Ethiopia and the Emperor also paid a visit to the province—both
signs that things were reasonably under control. Since then army
controls on the roads have also been relaxed and it has become
possible for outsiders to visit the province relatively freely. But not
all surrendered, and the Front kept forces in the Delo highlands,
and in Genale. There is also some evidence to suggest that some of
their forces crossed the Wabe Shebelli River into southern Arussi
and western Hararge where they have since remained. Certainly
there was guerilla activity going on in this remote area in 1971–72
and it seems logical to suppose that it comes from the same source.

It appears in fact that the Liberation Front of Western Somalia
has reactivated itself under a new title—the Ethiopian National
Liberation Front. The situation as regards these movements is,
however, somewhat confusing for there is also a United Front for
the Liberation of Western Somalia operating a press office in
Baghdad. The Ethiopian National Liberation Front was set up
within Ethiopia after outside support was cut off. "The Liberation

Front of occupied Western Somalia has contacted all progressive revolutionary organizations throughout the Empire, who oppose the present treacherous regime. Delegates representing these organizations met at a National Conference held on the 27 June 1971 . . . From the 1 August 1971 the new name of the Front will be 'the Ethiopian National Liberation Front' ".[14] This suggests that the various Oromo and Somali liberation movements came together within Ethiopia. Certainly an Ethiopian National Liberation Front spokesman in 1973 claimed that a build-up for a new offensive in the southern areas was being prepared. However, like the E.L.F., they did nothing to distract the Army in the 1974 crisis. There is also some evidence to suggest that since these guerillas had no support from Somalia in 1970–72 (though the border tensions between the Somalia and Ethiopia may change this) and could not therefore use the Somali border, they had transport assistance from the Eritrean Liberation Front through Eritrea.[15]

Since 1970 they have had to depend upon their own efforts, and in consequence the strategy has been defensive. The fact that the Ethiopian National Liberation Front is a revolutionary socialist group is significant and presupposes that the defeats of 1970 have caused a reappraisal of both aims and strategy. Certainly the former Liberation Front of Western Somalia was not particularly socialist.

Another area that deserves consideration at this point, where nationalist feelings have surfaced at intervals over a long period, is in the south east where the inhabitants are Somali. A large part of this area was reserved by the British in 1941, when they put most of the Somali-inhabited areas under one administration—with the exception of the French-controlled area around Djibouti. In the 1940s the British also floated the idea of a Greater Somalia comprising all areas inhabited by Somali groups which included southeastern Ethiopia, Djibouti and part of Northern Kenya as well as the former Italian and British Somaliland. After a considerable debate in and out of the U.N. it was decided that former Italian Somaliland should be handed back to Italy in 1950 on a mandate for independence in 1960.[16] In 1955 Britain gave the reserved areas and the Haud back to Ethiopia though not entirely to the satisfaction of the inhabitants. A delegation was sent on their behalf by Somalis in British Somaliland to London and the United Nations was also petitioned. It was claimed that indignation in British Somaliland was high because the transfer took place at a time when seven Ethiopian Somalis were executed by slow strangulation in front of their families, after a riot that had taken place four years before. The leader of the delegation explaining the reasons said: "The people of Ethiopia were our traditional foes and were among the people from whom we sought protection. Then years after, Great Britain has given away a substantial proportion of our territory without our knowledge or consent . . .. We had no other recourse but to petition the U.N. General Assembly".[17] The protests were, however, rejected and Ethiopia has held the areas since 1955.

The early troubles that occurred in the area were relatively small-scale. There was a clash in April/May 1942 in the Gursum and Gojjiar district of Hararge. *Shifta* attacks were carried out on the road and attempts to arrest those responsible led to an attack on the recent Amhara settlements in the area. Gojjiar was sacked and shortly afterwards Gursum, Giarso, Saiarre, Funyambira and Babile were also pillaged and burnt. The Somalis were however defeated at the Errer River; and with the arrival of reinforcements from Addis Ababa things rapidly quietened down.[18]

There were renewed disturbances in Hararge in 1948 and these involved demands for the independence of the whole area. The disturbances continued for some time and merged into the resistance to tax collection. Considerable force was employed to pacify the area and the killing mentioned above was one episode. There was another violent clash over the seizure of water holes not far from Dire Dawa in 1955. Since then there has been an almost continuous series of incidents in the Ogaden. The Liberation Front for Western Somalia claimed responsibility for a lot of them though it is uncertain how much support it had there and how much activity actually depended on it. Its main field of battle during the last decade appears to have been Bale.

Once British and Italian Somaliland territories became independent and united in 1960 the situation, from the Ethiopian point of view, deteriorated. The newly-independent Republic of Somalia was prepared immediately to be responsive to requests for unification from the Somali minorities in Ethiopia, Kenya and Djibouti. The problem was also confused by the fact that the boundary (especially in southern Ethiopia) is not carefully defined and the Somali nomadic tribes of the area cross it at will.[19] For some years a state of undeclared war existed along the frontier but in 1967 the tensions began to lessen. This was unaffected by the military revolution in 1969 and until 1971 the border was relatively quiet. Since then the tension has risen again as Somalia has come near to military parity and there has been the discovery of oil and gas in the south of Bale.

Although there was an apparent halt in the late 1960s Somalia has also shown a willingness to assist movements within Ethiopia, as well as beaming propaganda in both Somali and Oromo. The main effort was put into helping the Front for the Liberation of Western Somalia—that is for the liberation of Somalis in Bale and also the Oromo there. This support was withdrawn in 1969 and the Front for the Liberation of the Somalia Coast (i.e. in Djibouti) also lost backing. Later developments, however, suggest that Somalia may well take a much stronger line about the Somali minority in Ethiopia. In mid-1973 the O.A.U. was nearly disrupted by loud disagreements over the border; and although there was a considerable attempt at mediation little has yet come of it.[20] In January 1974 Somalia also announced her full support for the creation of a revolutionary Eritrean Government should the Eritrean people desire it. It is therefore possible that the recent reactivation of the Ethiopian National Liberation Front movement in Bale and Hararge will enjoy renewed Somali support. It is not, however, clear if the Liberation Front for Western Somalia still operates as a separate organization for the liberation of Somalis within Ethiopia or whether it is united with the Ethiopian National Liberation Front.

Whatever the state of the various liberation fronts, the fact remains that they can count on a considerable amount of support from Somalis within Ethiopia, both because of bad government and on ethnic grounds. There have been numbers of complaints and accusations against the Ethiopian administration in the Ogaden similar to those in Bale. These are impossible to verify—most of the area is closed to outsiders—but it does seem that a substantial amount of the 3rd Division's time is spent in tax collecting. Haile Selassie's attempts on his visits to bind the people more closely with money, titles and land does not appear to have been successful. The problem is unlikely to be solved using such traditional methods in the face of an ethnic, cultural and religious identity; and it can be assumed that demands for union with Somalia will continue to appear at regular intervals; and they are likely to be coupled in the future with revolutionary socialist ideology.

Although Bale has been relatively quiescent since 1970 the causes of the original discontent have not been removed, though some efforts have been made to reduce animosities. Before 1970 the entire administration was geared to Christian Amhara domination, organized from Addis Ababa. The provincial governor of this period, *Dejazmatch* Merid Beyene, a member of the Imperial family, spent relatively little time in his province; he was often found in Addis Ababa or abroad. The *awraja* and *woreda* governors, who are more relevant locally, have been the target for criticism and accusations of corruption and malpractice. A well-known case was that of a district governor, who on a salary of Eth. $100 per month, managed to save Eth. $18,000 in three years.[21] This case actually came to trial, but it appears to have merited only a transfer to a higher post as *awraja* governor in another province. It has not been the only case of its kind.

The most sensitive area has been taxation and tax collection. The two main taxes were the land tax and tithe, and the cattle tax for nomads. Both were unpopular and often refused. The history of this goes back to the early 1950s. The Ministry of Finance estimate for uncollected taxes 1952–57 amounted to Eth. $3 million. Two years later the Ministry of the Interior calculated that there were over 6,000 people in one *awraja* who could be brought to court for tax evasion. The situation was such that an investigation committee was set up in 1961. This found that the fault lay to a substantial extent within the administration itself and a number of officials were brought to trial and relieved of their posts for negligence and irresponsibility—a fairly generous way of looking at it. The committee also found that large amounts of land had been confiscated for failure to pay the land tax—nearly 8,000 *gashas* in Wabe, and in Delo, and between 3,000 and 4,000 *gashas* in the *awraja* of Fasil and in Ganale. There is a strong feeling that most of this land was confiscated by "irresponsible" officials before any court had ruled on the matter.

The problems inherent in this were apparently worsened by the Emperor's visit in 1964. A proclamation was published stating that he was allowing the taxes for 1952 to 1961 to be used for development projects in the province. He also said that people whose land had been confiscated could reclaim it if they paid their taxes and if it had not been given to another person. This proclamation was not only misunderstood to imply that unpaid taxes prior to 1961 were being cancelled, but also it infuriated former landowners to discover that after paying their land tax much of the land had been given to Amhara officials and was thus ineligible for reclamation, even though these officials had in some cases been disgraced.[22]

Indeed the whole landowning situation of the province is unsatisfactory. Approximately 1,000,000 out of the 1,206,700 people in Bale are Oromo, but most of the best land is Amhara-owned. The best areas for mixed farming are along the road around Goba and in the valleys running east and south from the town. Since the town was the centre of provincial administration and was therefore filled with Amhara officials it is just these areas where expropriation most noticeably took place. Equally, very large areas of cattle land (Bale has approximately 2,000,000 cattle) used by the Oromo, are owned largely by absentee Amhara nobility.

Another area of widespread dissatisfaction has been over the judiciary, and not just for its corruption. The higher courts of the province have been entirely Christian-controlled and Moslem judges do not sit in the high court, only in the lesser *Qadi* and *Nayiba* courts. There is no equivalent in the Moslem judiciary of the high court. Salary distinctions have emphasized the discrimination. A high court judge gets Eth.$500 per month, the chief *Qadi* of Bale gets Eth.$150. An *awraja* court judge gets Eth.$250, a *Nayiba* judge, Eth.$50.

The same techniques operate in the educational system. The statistics of the provincial education office for 1970 show that there were 682 students at the only high school in the province at Goba of whom 86 were Moslem. In all the Goba schools there were 2,191 students of whom only 208 were Moslem. In the almost exclusively Moslem *awrajas* of Delo and El Kere there are practically no schools at all—in Delo there are only 378 students and in El Kere only 64.[23] Christian holidays are kept and Christian religious classes are held; Moslems do not have the same privileges. Out of the 93 churches in Bale, 44 are Government built and supported: none of the Mosques were Government built and none have received Government land grants for their support.

It is true that since the rebellion broke out some change and reforms have been effected, but it is questionable how much these amount to in practice. A Christian Oromo was appointed *Enderassie* of the province—Major-General Jagama Kelo. In addition two Moslems were appointed *awraja* governors; and another was made provincial adviser. Some efforts were also made to correct specific points—the followers of Wako Gutu, who were forced out of Boranna, have been allowed to go back. The back taxes of 1952–66 have been remitted. For the first time a number of development projects have been undertaken. The road system has been improved, largely in the process of putting down the rebellion, but it has had some effect on opening up the countryside. More schools have been built, a hospital opened in Goba and a larger one is being constructed. It should be mentioned that this is the only hospital in the province. The previous one was taken over by the provincial administration for offices some years before. Once the new hospital is opened it may be that the province will get more doctors—in 1970 the only non-military doctor in the province left Goba. None of these matters, however, deal with the major problems of taxation, landownership, and Government corruption.

In no other Oromo area has there been such extreme reactions to the unsatisfactory nature of the local government. In Arussi, another largely Oromo province, there have been continuous small-scale outbreaks for years. These have tended to be organized by men of local *balabat* status who have felt slighted by their failure to be given office in the local administration; but the major factor has been peasant discontent. There are exceptions to this, of course. One important one has been *Kengnazmatch* Taye in Arussi. Taye is the leader of a spirit possession cult which is widespread in Arussi and indeed much further, and he is revered as a Moslem saint. At the great twice-yearly celebrations held at Fericasa in Arussi, the number of people who attend has been estimated at about 50,000. The cult itself is a well-established movement—Taye inherited his position through his grandmother who was a well-known seer in Harar and Arussi in the earlier part of this century.

The religious basis of the cult is mixed—the spirits invoked include Christian and Moslem saints as well as pagan deities, though the emphasis is towards the pagan and Moslem. The organization owes nothing, however, to either the Christian Church or the Moslem leadership. Some people have to attend the celebrations in considerable secrecy as it would damage their reputations seriously in court or Government circles if their presence there was known. Even so, Taye's following in the last few years has grown to such proportions that the Government has felt it expedient to grant him a title. This gives quasi-recognition to his position and he himself is treated with considerable deference on his visits to Addis Ababa.

Spirit possession cults are by no means unique to Arussi; they are found almost anywhere among the Oromo, even in Addis Ababa. They are also found outside Oromo areas. The most notable is actually in the province of Kaffa. This is not exactly the same type of cult—it involves ancestral spirit worship and the high priesthood is hereditary to the family of the former high priests of the King of Kaffa. Today the chief priest, Idebe Godo, lives in Bonga, the former capital of Kaffa and his writ runs as far as the Uganda border.[24] Indeed his control is more effective than that of the Imperial Government and it is wise to get his support as well as the administrations' in most matters. The Government accepts this, albeit with ill-grace, though his position has not been recognized to the extent of giving him a title; nevertheless it is real for all that.

The fact that this and other spirit possession cults have spread so widely among the southern provinces, and not just among the Oromo, strengthens the argument that they are seen as a definite and conscious rejection of Christian Amhara rule. It is impossible to ascertain the figures, but there is no doubt that the number of followers has increased significantly in the last twenty years, partly because it is one of the easiest outlets to relieve the frustrations against the regime. This expansion is paralleled by an equally significant expansion of Islam among the southern Oromo. Again figures are hard to come by, but the Moslems in Bale are now about 85 per cent of the population of the province, helped no doubt by the presence of an important Moslem saint, Sheik Hussein, whose place of burial is a centre for pilgrimages from all over the southern provinces. In fact it is possible to say that practically none of the rural population of the southern provinces are Christian; most follow Islam or a spirit possession cult. According to the 1968 figures, approximately 7 million out of a population of 7·6 million fall into this rural category.[25] From travellers' accounts and Italian estimates it is clear that however cautiously one uses the figures, they represent a substantial switch from a loosly-defined animism to a more organized non-Christian religion or cult.

Another form of rejection can be seen in the very swift spread of the Mecha Oromo Self-Help Association founded in 1967.[26] Within less than a year the Association claimed 300,000 members. While this may be an exaggeration, the meetings were very well attended and they attracted at least one important figure who was not usually regarded as an Oromo, so well had he assimilated into the ruling elite, General Tadessa Biru. He addressed a number of meetings of the Association and while he accepted the community self-help basis of it, his speeches contained some very outspoken criticisms, outspoken enough for the Government to take warning. The moment an opportunity offered itself, following a bomb explosion in an Addis Ababa cinema, the General was arrested. He shot his way out before being re-arrested, and his trial was largely held *in camera;* he received a long term of imprisonment. Interestingly enough witnesses for the prosecution as well as the defence were also arrested after the trial and have been held since 1968 as well. Following this the Mecha Galla Association was dissolved by the Government and any similar organization among the Oromo was forbidden on the grounds that it encouraged tribalism. There is no doubt that whatever the true figure of membership, the Government took fright at the numbers who were by inference, if not vocally, dissatisfied with the administration in many ways.

The Oromo have, broadly speaking, shown a number of signs of dissatisfaction with the Amhara-dominated Government. Even in areas where assimilation has been practiced for generations, as among the Yejju, personal factors or bad Government can still lead to attempted revolts or bandit activity. When a figure such as General Tadessa Biru rejects his upbringing and whole career, and when the students can so strongly talk of an Oromo Nation, it is clear that assimilation has failed to achieve its main object. Of course, in many areas assimilation attempts have been non-existent or spasmodic and the rule has been corrupt and the Government exploitative. The reaction has been either a cautious rejection of the system through the support of non-establishment religious organizations or outright rebellion. These reactions have not been helped by the Government's response to such threats. The activities of the army in Bale certainly played a major part in turning an essentially peasant revolt into a national revolutionary movement. While nationalism has been a major factor among the Somali dissidents, its appearance has been limited among the Oromo. Since the mid-1960s, however, there are a number of signs that an Oromo national consciousness is beginning to appear. As yet the Oromo are still far more divided than united; but the appearance of a national and revolutionary socialist movement is a sign that things are changing.

CHAPTER VIII

Contradictions within the Ruling Class

It has already been made clear that a great deal of the opposition that the Emperor has faced has been national or regional in origin; and this applies equally to peasant revolts as well as aristocratic plots. Given the predominantly Shoan influence at the centre of the empire it might be expected that the Shoan aristocracy would have been the most loyal group. In practice that expectation has been offset by factors like the personalization of the imperial rule, the method of imperial selection and the route of the Emperor to power; all of which have tended to encourage conspiracies among the elite. Furthermore it is obvious that imperial and Shoan aristocratic interests have not always coincided. While the Emperor has undoubtedly been personally sympathetic to some of the opposition, which has been aimed at nullifying the effects of measures that he has felt compelled to enact, he has certainly had no feeling for attempts to limit imperial control. Any attempt to undermine the imperial position has been firmly dealt with.

The distinction made here between opposition from aristocracy with regional links and from those at the centre is not perhaps entirely valid, considering the cross-links between the various groups of nobility and their common class interests. Nevertheless the regional aristocracy has tended to emphasize the regional element, where their own power bases lay. By contrast there have been a number of conspiracies arising from contradictions within the regime, where this factor has been missing, where there has been no regional element as such. These are plots where the conspirators have had a base among the Shoan nobility or the army.

It should be mentioned at the outset that the most surprising thing about all the plots that have been aimed at the Emperor is that none of them has been successful. The degree of incompetence

that has been displayed is such that one is almost led to the conclusion that the authors did not seriously intend them to be successful
at all. Obviously this is, in part, due to the efficiency of the imperial
and Government security services. This is not, however, the whole
story and psychological factors seem to have operated as well. The
reiterated failures have given rise to myths of the Emperor's
personal invulnerability. It is also true that a lack of ruthlessness
has been apparent on both sides; some have of course been killed
but by and large the Emperor has been extremely lenient to those
who have plotted against him. Much in fact has been made of the
Emperor's magnanimity in this but it would be more accurate to
see this as a reflection of the aristocratic strength in the empire.
Indeed, the balance of power between the Emperor and the nobility
has largely precluded the exercise of excessive punishment. However
far the Emperor may have carried his policies of centralization,
he has never reached the stage where he could openly flout the
aristocracy in matters so closely affecting them.

Illustrative of all these factors is the life of *Blatta* Telke Wolde-
Hawariot who had a career that oscillated between high office and
imprisonment, with little in between. Tekle's attitudes are also
worth looking at for he typifies the individual and personal opposition to Haile Selassie. His opposition was a post-war phenomenon—
in the years before the war he was a strong, if occasionally critical,
supporter of the Emperor. He has also, since his death in 1969,
become something of a cult figure among the student radicals for
being one of the very few of the upper-class whose opposition to
the Emperor was never suborned by office and title.

Tekle Wolde-Hawariot, born 1900, was not a member of the
highest nobility but from a *balabat* family of Bulga in Shoa. He
did, however, marry into the Shoan royal family—his wife *Wo.*
Ascale Waldamanuel being a direct descendant of *Negus* Sahle
Selassie of Shoa. He originally came to prominence in the time of
Lij Iyasu, working in the municipality of Addis Ababa under a
follower of *Lij* Iyasu. In 1916, however, he sided with *Ras* Tafari
and the Shoans; his subsequent career depended upon Tafari; and
indeed the two became close friends. Before *Ras* Tafari became
Emperor, Tekle had already been a deputy governor in Kaffa, one
of the judges in the anti-slavery courts and Chief Secretary to the
Customs at Gore in the west. After the Emperor's accession he was
successively Secretary-General in the Ministry of the Interior,
and Director-General in the Ministries of Public Works, Transport

and Agriculture. He was thus one of the clique of relatively radical young men that Haile Selassie used in the pre-war years when he was attempting to set up a bureaucracy to help in the imperial policy of centralization.

At this stage of his life Tekle was undoubtedly a firm supporter of Haile Selassie and the Emperor recognized it. In 1935 he was promoted to *Blatta* and left as the director of the municipality of Addis Ababa when the Emperor went north. As such he had a responsible part to play in preparations for defence against the Italians. The first element of disillusionment seems to have occurred in 1936 when Tekle was one of only three members of the Crown Council to vote in favour of the Emperor remaining in Ethiopia to continue the fight against the Italians. Tekle himself did remain and had a successful career as a patriot. Indeed he has been called the greatest of the patriot leaders.[1] Certainly he was one of the very few who from the beginning of the war appreciated the necessity of guerilla warfare, and he had greater understanding than most of the techniques. He had even started training some volunteers before the Emperor left for Europe. As a by-product of this he was able to provide his own followers with a good selection of arms. This interest in guerilla tactics seems to have contributed to his loss of respect for the Emperor; his advice along these lines was continuously rejected in 1935–36.

Although Tekle was involved in numerous engagements during the resistance, his primary interest rapidly became political rather than military. He was appointed political secretary and co-ordinator at a meeting of patriot leaders in July 1937; he therefore had a lot to do with the outbreak of revolt that followed on from the massacres at Addis Ababa and Debra Libanos. More important in the long run was his enforced retreat to Khartoum in May 1938, for it was there that he became involved in, and may have instituted, a series of discussions on the future of the Ethiopian state. Republicanizm was one of the subjects that was talked about and Tekle apparently wrote to France for assistance in planning the setting-up of a republic. A number of other exiles shared his views though not all; Mesfin Sileshi, for one, copied the correspondence and forwarded it to Haile Selassie in England.

In 1939 the matter progressed farther than talk. Having sent one of his supporters to prepare the way in Begemeder and in the Debra Tabor area, he himself followed and in that year he travelled widely in the north west. He claimed to have Haile Selassie's support for the idea of a republic and he granted titles to many patriot leaders. A document was drawn up for the League of Nations which set out the views of some nine hundred *balabats* and patriot leaders on the future of Ethiopia. Tekle also gave some thought to the possibility of a federated status for parts of Ethiopia under Italian control. Negotiations were carried out on his behalf with the Italian commander at Gondar—General Frusci—with the general approval of the patriots around. The Italians, however, baulked at the idea of federation.

It is not altogether clear how much of a part republicanizm played in these negotiations with the Italians and in discussions with other patriot leaders, for there was a pretender to the throne operating in Begemeder. This was *Lij* Yohannis, one of the sons of the late Emperor *Lij* Iyasu. One of the things Tekle had done in early 1940 was to stop *Lij* Yohannis from accepting the Italian offer of the title of *Negus* and the governorship of Begemeder. Nevertheless Tekle also had ideas of using Yohannis as a figurehead in setting up a republic with Italian connivance,[2] or in the negotiations to gather support among the nobility of the province.

Not surprisingly the idea of republicanizm worried Haile Selassie who sent a letter to *Dejazmatch* Wubneh, one of the leading Begemeder patriots, condemning it. He also despatched Lorenzo Taezez to the province, and sent Mesfin Sileshi to Gojjam to stop it spreading. It is possible that private instructions were also sent to *Dejazmatch* Wubneh to get rid of Tekle, although internal conflicts between the patriot leaders may equally well account for Wubneh seizing Tekle in July 1939. Tekle was rescued from a hanging only at the last moment by another patriot leader. However the episode marks the apparent end of Tekle's flirtation with republicanizm and although he stayed in Begemeder for several months there was no more mention of it. This is not surprising. In the atmosphere of exile and revolt such aberrations might be discussed, but they were hardly practical politics in the Ethiopian highlands at that date.

In any case the possibilities of *Lij* Yohannis were much greater, either from an anti-Haile Selassie viewpoint or from the angle of negotiations with the Italians. Indeed the support that the sons of *Lij* Iyasu aroused during the war was considerable and contributed to the suspicion with which Haile Selassie regarded the patriots after the restoration. Groups of heavily armed and experienced fighters were bad enough without significant leaders who had imperial pretensions. Several of *Lij* Iyasu's sons were active between

1936 and 1941. *Lij* Yohannis in Begemeder actually took the title
of Emperor, with the throne name of Wolde, at one point. In 1941,
however, when Haile Selassie entered Gojjam he came under safe
conduct, with a thousand men, and submitted. He was apparently
promised the governor-generalship of Sidamo; it is possible that his
failure to get it helped persuade him into involvement in Tekle
Wolde Hawariat's 1942 plot. His half-brother, Melaku Tsehai,
operated in Shoa with Abebe Aregai. Melaku was given the title
of *Negus*—king—on 28 October, 1937, by the patriots of the area;
it was he who gave Abebe Aragai his title of *Ras*, which Haile
Selassie was to confirm implicitly in letters sent to him. Melaku,
however, died of a fever in 1938.

Two other sons of *Lij* Iyasu were also around at the time of the
invasion and the restoration. *Lij* Girma, formerly a prisoner of
Haile Selassie, was a patriot leader in the south-west in 1936–37.
He had to take refuge in Kenya at one point and was prevented from
returning by the British. He died early in 1941 from food poisoning
in his refugee camp. *Lij* Tewodros was another, and he surfaced in
the Gambella area in the west in 1941 claiming to be Emperor. His
efforts were short-lived and his group were defeated by the Belgian
troops in the area who had been operating against the Italians.
Tewodros was wounded and captured but what finally happened to
him is unknown. Finally, mention should be made of Menilek Iyasu
who lived among the Danakil. He was informed of his father's
death in 1935 and acknowledged as Emperor by some of the chiefs
of the area when he was living under the protection of the French,
at Tadjura. He was still being "protected" by the French in 1938
but he fell into Haile Selassie's hands in the early 1940s. He is still
alive and farms an area not far from Miezo, to which he is strictly
confined. These are not all of *Lij* Iyasu's children, but enough to
give some idea of why the Emperor looked on patriots who had been
involved with them with some disfavour.

Tekle Wolde Hawariat had also known *Lij* Girma in Kenya; in
1940 he was sent there to organize and train some of the refugees.
In fact he had trouble getting back into Ethiopia from there and
the British did all they could to hinder him. Nevertheless he succeeded in crossing the border in 1941, in time to fall into Italian
hands. He was held only for a short time, however, and got to Addis
Ababa at about the same time as the Emperor. Once there he was
given the significant offices of Governor-General of Shoa and Mayor
of Addis Ababa. Whatever the Emperor's suspicions of Tekle, he

was much too important a patriot and too dangerous to be left out of office in 1941. Moreover there is little doubt that the Emperor wanted him under his own eye. He apparently found Tekle a useful scapegoat in his dealings with the British Military Administration and blamed him on several occasions for things that the British objected to. It is also more than possible that Haile Selassie assumed that appointment to high office would satisfy Tekle as it was to satisfy most others.

Tekle, however, was one of the very few whom high office did not suborn from his attitudes. His post-war career was a series of continuous plots against the Emperor, interspersed with office, until the day he died, machine-gun in hand. There is no doubt that his wartime experiences and those of 1935–36 provided the main *raison d'être* of his opposition, which was essentially personal though it was linked both to republicanism, as in 1939–40, and to constitutionalism. He certainly advocated the calling of a Parliament in 1941 and in 1940 he, with *Dejazmatch* Adafrisau and Major-General Abebe Damtau, had queried the Emperor's post-war plans at a meeting in Khartoum. They demanded to hear the Emperor's views on the constitution and the Government that should be incorporated on his return. Among their suggestions was more power for Parliament and less for the Emperor—closer to a constitutional monarchy. The Emperor was evasive on these issues, but both Tekle and Abebe Damtau were rapidly dispatched to Kenya.

Tekle's post-war plots were not always clear-cut in terms of aims. His first effort came only a few months after his appointment to high office. It involved the attempt to divert the training of 2,000 soldiers for the new imperial Army and to utilize them with *Lij* Yohannis Iyasu to get rid of the Emperor. The plot was apparently discovered by the Minister of the Pen, Wolde Giyorgis; Tekle was jailed for two years. Another of the conspirators got ten years and *Lij* Yohannis was sent down in semi-exile to Jimma. Rumours at the time suggested that at least two other important patriot leaders— *Ras* Abebe Aragai and *Dejazmatch* Geressa Duki—were involved to the extent of having been prepared to support any move if and when it happened.[3]

There is no doubt that this was an attempt to capitalize on the fairly widespread feeling that it was time for a change. Tekle's suggestion to recall Parliament and to make it elective, not appointive, was symptomatic of a lot of patriot discontent. This was not just over the fact that rewards did not live up to expectations, but it also came from the extensive employment of collaborators that outraged many of those who had spent the previous five years fighting. By no means all patriots took kindly to the return, from relatively comfortable exile, of those who had left without any or little resistance in 1935–36; this helped to fuel an already considerable support for those potential Emperors who had remained behind—the sons of *Lij* Iyasu.

Tekle was released in 1945 and made deputy *Afa Negus*. His position was uncertain from the beginning as the Minister of the Pen, Wolde Giyorgis,was then at the height of his power and was one of Tekle's greatest enemies. He was almost immediately suspected of involvement in the Parliamentary plot of 1946–47. This was an attempt by a group of ex-patriots to force a genuine constitution on the Emperor and cut down his power. Several Army units were suspected of being on the edge of revolt and there were plans to march on the capital. The danger was such that the Emperor thought it necessary to raise the Army's pay. Even before the plot was fully uncovered Tekle had been posted off to the remote south as Governor of Boranna. There was in fact some trouble there and he was suspected of trying to raise an armed force. In the circumstances it was not hard to persuade Haile Selassie that Tekle was too dangerous to be left at large. Apparently no evidence was adduced that Tekle was involved in the Parliamentary plot but it looked remarkably like one of his efforts; it certainly incorporated some of his ideas.

In any case, evidence or no evidence, he went back into detention. He did not come back to office until 1954 when Wolde Giyorgis' power was lessening. Then he acquired the post of Vice-Minister of the Interior, and in this capacity played a considerable part in the organization of the overthrow of Wolde Giyorgis, with his cousin Makonnen Habtewold. After Wolde Giyorgis had gone he became *Afa Negus* and kept the position until 1961. He was not involved in the attempted coup—indeed he deliberately kept out of it, never having been particularly impressed with Germame and Mengistu Neway who organized it. Nevertheless in the nervous months afterwards he again found himself under suspicion and was sent back to house arrest in the provinces, where he was to stay for another five years.

When he was released he did not get another post but lived quietly in Addis Ababa. His final attempt to overthrow the Emperor came in November 1969. The plot was apparently to assassinate him by planting mines on a road over which the Emperor was due to pass.

The security forces arrested those responsible twenty-four hours before the plotters were due to strike. Eight people were seized, including two army officers, and a number of others were also taken after a gun battle lasting several hours on the outskirts of the city. Tekle was implicated by one of those arrested and police came for him on the evening of 27 November. He refused to surrender and after a siege lasting several hours he was either killed or committed suicide.

His death had a considerable impact, and there was a lot of criticism that it should have been necessary to kill so great a patriot. The student attitude put out in a pamphlet was stronger.

> . . . this great nationalist died after having been besieged by the government's Police Force beginning from around 5 p.m. up to 2 a.m. The death of this prominent patriot who was around 75 years old clearly shows that the deep contradiction and decadence of the government is not only felt by the younger generation and the masses but also by the members of the ruling class. We unequivocally condemn this atrocious and brutal action of the government . . ..[4]

Tekle Wolde Hawariat's career is of interest not just in itself but for the way it illustrates a number of points about the Ethiopian political scene, for he operated within the "traditional methods" of conspiracy. It is, however, noticeable that his ideas were not entirely traditional. Although he toyed with and ultimately rejected the possibility of a republic, he never sought to appeal to a mass power-base or to acquire popular support. His forte was conspiracy not revolution, and was based on personal attitudes rather than principles. He was, for three decades, the most important single individual who showed opposition to Haile Selassie. He was above all a nationalist, which was why Haile Selassie could continue to employ him, even though he might feel the need to watch him very carefully. Tekle was in fact a politician in a mould that the Emperor could thoroughly understand—being a more skilful example of it himself.

Tekle Wolde Hawariat was not the only one who made attempts on the Emperor's life or position. The Byzantine atmosphere of such a highly personalized court and Government has been conducive to it. Most of these conspiracies have been unimportant, and have in any case been intercepted fairly easily by the elaborate security forces of the Government, the bodyguard and the Emperor's own security units. As far as can be judged they have in nearly every case been individual and inefficient. The only exceptions to this were the attempted coup of 1960 (see below), which failed for largely similar reasons, and the crisis of 1974.

The only sector of the central power that has given the Emperor really serious anxiety is the Armed Forces. One of the effects of centralizing the military has of course been to make the possibility of a coup or a hidden take-over greater. The Emperor endeavoured to guard against this by his normal techniques of political manoeuvering, by dividing the units of the Armed Forces against themselves, by instituting tensions between the Bodyguard and the Army and by his choice of officers. By and large he judged it expedient to keep most of the very highest nobility out of significant Army posts, or balanced them by men of his own choosing whom he could expect to remain loyal to the person who had given them everything.

In fact the Emperor's choices have not been too successful. One post where loyalty is crucial is that of Commander of the Bodyguard. In 1941 he appointed Mulugetta Buli, who was to hold the post for fourteen years. Mulugetta was a Galla from Siamo province who had been an instructor at the Holeta Military Academy before the war. Unconnected, he was very much of a counter-weight to the powerful Minister of the Pen, Wolde Giyorgis, since he had control of an alternative power source. He was also very much an Emperor's man. In this position he was also well placed to try a coup and after Colonel Nasser's take-over in Egypt in 1952, a group of his officers pushed to make Mulugetta do likewise. In fact Mulugetta deliberately gathered around him a group of officers who would have supported such a move. It certainly seems that he considered taking action, but how seriously is not known. It would probably have been difficult until after the fall of Wolde-Giyorgis and when that happened Mulugetta was moved out of the Bodyguard and made Chief of Staff. He was replaced by another imperial protegée, Mengistu Neway, whom Mulugetta disliked. The feeling was probably reciprocated especially after Mulugetta accused Mengistu's brother, Germame, of being a communist. At all events Mulugetta's opportunity disappeared as he was shifted out of the military and made Minister of National Community Development in 1959—not long after there had been a military take-over in the Sudan. Had Mulugetta seriously wanted to try and overthrow the Emperor he probably could have done so; he controlled all the ingredients for a Nasser-type take-over and was probably popular enough to have made it work, but he never managed to take the decisive steps. It was Mengistu Neway who was to make the attempt.

Mengistu was from a much more significant background, being a member of a very important Shoan family—the Mojas. This family has played an important part in the administration of the Empire over the last fifty years, though not always loyally, and it has remained significant politically and socially. They claim descent from the imperial line of the fifteenth century and are large landowners both in Shoa and elsewhere in the country. Their genealogy gives some idea of the ramifications in the power structure and the posts that they have filled.

Although it was Mengistu who was in a position to attempt a coup in his capacity as Commander of the Bodyguard, it was his younger and more radical brother, Germame, who was the organizer and inspirer. The attempt began on 13 December, 1960, while Haile Selassie was out of the country. Although the planning had been going on for some time, the actual decision to act was taken in something of a hurry when it became clear there had been too many leaks.[5] Within twelve hours, control of Addis Ababa had been established and a number of leading figures detained including the Crown Prince, *Ras* Imru and various ministers. Certain key personnel had, however, either slipped the net or been ignored. These included the Patriarch, *Dejazmatch* Asrate Kassa—one of the leading noblemen, and Major-General Merid Mengesha—Chief of Staff Armed Forces, Major-General Kebede Gebre—Chief of Staff Ground Forces—as well as the Chief of Staff in the Emperor's Private Cabinet, the Commander of the Territorial Army and the Air Force Commander.

Several of these congregated at the 1st Division headquarters and during the following twenty-four hours had more troops airlifted into the city and organized the advance of the tank squadron towards Addis Ababa. The Council of the Revolution spent this period arranging a temporary Government under the auspices of the Crown Prince with *Ras* Imru as Prime Minister and Mulugetta Buli as Chief of Staff. Mengistu involved himself, against the advice of Germame and other leaders, in trying to persuade Major-General Merid and the others with him at the 1st Division headquarters to join in the revolt.

It was not until Thursday the 15th that Mengistu finally agreed to move against Merid, and by that time it was too late. The Bodyguard's attack was defeated and in the face of air attacks and the

advance of the tanks, they were steadily driven back. A last stand
was made at the Paradise Palace, and before leaving it, Germame
and the others machine-gunned the hostages, killing fifteen of them.
The Emperor arrived back in Addis Ababa on the 17th to find the
loyalists in full control. A week later Germame committed suicide
when arrested but Mengistu survived and was publicly hanged after
a trial in March 1961.

This brief episode has been seen as the first attempt at a revolution
in Ethiopia, and as a major turning point in Ethiopian history.[6]
While this has considerable validity if for no other reason than the
extensive psychological effects and the production of an awareness
of the possibilities of change, it must not be over-emphasized.
The coup as it actually took place appears to fit more into the
tradition of attempts against the throne, although Germame certainly had more radical views. Equally it must be noted that the
coup as it happened was a hurried and rather *ad hoc* affair. Events
started to go wrong very early and most of the actions of Mengistu
and Germame were obviously consequent upon this.

Nevertheless the political manifestos and programme of the
Council of The Revolution do not come over as particularly radical,
even within the context of Ethiopia at that time. The original proclamation recorded by the Crown Prince was the most radical document.
It emphasized the lack of progress, the stagnation, the dissatisfaction
and the selfishness of a few people. There was no mention of the
Emperor and the proclamation made the Crown Prince say that
he had agreed to serve as a salaried official under the constitution.
The manifesto of the revolution was broadcast on 14 December:

The new government has the following aims:

1. It is clear that the fantastic progress achieved by the newly
independent African States has placed Ethiopia in an embarrassing
situation. The new government will have as its aim to restore
Ethiopia to its appropriate place in the world.

2. The new government will adhere to all its international
obligations, and will continue its existing relations with friendly
nations and will strive hard for world peace.

3. Capital investments made by foreigners in Ethiopia will
not be disturbed in any way, if such investments contribute to the
well-being and progress of Ethiopia and its people.

4. New factories and industries will be set up and put into
operation to help the people improve their standard of living.

The Moja Family of Shoa and connections

Dej. Germame = Wo. Walata-Giyorgis (Moja)

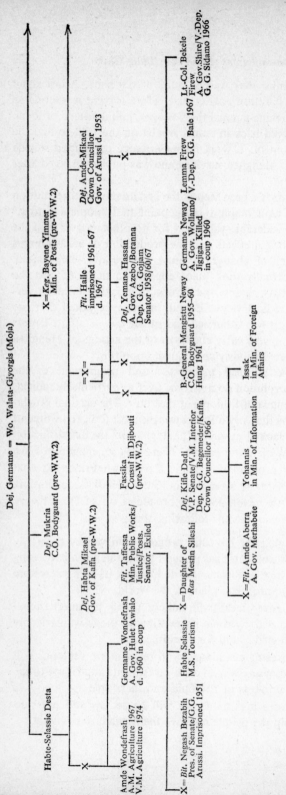

see next page

Abbreviations:
Bit.—Bitwoded
Dej.—Dejazmatch
Keg.—Kegnazmatch
G.G.—Governor-General
Dep. G.G.—Deputy Governor-General
Min.—Minister
M.S.—Minister of State
Di.—Director
D.G.—Director-General
C.O.—Commanding Officer
A.Gov.—Awraja Governor
A.M.—Assistant Minister
V.M.—Vice-Minister

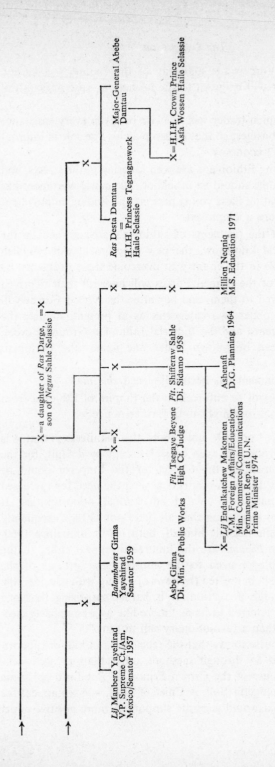

Moja family and connections.
This is a simplified genealogy,
and both personnel and positions
are incomplete.

Lij Manbere Yayehirad
V.P. Supreme Ct./Am.
Mexico)/Senator 1957

Balambaras Girma
Yayehirad
Senator 1959

Asbe Girma
Di. Min. of Public Works

X = a daughter of *Ras* Darge, = X
son of *Negus* Sahle Selassie

Fit. Tsegaye Beyene
High Ct. Judge

X = *Lij* Endalkatchew Makonnen
V.M. Foreign Affairs/Education
Min. Commerce/Communications
Permanent Rep. at U.N.
Prime Minister 1974

Fit. Shifferaw Sahle
Di. Sidamo 1958

Ashenafi
D.G. Planning 1964

Million Neqniq
M.S. Education 1971

Ras Desta Damtau
=
H.I.H. Princess Tegnagnework
Haile Selassie

Major-General Abebe
Damtau

X = H.I.H. Crown Prince
Asfa Wossen Haile Selassie

5. As agriculture is the mainstay of the country's economy, every assistance will be given to the farmers to raise agricultural production.

6. The Ethiopian trader will likewise be given every assistance to improve his business so that he can play his due role in improving the country's economy.

7. Many young Ethiopians are seen loitering in the streets, and these young people should be in school. The new government has the aim of educating these young persons and finding employment for those who are unemployed.

8. As one of the problems of Ethiopia's advancement is the lack of technical knowhow, the new government will establish technical schools in the country to overcome these problems.

9. Members of the Armed Forces will have all their deprived privileges restored to them, and hereafter the Armed Forces will not be known under two categories as at present, namely the Imperial Bodyguard and the Imperial Ethiopian Ground Forces. They will instead be known under one name—the Ethiopian Army.

10. The Parliament has been adjourned *sine die*.

11. A curfew will be enforced in the Empire of Ethiopia from 7 p.m. to 6 a.m. every night until further notice.[7]

The most obvious point to note about this manifesto is that it is not revolutionary nor is it even radical, except by default, for the failure to mention either the Church or the Emperor could be considered radical. Its main points deal with the need for increased economic development or related educational opportunities. It may be mentioned in passing that all these points have frequently been made by Haile Selassie himself, both before and since 1960. The most obvious *lacunae* are the failures to appeal either to the mass of the people or even to the non-Amhara sections of the Empire, some of whom greeted the news of a coup with considerable satisfaction, although no action. It is hardly surprising that one commentator has referred to its as "more like a Labour party election programme than a revolutionary call to arms".[8]

This is not of course to say that the rebels did not bid for support, but that they did so through methods other than revolutionary propaganda. The use of the Crown Prince, of *Ras* Imru as Prime Minister, and Mulugetta Buli as Chief of Staff, was an appeal for a broader base that would generate support. A more positive effort

was made on 15 December in another broadcast by the Crown
Prince which said that

> from this day onward every person will be given land according
> to his needs and will be able to live in peace. Moreover, those
> whose land has been taken away have, for a variety of reasons
> had but a little money cast in their direction. By returning this
> money they will from now on be entitled to take back their land.[9]

Increments were also offered to all Ethiopian soldiers; this offer
was immediately capped by a higher increase by Major-General
Merid on the Emperor's behalf. The proposal about land might
appear to be radical but in fact it was aimed primarily at people
in Addis Ababa and it did not go much further than the Emperor's
own statements that every Ethiopian should have his own land.

It is true that Mengistu in a speech to the students was much
more outspoken. He made references to land, privilege and the
failure of law. He said that he was prepared to destroy the hostages
and he felt, as he emphasized at his trial, that "Once we start the
fire, it will burn on by itself". Germame, his brother, went further.
His experiences as a Governor in the provinces in 1958 and 1959
underlined the attitudes he first acquired abroad. There is no reason
to doubt post-coup Government claims that he wanted to nationalize
all land including that of the Church; though the additional claim
that he had the intention of killing all Government officials, all the
aristocracy and all Army officers and soldiers over forty years old
is obviously nonsense.

Germame's more radical approach did not, however, surface in
the actual programmes put out during the coup and it is therefore
difficult to estimate how real it might have been in practice. There is
some evidence to suggest that he believed that once the coup had
started, there would be a very large swing of immediate support
from all the critics of the imperial regime as well as from the mass
of the people. Nevertheless Germame was a member of the Shoan
aristocracy, as were several other leaders. All were members of the
governing elite. Personal and family contacts obviously played a
large part in the recruitment. It is highly significant that when there
was discussion as to whether to arrest the Air Force Commander,
whose acquiescence was considered doubtful, one of the leaders
argued against it on the grounds that he was from the same part
of the country and there was no need for the man to be arrested.
It was certainly not a Moja family affair, but it did arise out of

contradictions within the ruling elite rather than out of any real revolutionary approach.[10]

In this sense the attempted coup of 1960 is closely related to other attempts upon the Emperor's position and life. Whether by design or necessity the leaders used the traditional elements of power to try and get support—the Crown Prince and certain members of the nobility. It was, as it happened, more of an attempt to overthrow Haile Selassie than an attempt to overthrow the imperial system. The parallel is with Tekle Walde Hawariot's efforts in 1942, with the Parliamentary plot and the conspiracy of *Bitwoded* Negash. What did add a new dimension was the unexpected violence of the finale and its near success; and for myth-making purposes they were reinforced by the suicides of Germame and another leader, Colonel Workneh, who made the comparison with the Emperor Tewodros' suicide, and the trial and death of Mengistu. Yet it is significant that there were no similar follow-ups. Rumours of new coup attempts abounded in the early sixties but nothing materialised, though the Army had to be placated several times with pay rises.

Considerable changes did, however, occur in the thinking of many, both inside and out of the Armed Forces. The amount of political awareness increased markedly and the attempt proved inspirational to many, especially to the students. The most obvious group that was affected were the armed forces themselves. Above all they were made fully conscious of the potentialities that their power gives them. Even so it was not until 1974 that they were prepared to move and then only against the Prime Minister and his clique, not openly against the Emperor. In the intervening period there was little indication of a general desire to get rid of the Emperor. Part of the reason for this was the deep divisions within the Armed Forces, especially in the officer corps. These are worth looking at in some detail because although the Armed Forces were relatively united in the February-March 1974 crisis, the divisions still remain.

The most generally applicable division among officers may loosely be called that between the traditional and the modern; and it correlates with age to a large degree. The traditional elements comprise most of the older and thus senior officers, many of whom fought in the patriot resistance or were in exile with the Emperor. As a rule they are substantial landowners partly through inheritance, partly through sizeable grants from the Emperor and the Government. They can be generally classified as loyal to the system, and to a lesser degree to the Emperor personally. They admit to the need for reforms but they qualify this by the desire for them to come through central Government and imperial auspices.

Most of the younger officers have come through the Harar Military Academy (founded in 1958) and staffed until recently by Indian Army officers. It acquired under them a not undeserved reputation for being more Sandhurst than Sandhurst itself. It is a very professional institution and has insisted on a high academic standard of entry and of education. For several years in the late fifties and early sixties the top percentage of secondary school graduates was conscripted directly into the Armed Forces for life and Harar acquired the majority of them. These men are now at the level of major and colonel—with some at brigadier-general after a number of promotions in 1973.

There is little sign of homogeneity among the younger officers as a whole, and several groups can be distinguished.[11] There is a considerable element who, while they may be critical of certain things, remain loyal to the Emperor in many respects. Most of them tend to come from the Holetta Academy which provides for short service commissions or for commissioning senior N.C.O.s as officers. Secondly there are a number of what might be called Nasserite officers in that they are strongly nationalistic though they have little loyalty to the imperial line *per se*. Indeed they tend to regard it as a brake upon progress and modernization, and are fully aware of the need for substantial social change. It was this group that gathered around Mulugetta Buli in the fifties, but they were not prepared to follow Mengistu in 1960, though it is possible that they had designs on taking the coup over had it been successful. A much larger group accepted many of these premises even while baulking at the removal of the unifying imperial factor. Until 1973 there is little doubt that they would have supported the claims of the Crown Prince; his succession was however thrown into doubt by his illness. Yet, while some of his supporters began to wonder if a monarchy was necessary, most held to the feeling that it did have value. There were also smaller groups who supported other candidates, for there were a plethora of these until the Emperor, in 1974, announced that the Crown Prince's son, Zara Yacob, was to succeed his father.

Care must be taken, however, not to exaggerate the cohesiveness of such groupings. The above picture implies that the whole officer corps is divided into well-organized and well-defined sections. This

is far from the truth. Cutting across all such attitudes are the series
of factors already familiar from the general political scene—family,
village, regional, national, educational, personal friendship and other
loyalties. All these provide networks of other linkages that can
dilute, as well as strengthen, attitudes. Given that the system has
revolved around the exploitation of such links it is not surprising
that the attribution of the concept of a "group" can be misleading.
The fact that the Government has also made it a practice to provide
land for the officer corps should again be emphasized here as it
militated against the more extreme anti-establishment attitudes.
Many of the senior officers come from the landowning class anyway;
those that do not have been deliberately incorporated as an act of policy.

This adds up to an officer corps that is faction-ridden and this
has been encouraged by the regime in the interests of security if not
of efficiency. The only large section of the Army that was homogeneous in the past was the Imperial Bodyguard before 1960, when
it was specifically seen as a special force, to the annoyance of the
Army as a whole. In the aftermath of the attempted coup it was
completely reorganized and its officers scattered, although a considerable portion of the guard in 1960 had been on service in the
Congo and were not involved. Since then there has been no such
equivalent although there are semi-elite groups—the tank battalion
and the airborne battalion—both of which tend to play a watching
role over other units. The airborne battalion is stationed near the
main airbase and while this may make military sense there is no
doubt that the Air Force believes that it is being watched. Feeling
between the two forces runs high and fights in the nearby town are
a common feature.

The most elitist unit today is the Air Force, and it is also the
most radical. It is not particularly large—2,250 to the Army's
40,940; and with thirty-seven combat aircraft in 1973.[12] The elitist
factor stems partly from its high standard of education and its long
involvement with foreign personnel—first Swedes and then the Americans. The students not only attend the flying school at Debra Zeit,
they also go through a series of more general courses some of which
are held at the university in Addis Ababa, providing a considerable
amount of contact with the students. The Force places a considerable
emphasis on civil action programmes, and the political consciousness
of the officers has perhaps been increased by the Air Force's part
in the putting down of the coup. If a similar situation were to occur
it is certain it would act differently. However, it should be noted

that the Air Force has played a vital part in the attempts to deal with the troubles in Eritrea, Bale and Gojjam, although its officers have been less enthusiastic than they might have been.

Besides the Army and the Air Force (the Navy is insignificant in strength) there are two other forces that should be mentioned—the Territorial Army and the Police. The Territorial Army is really a hangover from the pre-war period when Provincial Governors had their own armies. It is organized on a provincial basis though ultimately under the Ministry of the Interior, and with its higher officers appointed by the Emperor. In a given province the units are under the control of the Provincial Governor in most cases and it is used as an adjunct to the Police. Its active strength at any one time is around 10,000 and the highly unrealistic figure for full mobilization is 2 million: more accurate would be 50,000. The Territorials have not been used overmuch for they do little training and are not well armed; where they have been used as in Bale and Gojjam they have not been a great success. Their significance lies in their supposed loyalty to the Emperor personally though this has never been tested. It may be noted that there are training camps between fifty and 150 kilometres out of Addis Ababa on all the main roads. In certain situations it might therefore be an important force, though in 1960 its Commander, although he had the opportunity to do so, never got around too mobilizing them; nor did they play any part in 1974.

The Police are slightly different in that two elements are involved. There is the regular 30,000 strong force and the 7,000 strong Israeli trained Police commando—the Emergency Police. The latter which is very much the elite is a substantially armed unit with armoured cars. It was originally created for the Eritrean situation but has been used in Gojjam and elsewhere. It is essentially orientated towards counter-insurgency. Its creation has caused a certain amount of friction with the main Police Force which resents its privileged position, and feels that the Emergency Police are pampered. In general considerable efforts have been made in the last ten years to upgrade the Police Force, both by overseas training and through the Aba Dina Police College whose standards have been much improved. This has had the effect of increasing professionalism and also social awareness, especially among those who are stationed outside Addis Ababa where conditions are even worse.

Although both the Emperor and the Government of Aklilu

Habtewold encouraged these divisions, the potential political role that the Armed Forces could play became obvious to both ordinary soldiers and officers during the later 1960s. As it turned out it was the politicization of the former that finally brought trouble. In late 1973 and early 1974, as the rate of inflation really began to affect the soldiers, and the Government ignored warnings of possible trouble, the Army was prepared to act. A preliminary move was a mutiny at Neghelli in January 1974, by the soldiers and N.C.O.s over conditions; it was followed by complaints from the Air Force base at Debre Zeit in February. An attempt was made to defuse the situation in the Armed Forces by offering pay rises on the 24 February. But it was too little and too late.

On 25 February the 2nd Division in Asmara arrested many of its officers and took over the town. Shortly afterwards the 4th Division in Addis Ababa, the Air Force and the Navy also mutinied. While the impetus came from the deep dissatisfaction over pay and conditions—the original demands of the 2nd Division were almost entirely confined to this—the mutinies were rapidly orchestrated by junior and middle-ranking officers, though the soldiers remained a vital factor. Demands escalated to include more fundamental changes—free press, land reform, freedom for political prisoners, education for all children, improved labour legislation, political parties and the arrest and trial of corrupt Ministers.

In the first week of March, however, it became apparent that the second pay rise granted by the Emperor and the threat of total breakdown if demands went too far were causing second thoughts. Splits opened in the attitudes of the various units; the Air Force was prepared to push for the immediate removal of the Emperor and a military takeover. The other units were prepared to allow the new council of Ministers time to try and implement their promises of financial and social reform. In the last two weeks of March, Air Force co-operation was enforced by Paratroop occupation of the airbase; it was publicly maintained that this was actually a pre-emptive strike to prevent the Air Force attempting their own coup and precipitating civil war. Other officers were also arrested in some Army units.

This, however, did not presage unconditional support for the new Government. In mid-April, the 4th Division put the Prime Minister under notice that the arrest and trial of former Ministers was a necessity; and then acted themselves a week later. Significantly, a co-ordinating committee of the Armed Forces appeared publicly to explain this. The committee, which included representatives from all major units, in spite of some disagreements, was the controlling force behind the new Government. A communique issued by the military stated that the arrests "had been a necessary step to secure the peace and security needed to enable the new Government to carry out its programme of reforms. The Army and the Police had, with the will of the people, brought about changes in Ethiopia in February without bloodshed, but it had now become necessary to take steps to allow these changes to produce true social and economic change in the country".[13]

This made it clear to both the Emperor and to *Lij* Endalketchew Makonnen that there would have to be real reform and no more palliatives. The Armed Forces went back behind the scenes but after that they played a more positive role in policy formulation and in pressuring the Government into speeding up and implementing reforms. Two factors stopped a complete military takeover at this point: firstly the real threat of civil war. The Emperor made it clear that he would fight if pushed too far and intimated he could count on considerable support from the countryside and the landowning aristocracy. The second was the danger of the incipient divisions within the Armed Forces being too easily exploited especially by such a consummate politician as the Emperor.

These divisions, outlined above, still obtain within the Armed Forces. Their apparent unanimity by mid-1974 conceals them, but they have not disappeared. In certain situations they could easily resurface. Another potential danger is that the Forces could split along ethnic lines if the central Government collapsed. It has always been officially maintained that recruitment of both officers and men is without consideration of nationality or tribe. However, as seen in Chapter 3, the percentage of recruits to the Harar Military Academy from the northern provinces of Tigre and Eritrea has gone down substantially during the sixties. Certainly among the officer corps Amharas are preponderent. An analysis of appointments at the level of Divisional Chief of Staff and above between 1941 and 1966 produced the figures—62 per cent Amhara, 15 per cent Oromo; 9 per cent Eritrean; 5 per cent Tigre; 9 per cent others.[14] Two other estimates for the officer corps as a whole are given on p. 248.

As may be seen they do not entirely agree in detail, though both emphasize the predominance of Amhara. From other factors, it would seem that the 1972 figures are likely to be the more accurate. The main elements among the ordinary soldiers are Oromo and

TABLE 34.

Army Officers—Origins

Rank	Origin	1970	1972
Lt.-Colonel and above	Amhara	75	65
	Tigre/Eritrea	10	8
	Oromo	12	21
	Others	3	6
Below Lt.-Colonel	Amhara	65	60
	Tigre/Eritrea	10	—
	Oromo	25	30
	Others (includes Tigre/Eritrea)	—	10

Source: Personal information.[15]

Amhara, approximately 40 per cent each.[16] In the future this may well pose a serious problem for whatever Government is in power, as well as limit the Armed Forces' capacity for united action.

The least important section of opposition to the Government in terms of political power has been the student protest movement. However the education system took on a momentum of its own to expand further than originally anticipated, providing a dimension of protest that was not foreseen, and the most vocal opposition to the Government and the regime in the late 1960s and early 1970s came from the student body, both at the university and the high school level, and abroad as well as at home. The growth of this has been striking both externally and internally and student demands have escalated from very minor internal complaints to well-founded attacks on the whole structure of the Government and the society,

To a degree there has been an element of make-believe in the Government-student confrontations, in that the students know that the Government is their only potential employer; the Government is equally aware that the students provide the necessary manpower resources. Inevitably the vast majority of the student radicals have ended up in the Government as part of the bureaucratic machine, leading to accusations of opportunism from the next generation of radicals. The protests thus have an air of fantasy about them—not helped by the generalization of attacks, failures of both tactics and strategy, and deep division within the students.

Splits have pervaded the student organizations from the beginning; both in the overseas sections as well as in the Haile Selassie 1st

University.[17] Although the students are relatively well-organized abroad, with a World Wide Union with three continental branches (the North American, the European and the National Union in Ethiopia) this gives a false impression of solidarity. The North American Union split badly in the late 1960s over the Eritrean problem, over the right to autonomy by the nationalities, and the need for an effective world-wide organization, and these problems have continued. These splits which are based to a considerable degree on personality factors do also reflect strong ideological undercurrents. By the late 1960s, however, there was a general agreement that the whole movement supported revolutionary socialist theories—though there is considerable disagreement over which line actually to follow. Inevitably, the overseas students are more concerned with theory than with action, in comparison with the students within Ethiopia.

The latter have suffered from vigorous Government pressures including substantial force, a lack of materials for ideological study and divisions on personal and ideological grounds. These problems plus the continual turnover in leadership have produced only a small, really radical minority. This minority has been able to capitalize on deep-rooted discontents but only for brief periods. Nevertheless, the students have played a considerable part in demonstrating and underlining the division within the Ethiopian society and in politicizing the people to some degree.

Although students had demonstrated in favour of the attempted coup and agitated on internal university matters, a significant degree of protest emerged only early in 1965, after the University Students Union of Addis Ababa was set up. In that year they took to the street on the basis of their "Land to the Tiller" slogan. This was followed by annual demonstrations attacking the situation of the beggars in Addis Ababa ("Is Poverty a Crime?"), raising the question of the right to peaceful assembly and the Agricultural Income Tax Law. In March 1969, a comprehensive list of demands was produced including attacks on the taxation system, the cost and type of education, the need for more schools, the treatment of employees and on the Peace Corps teachers. Among the rash of pamphlets produced at this time was one that was addressed to various groups of the population and made an effort to identify the specific grievances that the soldiers, the workers, priests, farmers, clergy, and prostitutes might have.

Later in 1969, the student paper "Struggle" came out with an article by Waliligne Makonnen, "On the Question of Nationalities in Ethiopia". This has been one of the most significant student productions for it called for the various peoples of the empire to be allowed the right of self-determination. Shortly afterwards the president of the Student Union, Tilahun Gizaw, was assassinated, and on 29 December the Government, in an attempt to prevent the students holding a memorial march with the body, allowed the Imperial Bodyguard to storm the university campus. The resulting casualties were officially declared to have been three dead and ten wounded. More accurate unofficial figures were ten killed and at least one hundred wounded.[18] Major student demonstrations were not resumed until 1971 and then by the high school students in an attack on higher bus fares and prices generally, and had considerable effect in getting price controls in Addis Ababa. The following year in an attempt to pre-empt the troubles the Government hit first and arrested numbers of student leaders under Ethiopia's ninety-day detention order. Altogether about 1,000 were sent to various labour camps for three-month periods.

By 1973, the protests of students had finally begun to affect some of the teachers in schools and the University. All were involved in publicizing the cause of the famine-struck areas, and in organizing some relief; equally both were prominent in the crisis of February-March 1974. Students played some part in helping with labour demonstrations and strikes and held their own demonstrations attacking various aspects of government policy. Not surprisingly they also protested against certain members of the new Government and showed that they were far from satisfied with its make-up and with the pace of reforms in 1974.

Over the years since 1965, the students in Ethiopia as well as those outside have become progressively radicalized and have shown growing political maturity. This has been most observable in the change from the use of slogans relatively meaningless to the people of Addis Ababa to attacks on higher prices, famine and food shortages that are more immediately relevant. Contacts with the workers and labour unions have increased; and through the Ethiopian University Service (one year's practical work in the provinces as a part of the degree programme) they have also influenced individuals and other students in the provinces.

The most significant stand that they have taken both in and out of Ethiopia has been the support for each nationality in Ethiopia to have the right of self-determination. This is highly important, not just ideologically, but from the practical point of view. It has brought the students into supporting the position of the Eritrean Liberation Front and other guerilla groups. An apt if tragic illustration of this alliance was the attempted highjacking of an Ethiopian Airlines plane in December 1972, in which three of the seven persons involved (six were killed) were Eritreans. It has also brought reaction in areas hitherto untouched by such ideas. In March 1974, a movement appeared in the Wollamo *awraja* demanding the dismissal of Shoan Amhara officials and their replacement by local people; this has been paralleled in other areas.

Student influence is usually discounted as a political factor but in a society where unfavourable comment of any kind had been virtually impossible until March 1974, students have played a vitally important role. They have provided alternative ideas in a relatively public way and have focussed attention on some of the more glaring contradictions in the society and in the regime. Their tactics and strategy have not been above criticism, but the value of student protest has been unquestionable.

PART FOUR: CONCLUSION

CHAPTER IX

The Realities of Change

The Ethiopian empire in 1974 contains a heterogeneous mixture of peoples, some of whom have, or are acquiring, national ambitions of their own. It is ruled according to a structure of Government that is essentially feudal and shows some signs of remaining so. Nearly all of the specifics of a feudal society can be found, though with certain modifications[1]: the overlordship by a class of military figures who controlled a subject peasantry and evolved into a class of landed gentry; ties of loyalty and personal links of dependence and obedience; the fragmentation of power operating through the use of the service tenement or the fief in place of payment, though under the ultimate, if theoretical, power of a sovereign ruler; a mode of production in which serfdom imposed by either military force, custom or by law, was dominant.

This applied almost in its entirety to the Ethiopian state though the ties of loyalty were never enforced through the formal oaths of European feudalism. Serfdom also was never so classified as in Europe and the peasants were never bound to the land in the same legalistic way. Custom, force and economic circumstance, however, limited the opportunities for movement to near zero. Another limitation that operated was the resurrection of imperial power, as at the end of the nineteenth century, in the 1930s, and again in the period 1941–74. On the first occasion, during Menilek's reign, a typical attempt to centralize was enforced on the feudal nobility through a variety of methods—one of the most significant was through enforced residence in Addis Ababa which had the merits of cutting off the provincial lords from their power bases and of pressuring them economically.[2]

Since 1941 the position of course has changed in that the direct military arm of the nobility has been removed and both the army and the economic structure largely centralized. The nobility have, however, been used as governors in provinces they formerly had total power over, their fiefs have remained (until 1966 in law)—as have their private estates—and they have been able in a number of cases to enlarge them since the war, and the power of the lower levels of the feudal hierarchy have remained largely unaltered. The personal nature of the Government still continues the former ties of personalized dependency; and the subject peasantry still provide the basis of production. This remains production for use rather than for sale and is essentially a use of traditional methods and low output. There is a small and narrow market structure with underdeveloped trade. The peasantry's situation may still be categorized as serfdom enforced by military force, as in the crushing of numerous attacks on landlords; and by custom, sanctified by one of the largest landowners, the Church.

Equally, the feudal nobility have been used to staff most of the modernization of the Empire thus ensuring that the feudal and personal links remain the major binding force in Government and administration. The existence of an aristocracy of birth, divided though it may be into several degrees, makes certain that the power of position is limited. To maintain that *gult* lands and titles have been non-inheritable misses the point. In practice inherited status and with it *rist* land form the base of the position of the great aristocratic Amhara and Tigre families. It may in any case be noted that until 1941 titles and positions were given by any great lord to his sons and relatives. While it is true that governorships and *gult* lands were not theoretically inherited, in practice it is clear that they normally were. A powerful Emperor might insist on a show of deference first, or hold the process up for a time, but since the nobles did have alternative power sources and legitimacy of their own, the expected positions and inheritance would usually materialize.

Not only was this pattern all-pervasive at the local Government level but it permeated central Government. It has been further positively encouraged through the imperial and central policies of land grants. Given the government's attitude towards nomadic and all non-settled lands, there is an enormous reservoir from which grants can still be made. To make certain that the newer members of the elite—brought in to cope with bureaucratic norms—were tied into the pattern, all received grants. Not perhaps large ones, but the higher the position the larger the grant. Titles would go with the grants, as would tenants, if anybody happened to be farming the land already. Both Government administration and the army were tied in this way, through *maderia* grants, and further, through the extension of the right to transfer *maderia* to *gebbar*, private tenure.

The emphasis laid by the Government on the cancellation of the extra-Governmental rights that were incorporated in *siso*, *gult* and *rist-gult* holdings would be valid if there were signs that the situation had in fact changed. The evidence suggests, however, that the effects have been minimal. This differential between theory and practice is hardly surprising as the local judiciary and Government organization are staffed by the very men such measures would dispossess. The example set by the imperial family of ignoring the legal situation, appears to have been widely followed.

Some of the contradictions that arise under this system have been developed in the preceding chapters. Significantly they have not been confined to any one area of the Empire; and their dual aspect must be emphasized—on the one hand internecine conflict between members of the landowning classes, and on the other peasant discontent and rebellion. In recent years a national dimension has been added to some of these conflicts but the immediate element for most of them has remained agrarian disputes.

Part of the trouble in Bale was over land seizures; and there is a long record of action against dissident peasantry on a small scale, as well as in more sizeable operations. Peasant unrest in Wollo led to "the eradication of a chain of villages" in 1958;[3] Illubabor in the mid-1960s, Wollega in 1968, Wollo in 1970 were all the scene of repression of over-taxed peasants as had been Begemeder in 1944 and Arussi on several occasions in the 1940s and 1950s. In Sidamo, and Bale provinces in the 1960s it has been reported that there were many people killed objecting to land seizures; similarly evictions have led to several actions in the Sheshamane area, and in Wollega in the last three years. Examples of further incidents could be provided in all provinces.

In passing it might be noted that there is a tendency in many areas of Ethiopia, especially the southern provinces, to accept that the only way to get a necessary change is to break into an outright revolt. If this becomes serious enough to attract the attention of the central Government then palliatives may be offered—as in Bale in 1970–71, Gojjam in 1968–69. In this sense it can be argued that revolt has been accepted into the fabric of the present state as a method of opposition. The necessity for this is conditioned by the fact that there is no other method of drawing attention to a problem. Much has been made of the point that the Chamber of Deputies represents the provinces in the central Government. Within limits this is true, but this function, largely because of the electoral support they have received from the "big men" of the district, is to push for the provision of roads and bridges, not to draw attention to the situation of an overtaxed peasantry. In any case the Deputies, by and large, belong to the landowning class.

Linked to this has been the non-assimilative nature of the imperial state. The evidence is incomplete, but the history of the royal house of Wollo certainly suggests a failure even at the highest levels. Incorporation is frequently mistaken for assimilation; and feudal marriage alliances should not be mistaken for it either. National feelings have been a central feature of the Eritrean revolution and have appeared among the Oromo; it is also clear that complaints against Shoan Amhara rule, which are widespread elsewhere, imply a stirring of national feelings in Bale and the south. Even the land-owning classes for all their manifold connections have made this clear in a number of revolts. To a certain degree the imperial Government has recognized this and even tried to use it as a Govern-mental technique—significantly however such attempts are con-fined to Tigre and to a lesser degree, Wollo. In the southern areas where Amhara control has been the result of conquest, participation by the local aristocracies has been correspondingly less.

This assimilatory failure can be most clearly seen in the ethnic distinctions that are still alive in Ethiopia. They go back a long time and operate in the highlands, witness the continued isolation of the Falashas in Begemeder, as well as elsewhere. Theoretically, since any child of an Amhara parent can be considered as Amhara, it might be expected that inter-marriage in conquered areas would provide for considerable assimilation within a few generations. In practice certain other factors operate and there is in the peasant communities a strong preference for marrying within their own area and their own group. This is especially the case in *rist*-owning areas, for the marriage provides a whole new series of *rist* claims. Equally many of the inter-marriages came in the southern conquest provinces and the potential assimilation that might have arisen was negated by the distinction between conqueror and conquered. Even today the towns in the south are essentially Amhara towns, and the other peoples have alternative settlements. Furthermore the *rist* claims that might come out of such marriages operated in the central and northern highlands and were virtually unobtainable, and the lands that were in the south were, at the time of the conquest and until after the war, held largely on *maderia* tenancy which could not be inherited. So inter-marriage at the peasant level did not provide a way up the social ladder.

Assimilation was thus essentially an individual factor. It was never institutionalized as a policy except through inter-marriage at the highest social levels and this was not particularly successful. The growing numbers of revolts that have had specifically anti-Amhara elements in them must be seen as a rejection of the post-war efforts to provide Amhara acculturation. The distinction should be made between Amhara and Ethiopia for the two are not synonymous. However as the administration is largely Amhara, especially in the south, the two have frequently been identified. As there have been many valid complaints against the quality of the administration, there have been few reasons to identify with it. As noted earlier the Church hardly impinged in the conquered areas and there was no attempt until the late 1950s to provide education. Obviously people learnt some Amharic, but it is wishful thinking to believe that this provides evidence of more than necessity.

Equally, within the Amhara areas themselves, while there is commitment perhaps to the Empire of Ethiopia, there is little love for the Shoan Amhara Empire. Gojjam has shown itself fiercely resentful of Shoan governors and has demonstrated very strong regional emphasis even as recently as 1968. The concept of the Empire of Ethiopia as a reality has operated much more internationally than internally—for the average peasant it is still "my village, my district, my province, region or people", and only as a fourth best "my country".

The failure of assimilation is also clear in its most seriously attempted form—education. Pressure from Eritrean students has enforced an acceptance by the University that they should be granted exemptions in Amharic entrance qualifications. The growth of interest in Oromo writings among the student body also exemplifies this. Student feelings in this direction have begun to polarize. Ten years ago, especially to a foreign enquiry, "I am an Ethiopian" was the response. Today it is more likely to be "I am an Eritrean" or, "I am an Oromo". This response is limited to politically-orientated students, and should not be overstated. It is, however, a significant trend in intellectual thinking. The most radical students have come to accept the postulate that there are a number of different nationalities in Ethiopia and to accept that these have the rights of self-determination. How far this acceptance goes even among the most radical is another matter. To an extent it is a necessity to help unite the fragmented opposition to the regime. As yet no test of it has come, and it is likely that many will reject it ultimately, if it means the dismemberment of the country. There is a feeling—not necessarily valid—that these potential nationalities will obviously opt for remaining within the Ethiopian state. If this hope was exploded the nationalities problem could rear its head in a much more violent form than we have seen so far. This is especially likely given the somewhat optimistic hope that a socialist Ethiopian state can hold the minorities freely. The gap between theory and practice may prove wide.

Sophisticated theory of this kind has perhaps had little effect on the people of Ethiopia as a whole, even in the areas where revolutionary movements have actually operated—Eritrea and Bale. In general the life of the tenant and peasant farmer has remained geared to his own concerns of extracting enough to eat—not always successfully. A peasant, tenant, small landowner is circumscribed by the conditions under which he holds his land, the amount that he has to pay in tax and his relationship *vis-à-vis* the great landowners—those that he is dependent upon—and officials of his neighbourhood. For most peasants the only change of the last thirty years that has impinged on his daily life is the steadily growing use of money, and even that is related essentially to the market and the taxation system, and hardly operates for most peasants.

For the individual tenant farmer or peasant the effects of modernization have been negligible. In this sense the material benefits are less important than the possible structural and social changes that could have occurred. This is true in whatever part of Ethiopia is taken as an example—with the minor exceptions of small areas where traditional land tenancy arrangements have been swept away to make room for commercial agriculture. But even here the traditional feature of dependency has remained largely unaltered. This is not surprising for dependency still remains the major necessity for the peasant farmer or indeed any individual. Whether in the city or in the province a person finds another to attach himself to. Such a factor is an integral part of a feudal society and is reinforced throughout the system—in literature, customs, upbringing and education.

The system of dependency and the counterpart of domination extends vertically throughout the whole of Ethiopia. Society relies on an individual relationship "between superior and subordinate, with the subordinate existing essentially as an extension of the ego of the superior".[4] The most obvious example of this has been the imperial method of Government; but it operates in every situation. It is significant that it operates fully even within the supposed modernizing sector. This is perhaps an adaptation in that it is a more free-flowing relationship than can possibly be allowed within the enclosed provincial land circle. It is not, however, different in kind, especially since both the patrons and clients in the modernizing sector usually come from the landowning class.

As an adjunct to a system of vertical domination and dependency there is a lack of cohesiveness on the horizontal class level. Mutual aid groups and associations are relatively few; and where they exist they have been subject to strict Government control. Obviously in a society based on domination by a feudal class one of the most serious threats would come from village or district cohesiveness at the peasant level. The energies of the society are thus directed against any such groups, and towards the encouragement of the individual.

The actual nature of the peasant in Ethiopia as described by a number of observers is of course related to this. Dr. Levine in *Wax and Gold* isolates two particular qualities he ascribed to the Amhara peasant—oral ambivalence and physical aggressiveness. The former is manifested in "wax and gold", the use of phrases that allow thoughts to be put into words that conceal the real feelings; to insult without specifically giving insult. Also it appears in the continual and continued ambiguity that allows for no direct answer, no direct commitment; it puts things off from day to day or gives the answer that is required by the questioner.

The lack of preciseness, or the refusal to answer direct questions with direct answers is carried a long way. An investigator who enquires about the number of children a peasant has is unlikely to receive a specific answer or even an answer at all. This is not entirely due to the very natural desire to annoy inquisitive and rude foreigners; it applies to Ethiopian enquirers as well. It is based on the attitudes of the peasant to the Church and the state. He is not prepared to specify what God has given to him nor does he see why the Government should know. Information tends to bring some sort of Government reaction. Tell a Government official how much corn was grown and he will tax one more heavily. The correct number of children, cattle, goods, whatever, may have the same effect. Unless the answers are ambiguous, or inaccurate, the giver of the information will suffer.

A number of reasons have been put forward to explain this attitude ranging from the suggestion that it provides an outlet in a society where public opinion is non-existent to seeing it as an outgrowth from a situation where the emphasis is on a transient life in the religious sense and therefore nothing is totally absorbing.[5] Another answer emphasizes the total insecurity of the peasant: "centuries of isolation, centuries of grinding poverty, centuries of insecure tenancy of land have left their mark on the Abyssinian peasant and, willy-nilly, all Ethiopians are peasants".[6] This explanation has the merit of providing parallels with other peasant societies, There is little doubt that duplicity is a necessity for life wherever there is a peasant society that is in a similar situation. Trickiness is the standard most admired. The exemplar is the person who can go furthest in fooling the pompous official, the landlord, the priest, etc. Any number of studies on the landlord/tenant situation in the Middle East, Central and South America and Europe supply examples.

It is a very individual approach partly because of the need to preserve the individual's own position and place. The insecurity is such that only a threat to matters of prime importance will provide a *raison d'être* for common action. It is not surprising to find that a major interest of the small landowner within the *rist* system of Gojjam, Begemeder, Tigre, Shoa and Wollo is in legal cases over land. There is a continual need to hold on to, or to try and acquire more land. Individual aggressiveness comes out most clearly in this. Indeed individuality can only be provided for in this way in so highly stratified a society.

It may be objected that Ethiopian society is not as rigid as this implies. There are possibilities for low status individuals to rise to important positions, especially in military terms. Obviously there is a certain amount of social mobility, though within Ethiopia it tends to be ethnically based, that is, it is easier for an Amhara. Indeed no society is ever totally enclosed, and exceptions can of course be found. Military excellence is almost always a method of upward mobility in a society dedicated to martial categorization. A number of examples may be adduced but they are uncommon enough to be remarkable. Many cases, for instance, that of the Emperor Tewodros, turn out to be a change in political fortune of a member of the nobility which is hardly the same thing.

While the system induces insecurity, and underlines the need for individual efforts, it also provided a possible parameter for unified action when a direct threat was posed to the family livelihood as a whole. Such threats, or other threats to the land of a peasant do give rise to community action. Circumstances can enforce a situation where revolt is seen as the only alternative. In normal times the threat to the *rist* lands of a peasant family in Tigre, Begemeder, Gojjam, Wollo and Shoa will therefore produce a horizontally interactive group in response to an outside threat. In times of acutely bad Government, or a threat to an area, the interaction will spread much further as in Gojjam 1967–68, Tigre 1943–44 and so on. In southern areas it may, however, be noted that community action has survived to a greater extent—as an imperative in the face of the threat posed by Amhara officialdom.

Nevertheless, it is worth noticing that in terms of associations, the various community groups that do exist in Ethiopia exist largely outside the peasant milieu and are to be seen as essentially of post-war or war-time origin and as city-based. The earliest of these associations appears to be the *eder*, which operates as a welfare institution, largely to assist with the cost of burial and to help at times of death. As far as can be established the *eder* first appeared in Addis Ababa in the early part of the century, but became significant only during the Second World War. It may be assumed that they were a substitution in the town for the mutual aid operations that any village in the countryside would provide through the family. The enlargement of the urban population with the first industrial establishments, plus the lack of links or kin that an individual might have, provided the impetus.

A similar type of organization though much larger in size and scope, is the regional or ethnic association—*mehaber*. The first of these to be set up was the Gurage association which has been devoted to the collection of money for self-help projects in the Gurage area. In particular the construction of roads and schools has been financed, sometimes in conjunction with other *mehabers*. The Gurage association has remained completely concerned with development projects and totally eschewed politics. One association, the Mecha Oromo, that flourished briefly in the mid-1960s, did show signs of being political—General Taddesse Biru was deeply involved in it. After his arrest the association was immediately disbanded by the Government, and other *mehabers*, though not broken up, were regarded with considerable disfavour. In fact there are now a considerable number of these representing areas from all over the Empire. They have taken care to steer clear of politics but the possibilities are there as the Mecha Oromo *mehaber* showed. It will be surprising if they are not used more openly for politicizing—they already involve some significant figures from the given region who

264   *The Dying Lion*

can bring the *mehaber's* views to the people who matter or to
Deputies in Parliament.

These types of organizations are essentially city-based even if they
do have regional connections. Other organizations such as professional associations and the labour unions are also urban-based.
They have had little effect on the formation of significant potential
pressure groups outside the cities. In general they have fitted into
the common social pattern, and the accepted norms of deference
and obedience operated within them at least until 1974. The crisis
of February and March, however, did bring certain organizations,
especially the teachers and the Confederation of E.L.U., on to the
political scene. It may be assumed that the *eder*, and the professional
organizations will be prepared in future to operate more freely and
no longer stay within the limits carefully laid down by the Government, and interpreted by the presidents and committees of the
associations.

One other type of association that has been growing in recent years
in the provinces—though not in the Amhara areas—is the co-
operative society. These are organized by the Co-operative Societies
Proclamation of 1966 and have a Department of the Ministry of
National Community Development to look after them. The growth
in the number of these societies has been very marked since the
proclamation when there were less than twenty. As of 1970 there
were 101 though only 34 were registered; registration gives the
societies the right to own property, be sued, and have full legal
recognition. However the numbers involved are not very large, on
average 145 per society—though the registered societies with better
facilities for credit averaged 276 members. There was a total membership of only 14,697 people in 1970 but it was relatively widespread,
eight provinces having eight or more societies.[7] It would seem that
the spread of such societies, and of other associations, suggests there
is a need for them even without any political attachments. Indeed
they fill a gap where there are no social services, and where the
Government does not release funds for development. Organizing
mehabers is an invaluable way of helping self-help groups, especially
in rural areas. These are now much used by the Government though
judging by the amount of quiet complaint the original voluntary
element has tended to get lost.

The modern history of Ethiopia has usually been seen as almost exclusively centred around the personality, character and power of one man—Haile Selassie I. Since 1916 he has been at the centre of the political scene; and throughout this period he seldom allowed his grip to slacken, except for the brief Italian interlude, until recently. By any standards he has been a superlative politician and proved his mastery of both international and domestic politics. Inevitably the total control lessened in the 1960s and 1970s as the Emperor aged. No longer were all appointments made personally; no longer did he visit all schools, discuss all activities. Complexity and no doubt his age lessened the immediate day to day impact. Nevertheless, the ultimate control lay where it had lain for forty-four years, in the hands of the Emperor whose position at the top of a hierarchical pyramid was unchallenged until the events of early 1974.

Haile Selassie's main achievement was to build up the position of the Emperor—that is, his own power. While he never tried to break the power of the feudal aristocracy, he suborned it to his own controls and removed some of their functions. In return he had to allow them to take critically important posts in the Government and bureaucracy; and he also had to accept, and indeed encouraged, the development of a certain number of capital ventures in which both he and they took and held primary shares.

At the local level he allowed the traditional forces to survive unchecked, much to the frustration of Ministries who wanted greater efficiency. The contradictions between the growing needs of finance for the central Government and the traditional landowning control of local taxation were left more or less untouched. Haile Selassie made no effort to enforce collection from those who could pay and continued to accept the basic inequality of the tax burdens; the ever-increasing nature of these burdens inevitably led to greater peasant discontent.

It is often argued that the Emperor has modernized at the best speed to avoid trouble. Leaving aside the whole question of modernization itself, a judgment on the time taken can be given by comparing his own actions before and after the war. The pace was far faster from 1930 to 1935 than at any other time. Certainly, the speed of modernization has not avoided trouble—one twelve-year revolt still going on, another seven-year struggle and multifarious outbreaks of violence. The most obvious example has been in February 1974, when the crisis came out of a dissatisfaction with corrupt and inefficient Government, over-taxation, starvation, famine and land seizures.

Given his high degree of personal control and interest over all matters of detail, it is arguable that all significant developments that have taken place in Ethiopia between 1941 and 1974 have been essentially at the Emperor's desire. In this sense a judgment of him depends on how one sees his achievements. Here lies a paradox. His reputation is enormous, his admirers are world-wide. He is seen as a great modernizer, as an international statesman, as a foresighted monarch. Yet Ethiopia remains one of the least developed countries in the world, operating under a feudal system that still permeates both Amhara and non-Amhara parts of the country, with a more or less continuous series of internal troubles over the last thirty years. His powerful personality explains it in part—he is an immensely dignified person with great presence. In addition he symbolized, in 1936, with his great speech to the League of Nations, opposition to Fascist dictatorships, which appealed especially to the United Kingdom and the United States. And he has seemed almost indestructible. Finally it must be acknowledged that his public relations are first class; the details of the internal control operated within Ethiopia have been well concealed.

His achievements can however be looked at in two ways. On the one hand can be listed the numbers of schools, factories, hospitals, roads, the ministerial system, a centralized bureaucracy, a Parliament, and a modern army and tax structure. By comparison with what there was when Haile Selassie became Crown Prince the contrast is great. Another way of looking at it is to say that only 8 per cent of the school-age children were in school in 1970, there is only one hospital per 300,000 people (and most of these are in the cities of Addis Ababa and Asmara), most of the country is still without roads, the Parliament is a rubber stamp, the Army largely involved in putting down revolts caused by bad Government, taxation hardly touches the wealthy and famine in 1973 killed 100,000 people. This has taken fifty-eight years to achieve. Both ways of summing up the achievements of Haile Selassie's rule are valid—one's choice depends upon one's own prejudices and priorities.

Within the traditional Ethiopian milieu Haile Selassie has been undoubtedly a great ruler, even though he failed in war. Historically, innovation came from the Emperor—this he has provided; but only up to a point. The obvious comparison is with the benevolent despots of eighteenth century Europe; specifically perhaps with Joseph II of Austria, who was a man of immense industry and energy yet who never realized that the major weakness of his Empire lay in his method of governing it. There is every reason to believe that for Haile Selassie the imperial position is equated with the good of the Empire and its peoples.

While this, in theory, might suggest a commitment to a perpetuation of the imperial system, Haile Selassie has in fact weakened this possibility very seriously by his failure to associate the Crown Prince or any other alternative with himself until he made the line of succession clear in 1974. This inevitably leads to the conclusion that he had given relatively little thought for the future of Ethiopia after his demise. It is also implicit in the argument that his main preoccupation has been his own survival as Emperor. It is true that his own authority as Emperor at the head of a system that has been generally accepted for whatever reasons as legitimate by the majority of the people, provides in itself an available theory of continuity. This continuity is also provided for in the constitutional requirements for succession. It presupposes, however, that Government policies and attitudes of the last twenty years have successfully solved the problems that have grown out of attempts to provide a modern façade to a feudal landowning state.

In 1973–74 the total failure of this whole approach to Government and administration was shown firstly by the lack of response to the famine and then by the upsurge of discontent that swept away his Prime Minister and Ministers. By definition the accusations of corruption and inefficiency levelled at them were also aimed at the Emperor. Allegations have not been confined to Ministers but have involved numbers of civil servants and lower officials. These attacks highlight the magnitude of the problem which has been compounded by thirty years of neglect. Unless the facts of the basic contradictions within Ethiopia are accepted and the dangers realized, the future will be increasingly difficult. The new Government, and its successors, whether military or civilian, face the necessity of large-scale and fundamental economic, social and political change.

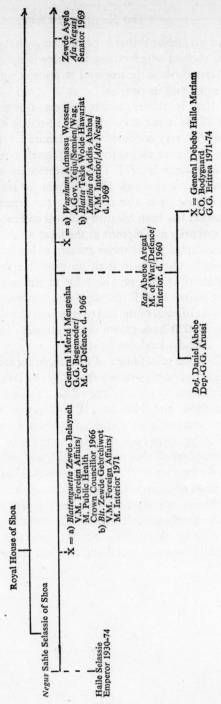

Addisge Family and Connections

This is a simplified genealogy and both personnel and positions are incomplete

Royal House of Shoa

Negus Sahle Selassie of Shoa

Haile Selassie
Emperor 1930–74

X = a) *Blattenguetta Zewde Belayneh*
V.M. Foreign Affairs/
M. Public Health
Crown Councillor 1966
b) *Bit.* Zewde Gebrehiwot
V.M. Foreign Affairs/
M. Interior 1971

General Merid Mengesha
G.G. Begemeder/
M. of Defence. d. 1966

Def. Daniel Abebe
Dep.-G.G. Arussi

Ras Abebe Aregai
M. of War/Defence/
Interior. d. 1960

X = a) *Waqshum* Admassu Wossen
A. Gov. Yejju/Semien/Wag.
b) *Blatta* Tekle Wolde Hawariat
Kantiba of Addis Ababa/
V.M. Interior/*Afa Negus*
d. 1969

X = **General Debebe Haile Mariam**
C.O. Bodyguard
G.G. Eritrea 1971–74

Zewde Ayele
Afa Negus/
Senator 1969

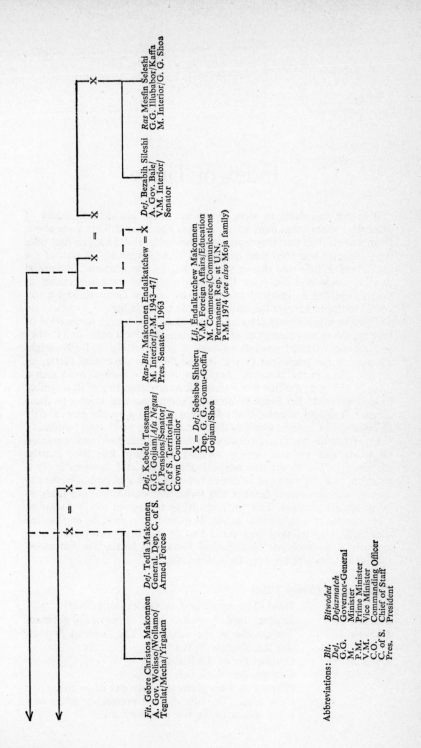

Flt. Gebre Christos Makonnen
A. Gov. Wollso/Wollamo/
Tegulat/Mecha/Yirgalem

Def. Tedla Makonnen
General. Dep. C. of S.
Armed Forces

Def. Kebede Tessema
G.G. Gojiam/*Afa Negus*/
M. Pensions/Senator/
C. of S. Territorials/
Crown Councillor

Ras-Bit. Makonnen Endalkatchew
M. Interior/P.M. 1943–47/
Pres. Senate. d. 1963

X = *Def.* Sebsibe Shiberu
Dep. G. G. Gomu-Goffa/
Gojiam/shoa

Lij. Endalkatchew Makonnen
V.M. Foreign Affairs/Education
M. Commerce/Communications
Permanent Rep. at U.N.
P.M. 1974 (*see also* Moja family)

Def. Bezabih Sileshi
A. Gov. Bale/
V.M. Interior/
Senator

Ras Mesfin Seleshi
G.G. Illubabor/Kaffa
M. Interior/G. G. Shoa

Abbreviations: *Bit.*   *Bitwoded*
            Def.   *Dejazmatch*
            G.G.   Governor-General
            M.   Minister
            P.M.   Prime Minister
            V.M.   Vice Minister
            C.O.   Commanding Officer
            C. of S.   Chief of Staff
            Pres.   President

Index of Titles

It is not surprising in view of the extremely hierarchical nature of Ethiopian society that titles are numerous. The most striking thing about them was the fact that they were non-inheritable. It did happen that titles were assumed and then later recognized by an Emperor, but part of the validity of a title was that it was granted by the Emperor. Provincial nobility could and did grant titles extensively but these were never as highly regarded as imperial grants. Under normal circumstances a son would aspire to and get the equivalent title of his father.

Titles were given essentially on a dual basis. One was in recognition of loyalty; the other recognition of the position in a local community. They brought no material rewards (though a governorship and *gult* might accompany the grant) but they gave, and this was the crucial factor, an assured place in the hierarchy. Members of certain families hold such a place in any case; the title was merely a formal verification of it; a symbol to everyone that the Emperor accepted something well known to those around. It should be noted that titles were and are normally granted only to members of specific families, that is *balabat*, or *mekwanint* families.

Since then the position has changed to the extent that the Emperor granted all titles; and the traditionally military ones have lost their martial significance. The Court and administrative titles still however imply a function. A distinction can be drawn between titles that normally went to *balabat* and *mekwanint* families and those that would be more likely to go to royal favourites. This tradition, while it was not totally exclusive, still operates to a substantial extent. It should, of course, be emphasized that traditional military titles could also go to the non-aristocracy, particularly if the recipient distinguished himself in battle. To that extent their origin has still not been forgotten today.

Traditional Military Titles

Ras	Head of an army; held by the leading nobility
Dejazmatch	General; held by various levels of provincial governor
Fitawari	Commander of the vanguard. The Imperial *Fitawari* was the Minister of War
Kegnazmatch	Commander of the Right
Garazmatch	Commander of the Left
	(These two were given to governors of *awarajas* and other areas. The title did not necessarily relate to a command or to the size of a district.)

Balambaras   Commander of a Fort
Basha   Commander of a Rifle group
Shalaqa   Commander of a Thousand
These are all in use still but as honorifics, without the military connotations; but the relative importance remains the same.

Court Titles

Negus   King; the Emperor's title is actually *Neguse Nagast*— King of Kings
Leul-Ras   Prince
Bitwoded   Chief counsellor of the Emperor
Blatengetta   Administrator of the palace
Tsahafe Taezaz   Royal secretary; Minister of the Pen
Bajirond   Treasurer; applies to any treasurer
Liqemokas   Emperor's double
Ligaba   Chamberlain
Aggafari   Chief steward
Lij   Literally child; honorific for the children of important nobility

Administrative Titles

Afa Negus   Mouthpiece of the Emperor; Lord Chief Justice
Azaj
Womber } Royal judges

Kantiba
Shum } Titles given to specific governors, e.g. the *Wagshum* of Wag and Lasta. *Nagash* is obsolete; *Kantiba* is now
Nagash applied to the mayors of cities and towns

Enderassie
Teklegnia
Melkenya } Official representatives of higher authority within a province, sub-province or district. *Enderassie* applies usually to a deputy governor-general, one who is the
Meslenie
Ferasegna Government's (or the Emperor's) special representative

Atbia Danya   Local judge
Chika Shum   Village or parish chief; lowest official position
Negadras   Customs collector; chief of merchants

Church Titles

Bezu   Holy one; Patriarch
Abuna   Historically used for the Patriarch, now used for any bishop
Ichege   Until 1950, the administrative head of the Church
Neburae'ed   Ruler of the city and district of Axum where the cathedral of St. Mary of Sion is. Could be held by a layman as well as by a cleric
Liqe Kahenat   Head of the clergy of a province or any large area
Aqabe Sa'at   Organizer of the ecclesiastical calender

Liqe Debterra	Head of the *debterras*
Liqe Mamiher	Head of the *mamiheran*, the learned men of the Church
Aleka	Head of a large monastery or an important Church, with considerable administrative functions
Abba	Title for respected clergy
Qes	Priest

Glossary

Amba	a flat-topped, steep-sided mountain
Amoleh	salt bar; used as currency in the nineteenth century
Ashkar	retainer, follower
Ato	equivalent to 'mister'
Awraja	a sub-province
Balabat	literally one who has a father; a member of the landed gentry
Balderas	land for horses and mules, belonging to the Government
Bet Iqa	land reserved for mules used for war-time transport; the land users were regarded as part of the army
Diesa (Shehena)	communal land in Eritrea; divided every few years among the inhabitants of a village or district
Ekub	a social organization for saving; found in urban areas
Gann gebb	land for the preparation of food for the palace or for soldiers; divided into twelve sections—one for each month
Gasha	a measurement of land; theoretically forty hectares but varies widely
Gebbar	historically a serf in the southern provinces; also term given to land that is held in freehold and which pays the land tax
Gebretel	land taken by the Government for non-payment of taxes
Ge'ez	classical language, ancestor of both Amharic and Tigrinya; used in the liturgy of the Church
Guebbar	a feast, particularly one held by an important figure
Gult	a fief, granted by the Emperor for a period of years or for life in return for certain duties; abolished legally in 1966
Gult-gej	ruler of a gult area
Haimanote Abew	an organization of the Church, orientated towards youth; it means 'the original truth'
Hudad	land used to provide grain supplies for the imperial palaces; farmed by a group of tenants
Kitet	the call to arms, beaten out on the drums that were a sign of position
Maderia	land leased out by the Government especially to civil servants and military; no land tax is paid on it

Mehaber	an organization for social purposes with regional connections and a regional origin
Mekwanint	literally an office holder, but used to refer to the lesser nobility
Mengist	land whose title is vested in the Government; it is the reserve for Government land grants. Once the grants are made the land becomes *maderia*, etc.
Mesafint	princes, the highest nobility
Metekel-woreda	a sub-district
Nayiba	a Moslem judge
Nech-libash	servants of an official, though more usually used to describe the C.I.D. in urban areas
Qadi	a Moslem judge
Restegna	a member of the *rist* owning class, implies a certain status especially in the northern provinces
Rist (Resti)	land that is owned by an extended family and which is heritable
Rist-gult	a fief that is heritable; granted by the Emperor and usually to members of the imperial family. Legally abolished in 1966
Semon	land over which the Church has usufructuary rights and privileges
Shifta	bandit; used to describe all those who act against the Government, whatever the motives
Siso	land that the original nobility of the southern provinces were allowed to keep after the conquest by Menilek
Teklay guezat	province, governorate-general
Willayas	military areas of the Eritrean Liberation Front
Woreda	a district
Woregenu	land on which cattle were fattened for the palace
Woyane	name given to the revolt against Haile Selassie in Tigre in 1943
Woizero	a married woman, equivalent to 'Mrs'
Zar	a spirit or devil, usually used with reference to spirit possession cults

Notes

Preface

1. *Addis Zemen*, *Pagme* 1 1966 (6/9/74).
2. *Addis Zemen*, *Maskaram* 3 1967 (13/9/74).
3. Addis Ababa Home Service in Amharic. 1700 GMT 12/9/74. BBC Summary of World Broadcasts. Part 4, Second Series ME/4703 14/9/74.
4. Addis Ababa Home Service in Amharic. 1100 GMT 24/9/74. BBC Summary of World Broadcasts. Part 4, Second Series ME/4713 26/9/74.

Chapter One

1. Suspicion of foreigners has always been a marked characteristic of Ethiopia; this episode reinforced the feeling and it was not until the mid-nineteenth century that any substantial number of foreigners were allowed to visit the country.
2. The main reason behind this custom (which finally came to an end in 1950 when the first Ethiopian Patriarch was appointed) was the desire of the Alexandrian Patriarch to keep control of the Ethiopian Church. It also had a certain usefulness for the Ethiopian Church in that it helped to control disputes between the great monasteries.
3. *Amba* is the name given to a steep-sided and isolated mountain, of which there are many in Ethiopia.
4. See p. 16.
5. The *Kebra Nagast*, the Glory of the Kings, was written during the reign of the Emperor Yekuno Amlak *c.* 1270–85. It contains the story of the Queen of Sheba, her visit to Solomon and the birth of their son, Menilek I. The *Fetha Nagast*, the Law of the Kings, is the traditional law compilation, mainly based on the Bible and on the early church councils. It was put together in Egypt and deals largely with ecclesiastical law and disputes. It is not really a code though it was used as such for both ecclesiastical and secular affairs.
6. This is a rather over simplified account of the land system in Ethiopia. For further details see Chapter IV.
7. In ethnic terms the Amhara are probably a mixture of the indigenous population and the Semitic invaders of the north of Ethiopia in the first millenium B.C. The same is true of the Tigre people. The division between them probably occurred during the supremacy of the Zagwe dynasty who were Agau—an indigenous Cushitic people who have

managed to preserve themselves in many parts of the central high-lands. To the south of the Amhara areas lay a large number of other Cushitic groups, collectively referred to as the Sidama. In the period when the medieval Empire came into being around 1300, the Sidama were also setting up their own kingdoms, one of which at least, Kaffa, lasted until the end of the nineteenth century.

8. The Galla, as they have been usually called, refer to themselves as the Oromo people. Therefore Oromo has been used throughout this book.

9. Genealogies of this kind must of course be treated with care; but as they are the basis for all *rist* claims and are much in use, there is a reasonable check on their accuracy.

10. The Scottish traveller, James Bruce, was in Ethiopia at the time and left a very vivid account of the court and its intrigues. J. Bruce, *Travels to Discover the Source of the Nile 1768–73*, Edinburgh, 1790.

11. See map on p. 19.

12. In the nineteenth century these Oromo chiefs became rich enough from the trade in gold, ivory and slaves to set up five small Moslem kingdoms, the most important of which was the Sultanate of Jimma.

13. The kingdom of Kaffa appears to have come into being in the sixteenth century, a little later than the other Sidama states. It was at its most powerful about 1800; but it suffered very severely for its fierce resistance to Menilek in the late nineteenth century.

14. The Oromo have never in any real sense been united. They can all understand each other, but since the old institutions have begun to break down they have little in common except language and a consciousness of themselves as Oromo.

15. For details of Muhammed Ali and his influence on Ethiopian affairs see M. Abir, *Ethiopia—the Era of the Princes*, London, 1968, Chapters 1 and 3.

16. R. Pankhurst, *The Economic History of Ethiopia*, Addis Ababa, 1968, Chapter 1; and "Misoneism and Innovation in Ethiopian History," *Ethiopian Observer*, Vol. VII, 1964. S. Rubenson, *King of Kings, Tewodros of Ethiopia*, Addis Ababa, 1966. Margaret Morgan, "Continuities and Traditions in Ethiopian History: an investigation of the reign of Tewodros", *Ethiopian Observer*, Vol. XII, 1969, No. 4, pp. 224–69.

17. Yohannis IV was descended from two of the greatest Tigre families —the *Shums* (rulers) of Tembien and Agame. His position also gave him control over the Agula valley which was the main salt route and he thus controlled the distribution of the *amoleh*, the salt bar currency of the nineteenth century. M. Abir *op. cit.* especially pp. 44–50.

18. There are grounds for thinking that *Ras* Tafari's mother was also a relative, albeit a fairly distant one, of Mikael of Wollo.

19. Matewos was an *Abuna* in Ethiopia from 1879 until his death in 1926. A conservative figure, he is also supposed to have served Menilek as an adviser in foreign affairs. In this connection it should be noted that *Lij* Iyasu had upset the British, French and Italians by his leanings toward Turkey and Germany. They were even contemplating active intervention by 1916.

20. The word *gebbar* actually means one who pays tribute; and it strictly refers to free peasant cultivators. In practice, as mentioned, their burdens were very onerous and abuse was common; so their position was only marginally better than that of serfs, although they did have more freedom of movement. In the south their position was much closer to that of serfs as their labour was given to officials for life and was almost impossible to break away from.

21. Quoted from R. Pankhurst, *State and Land in Ethiopian History*, Addis Ababa, 1966, pp. 17–18.

22. See D. Crummey: "Tewodros as Reformer and Moderniser," *Journal of Modern African History*, Vol. X, No. 3, 1969, pp. 457–69.

23. Quoted from R. Pankhurst, *State and Land, op. cit.*, pp. 74–76.

24. Quoted from Dr. Harold Marcus: "The organisation of Menilek's palace and Imperial hospitality". *Rural Africana*, Spring 1970.

25. This was supposedly in return for Church support for a usurpation by the Prince of Tegulat in Shoa which overthrew the Zagwe dynasty in about A.D. 1270.

26. The major reason was the land system itself, and of course those who operated it, were not going to allow any changes. Trade was also exorbitantly taxed and there was a multiplicity of customs posts. Given the Amhara dislike of anything non-military, and the ring of Moslem states around the empire it was not surprising that trade fell easily into Moslem hands.

Chapter Two

1. Ephraim Isaac, "Social Structure of the Ethiopian Church". *Ethiopian Observer*, Vol. XIV, No. 4, 1971, p. 255.

2. According to the Governor of Eritrea's report on conversations held with *Dejazmatch* Haile Selassie Gugsa in May 1934 the reasons were: that his father had decided in the last few months of his life to support Italy and Haile Selassie felt he ought to follow his father's wishes; that the population of Tigre could have no hope in the government of an Emperor who intended to use the province only to provide wealth for his friends; that the Emperor encouraged dissensions between the leading Tigre nobility so as to incite disorders; that he wished to restore to Tigre the glories of Yohannis IV's reign; that he hoped Italy would free the people of Abyssinia from the tyranny of the Emperor Haile Selassie. ASMAI 54/38/158 Governor Eritrea (Asmara) to Ministero delle Colonie.

3. See S. Hoben, "Situational Constraints on Semantic Analysis: An Amharic Case", Ph.D. Thesis, University of Rochester, 1972, unpublished.

4. The courts of the *mesafint* and other nobles were copies of the imperial court, including such officials as the *Ligaba*, the chamberlain, and so on. As far as wealth allowed, the resemblance was perfect. Similarly, the *mesafint* gave out titles, especially to their sons, and provided weapons, and money out of the taxes they received. Their chief source

of patronage was the distribution of governorships and offices such as *chika shum, mislenie* and the like.

5. This was equivalent to approximately £30,000 at that time. The exchange rate was fluctuating between 18 MT$ and 10 MT$ to £1 at this period. MT = Maria Theresa (see p. ix).

6. Haile Giyorgis' wealth is difficult to calculate. He earned approximately 100,000 MT$ per year at the turn of the century and increasing amounts in the following years up to 1916. He certainly owed the Emperor Menilek 75,000 MT$ in 1910, a sum which probably represented two years' income at most from his position as *Negadras* of Addis Ababa.

7. The first Governor of the Bank of Abyssinia, MacGillivray, believed *Ras* Makonnen, Haile Selassie's father, to be richer than Menilek. Makonnen was able to take a share out of the Harar customs receipts that amounted to about 80,000 or more MT dollars. R. Pankhurst, *Economic History, op. cit.*, pp. 496, 533ff.

8. Quoted from Cheesman, "Report on Provincial Administration" to the British Ambassador, Sir S. Barton, 29/7/33. F.O. 371/16989/ J1995/32/1.

9. See genealogical charts on p. 32 and on p. 183.

10. These figures are partly based on a very valuable index of appointments compiled from the *Negarit Gazette*—the official government publication—by Dr. C. Clapham to whom I am greatly indebted for their use, supplemented by: *Administrative Directory of the Imperial Ethiopian Government*, 1966, 1969, Imperial Ethiopian Institute of Public Administration, Addis Ababa.

11. Many of Mikael's descendants lost power in the wake of *Lij* Iyasu's defeat. However, by the end of the 1920s they were already well ensconced again. The Crown Prince, who was a son of the Empress Menen, a grand-daughter of *Negus* Mikael, was appointed the Governor of the province partly in order to soothe the susceptibilities of the Wollo people. When he actually rode into Dessie for the first time the people turned out to welcome him and cheered "the son of our Emperor, *Lij* Iyasu"—according to the Italian consul who was present.

12. The *chika shum* frequently got 2 per cent of the land tax collected in an area—especially in *rist*-owning areas. This is not however done by law and it is not completely applied. There are other possibilities for rendering the position worthwhile, since it carried certain weight in local affairs.

13. *Atbia danyas* were set up by Proclamation No. 62 of 1947. They were given civil and criminal jurisdiction in minor cases; though in the case of civil matters only if the contending parties agreed to use them.

14. The current legal system provides for a Supreme Imperial Court for appeals; a high court with divisions that sit in the provinces; *awraja* and *woreda* courts. Provincial courts still exist for civil cases, as do *metikel woreda* courts. Theoretically both have been abolished although they still exist in some areas. The modernized procedures provided for in the various codes are an amalgam of traditional customary law and western law codes. In the provinces customary law is still in fact widely used.

15. Report on conditions in Ada district, 1969.
16. *Atbia danyas* are paid by the fees they collect from applicants to them. Their official income may thus be very low.
17. For further details see T. Geraghty, "People, Practice, Attitudes and Problems in the Lower Courts of Ethiopia", *Journal of Ethiopian Law*, Vol. VI, No. 2, 1969, pp. 427ff.
18. There are 99 *awrajas*, more than 400 *woredas* and some 1,300 *metikel woredas* in the Empire, though as noted earlier the last are only partially functional.
19. Clapham, *Index of Appointments, op. cit.*
20. This is an estimate extrapolated from my own calculations on the basis of travel in these provinces—especially Wollega, Illubabor, Kafa, Sidamo and Arussi.
21. See A. Orent, "Lineage Structure and the Supernatural: The Kafa of Southwest Ethiopia", Ph.D. Thesis, Boston, 1969, unpublished.
22. J. Stauder, *The Majangir: Ecology and Society of a Southwest Ethiopian People*, Cambridge, 1971.
23. This estimate comes from a relative of the *Ras*; but that is no guarantee of its reliability.
24. See P. Schwab, *Decision-making in Ethiopia*, London, 1972, pp. 175–80.
25. Moslem courts were set up by Imperial proclamation in 1945. There is considerable complaint at the disparity between the salaries of *Qudi* and *Nayiba* court judges and those of the government judges.
26. Ephraim Isaac, *op. cit.*, p. 255.
27. Sir E. A. Wallis Budge, *The Queen of Sheba and Her Only Son, Menelek I*, London, 1932. This is a translation of the *Kebra Nagast*.
28. Figures quoted in J. C. D. Lawrence and H. S. Mann, "F.A.O. Land Policy Project", *Ethiopian Observer*, Vol. IX, No. 4, 1966.
29. Alan Hoben, *Land Tenure among the Amhara of Ethiopia: the Dynamics of Cognatic Descent*, Chicago, 1973.
30. The last *Ichege* was the man appointed Patriarch in 1950; the offices of *Abuna* and *Ichege* were therefore amalgamated.
31. *Zar* is a spirit possession cult, widespread in the highlands; other varieties are found among the Oromo and non-Amhara peoples. S. D. Messing, "Group Therapy and Social Status in the Zar Cult of Ethiopia" in *Culture and Mental Health* (Ed. Opler, M. K.), New York, 1959, pp. 319–32. Also A. L. Morton: "Some Aspects of Spirit Possession in Ethiopia", PhD. Thesis, L.S.E., 1973, unpublished.
32. Quoted in Ephraim Isaac, *op. cit.* An English translation of the *Fetha Nagast* was published by the Law Faculty of the Haile Selassie I University in 1971.

Chapter Three

1. The rights that the people have may be considerable but the limitations on them have increased in recent years. The most obvious example is in the Public Safety and Welfare Order No. 56 of 1969. This was supposed to last for six months, but it has been reactivated steadily

since. It allows for the Minister of Interior to order the detention in any place he chooses, of any person, "if he shall have reasonable grounds . . .". Initial detention can last for up to three months but it can be renewed for further 90 day periods at will. Suspicion is all that is necessary and there is no appeal. The obvious parallel is with the South African detention law.

2. The literacy test alone would disqualify most people. Illiteracy is estimated at well over 90 per cent officially; and is probably around 95 per cent.

3. C. Clapham, *Haile Selassie's Government*, London, 1969, p. 143.

4. J. Markakis and Beyene Asmelash "Representative Institutions in Ethiopia", *Journal of Modern African Studies*, Vol. V, No. 2, 1967, pp. 193–219.

5. The number of Deputies actually holding titles has fluctuated: 26 per cent in 1957, 14 per cent in 1965 (Clapham, *op. cit.*, p. 143), and 29 per cent in 1973 (Ethiopian Herald, 7/7/74). As noted however these figures conceal the hold of the local nobility. *Mekwanint* and *balabat* families retain their local influence and this certainly carries over into Parliamentary elections.

6. For a full discussion of this legislation see P. Schwab, *Decision-making in Ethiopia*, London, 1972, pp. 89–140.

7. See Chapter IV for the 1973 draft proposals.

8. This calculation is based on my own researches in 1971/2, and does not apply to the 1973 Parliament, which has shown itself much more radical in outlook since the crisis of February 1974.

9. Speech to the joint session of Parliament on the thirty-first anniversary of the coronation—2 November 1961.

10. The duties of Ministers were originally laid down in the Order to define the powers and duties of our Ministers, No. 1, 1943 and an Amendment Order No. 2, 1943. The Revised Constitution of 1955 and the Ministers (Definition of Powers), Amendment Order of 1966 make further changes.

11. "No longer shall you shirk your duties. No longer shall we accept your responsibilities, when we have given power to you . . . If you encounter difficulties, We have appointed Our Prime Minister to aid you. His primary function is to co-ordinate work among the Ministries and see that the execution of Government programmes is facilitated." Speech to the Ministers, 14 April 1961.

12. C. Clapham, *op. cit.*, figure 5.

13. R. Greenfield, *Ethiopia*, London 1965, p. 297.

14. Aklilu also used his own family and the family of his brother's wife. His brother Akalework has been Minister of Health, Agriculture, Education and Justice. Other relatives have been Assistant Minister of Education and Vice-Minister of Public Works, and Director of the Haile Selassie I Prize Trust.

15. For a full account of these distinctions see C. Clapham, *op. cit.*

16. A personal communication from Peter P. Garretson.

17. The Third Five Year Plan stated that "attempts will be made to decentralize head office responsibilities down to governate-general

level . . ." Part of the aims of the committee that was set up were that "the Governate-general's office will be responsible for all the executive and administrative functions of the Ministry (of the Interior) including intersectoral development programme co-ordination. The *awraja* self-administration . . . in itself is an important institution for the integrated regional development programme, which will be initiated primarily on the basis of such local self reliance."

18. The Ethiopian Army. 1973

	Paramilitary	
4 Divisions of Infantry (8,000 each)	Territorials (active	
1 Tank battalion	strength)	9,200
1 Airborne Infantry battalion	Mobile Emergency	
4 Armoured Car squadrons	Force	6,800
4 Artillery battalions	Frontier Guards	1,200
2 Engineer battalions	Commando Force	3,200
50 Medium Tanks/20 Light Tanks		
about 40 Armoured Personnel Carriers		
86 Armoured Cars. 6 Helicopters		

Source: "The Military Balance 1973/4", International Institute for Strategic Studies, London.

19. D. Levine, "The Military in Ethiopian Politics: Capabilities and Constrants," in *The Military Intervenes*, ed. by Henry Bienen, New York, 1968, p. 15.
20. Figures supplied by an instructor at the Harar Academy.
21. There have been several other occasions when the armed forces have successfully demanded pay increases. Individual units also get attention promptly. The mutiny of NCOs and other ranks in January 1974, at Neghelli (in Sidamo) where a brigade of the 4th Division is stationed led to an immediate visit by the Chief of the Chief of Staff and other officers. The men had arrested all over the rank of sergeant; their dissatisfaction was over high prices and low pay. This was the first of the series of mutinies in early 1974, and it was the Government's failure to cope with the problems that led to the others in February and March 1974.
22. C. Clapham, *op. cit.*, pp. 19–21.
23. Tadesse Tereffe, "Progress, Problems and Prospects in Ethiopian Education", *Ethiopian Observer*, Vol. VIII, No. 1, 1964, pp. 6–18.
24. See Report on the organization of Education in Ethiopia 1971–73 and Report on major trends in educational development: Ministry of Education and Fine Arts, Addis Ababa, June 1973.

Chapter Four

1. Agriculture provided 58 per cent of the Gross Domestic Product in 1971 and an estimate for 1973 puts it at 65 per cent (*African Development*, May 1973). 92 per cent of the population live in rural areas; and nearly 88 per cent of the workforce are employed in agriculture. It provided 89 per cent of exports in 1971.
2. Third Five Year Plan, Addis Ababa, 1968, Chapter XI.
3. See A. Hoben, *op. cit.* and P. Schwab, *op. cit.*

4. See also A. Hoben, *op. cit.*, who calculates that one third of land is acquired in a life time. My own researches in Tigre suggest that a higher percentage is inherited directly. This is supported by the fixture of the *chika shumates* within certain families (which does not apparently apply in Gojjam—though it does in Begemeder and Wollo).

5. Quoted from F.O. 371/41470/J594/16/1. Enclosed in Howe to F.O. 29/1/44.

6. S. F. Nadel, "Land Tenure on the Eritrean Plateau", *Africa*, Vol. XVI, January 1946, pp. 1–21, 99–109.

7. Families that were regarded as *balabat* families comprised some 15–20 per cent of the *rist* owners in areas of Hauzien and Agame that I visited. There were also other divisions between pre- and post-war arrivals that related to social status among the other 80 per cent. By and large the latest arrivals held the least amount of land.

8. Balambaras Mahteme Selassie Wolde Maskal, "The Land System of Ethiopia", *Ethiopian Observer*, Vol. I, No. 9, 1957, pp. 283–301.

9. Quoted J. C. D. Lawrence and H. S. Mann, "F.A.O. Land Policy Project", *Ethiopian Observer*, Vol. XI, No. 4, 1966, pp. 283–336.

10. D. Sandford, "Memorandum on Land Tenure, Registration and Measurement in Ethiopia", enclosed in Howe to F.O. 29/1/44, F.O. 371/41470/J594/16/1.

11. The districts held as *gult* by *Ras* Seyoum were noted by the Italian consul in Adwa when *Ras* Seyoum obtained them.

12. In Tembien, Agame, Adua, Gheralta, Hauzien and Atsbi Dera in 1971, I found very few people who were in any sense aware that *gult* ownership had been abolished. There were frequent references to *gult gejs* and to their authority and functions.

13. For details of the various tenures see Balambaras Mahteme Selassie, *op. cit.* Also Berhanou Abbebe, "Evolution de la Propriété Foncière au Chao (Ethiopie) au Règne de Ménélik à la Constitution de 1931" Paris, 1971. This covers various aspects of Shoan land tenure in detail.

14. Decree No. 2 of 1942.

15. J. C. D. Lawrence and H. S. Mann, *op. cit.*, pp. 323–4.

16. Gebre-Wold-Ingeda Worq, "Ethiopia's Traditional System of Land Tenure and Taxation", *Ethiopian Observer*, Vol. 5, No. 4, 1962, pp. 302–39.

17. Ministry of Land Reform and Administration, "Report on a Land Tenure Survey of Shoa Province", May, 1967.

18. P. Schwab, *op. cit.*, p. 33 quotes Silashi Wolde-Tsadik ("Land Taxation in Hararge Province", *Agricultural College Bulletin*, June, 1966), who found 22,271 *gashas* of untaxed *rist-gult* in Chercher *awraja* in Hararge province; and a further 11,000 *gashas* on which the land tax was under Eth. \$10,000—exactly one-fourth of the stipulated tax. There is a strong presumption that these are imperial lands, especially in Chercher, as both the Emperor and Empress had very extensive land holdings there before the war.

19. For the view that *hudad* and *woregenu* lands should be regarded as government lands see J. M. Cohen, "Ethiopia after Haile Selassie", *African Affairs*, October, 1973, pp. 365–82. This interpretation of

government lands conflicts with the more traditional divisions to be found in Balambaras Mahteme Selassie, *op. cit.* and Gebre-Wold-Ingida Work, *op. cit.* and Berhanou Abbebe, *op. cit.*

20. *Gebbar* is used in two senses: (a) as a form of individual ownership of land and (b) as a word to describe the serfs who lived on the land. This latter usage is an historic one and no longer applies.
21. For further details of the orders see J. M. Cohen, *op. cit.*
22. J. M. Cohen, *op. cit.*, estimates that an average of $500 is necessary.
23. Cohen, *op. cit.*, p. 378. It should be emphasized that these figures are probably underestimates rather than overestimates.
24. Figure provided by a civil servant in the Ministry of Land Reform and Administration in 1972.
25. For arguments concerning the legality of this viewpoint see Billign Mandafro, "Agricultural Communities and the Civil Code", *Journal of Ethiopian Law*, Vol. VI, No. 1, 1969, pp. 145ff.
26. The total amount of government land is impossible to calculate entirely as so little is measured. Cohen, *op. cit.*, estimates that 46·6 per cent of the total 122,000,000 hectares and 11·8 per cent of the 84,000,000 hectares of arable land is governmental.
27. See S. F. Nadel, *op. cit.*, and Billign Mandefro, *op. cit.*, for details of this system. It may also be noted that Eritrea's system of land tax is different from the rest of the Empire, an agricultural income tax but no actual land tax and tithe. The province is also distinguished by being exempt from the 1952 order granting one half a *gasha* to all Ethiopians; and this was not adjusted when the Federation ended. Government title to land in the province depends upon an Italian decree of 1926 which had taken over *inter alia* the lowlands uninhabited by sedentary peoples; subsequently all land below 850 metres in height in the west, and 350 metres in the east were added.
28. The Ministry of Land Reform and Administration Land Tenure Surveys have been used for the following section; as have the Central Statistical Office Sample Surveys of the Provinces. The relevant volumes have not been individually acknowledged.
29. The Ministry of Land Reform and Administration, "Field Study in Systems of Land Tenure and Landlord Tenant relationships, Tabor Wereda (Sidamo)", Addis Ababa, 1966.
30. Michael Stähl *Contractions in Agricultural Development*, Scandinavian Institute of African Studies, Research Report No. 14, Uppsala, 1973.
31. Civil Code articles 2996, 3007, 3011, 2979.
32. Ministry of Land Reform and Administration, "Study of Agricultural Land Disputes in Kuni *Woreda* and Chercher *Awraja* Courts (Harar Province)"—quoted by Dessalegn Rahmato in *Challenge*, Vol. X, No. 2, 1970, pp. 25–49.
33. J. C. D. Lawrence and H. S. Mann, *op. cit.*
34. Figures quoted in Michael Stähl, *op. cit.*, as are the calculations for evictions in the following paragraph.
35. For details of CADU's development see: Henock Kifle, "An Analysis of the CADU Credit Development Programme 1968/9–1970/1" (CADU publication number 66), 1971. Also B. Nekby, *CADU, an*

Ethiopian Experiment in Developing Peasant Farming, Stockholm, 1971.
36. Confidential Report quoted by M. Stähl.
37. WADU originated as a project started by the district government and largely financed by the people of Soddu with Israeli advisers. See Schwab, *op. cit.*, pp. 173–75.
38. J. D. MacArthur, "Some Aspects of Land Policies in Ethiopia", November 1971. These figures refer to the FAO/Ethiopian Government credit scheme.
39. Information from civil servant in the Ministry of Land Reform and Administration. See also J. D. MacArthur, *op. cit.*
40. The Ministry of National Community Development controls a number of settlements in the south and west of Ethiopia, e.g. Wajito in Gamu Gofa and Dimtu in Wollega. None has been particularly successful due to the scarcity of the ministry's resources.
41. J. D. MacArthur, *op. cit.*
42. *Commercial Bank of Ethiopia Monthly Bulletin*, January 1973.
43. Figures from the *Ethiopian Herald*, 18/2/73.
44. P. Schwab, *op. cit.*, has a detailed analysis of this.
45. Michael Stähl, *op. cit.*

Chapter Five

1. Eshetu Chole, "The Mode of Production in Ethiopia and the realities thereof", *Challenge*, Vol. XII, No. 1, November 1971, pp. 3–29.
2. Cook to F.O. 6/7/45. F.O. 371/46048/J2336/4/61. Howe to F.O. 13/9/44. F.O. 371/414714/J3389/16/1, etc.
3. U.N. Adviser—quoted in *African Development*, May 1973.
4. Eshetu Chole, *op. cit.*, p. 15.
5. *Coffee Policy-making in Brazil, Uganda and Ethiopia—some Implications in Economic Development*, Commercial Bank of Ethiopia, Market Report, October/November 1972.
6. There is a meat extract factory going up at a cost of Eth. $24 million. It is wholly government-owned, but it is being put up by a Japanese firm under a management agreement. It should be complete by 1975.
7. Economic Commission for Africa, *Summaries of Economic Data*, Ethiopia 1971. Compiled January 1973.
8. "Ethiopian interests, however, and particularly the Palace, formed companies for the operation of the 'Colonalpi' mill mentioned (a flour mill producing biscuits and macaroni), a brewery and alcohol distillery and a shoe factory, all in Addis Ababa." Howe to F.O. 7/5/43. F.O. 371/35612/J2572/13/1.
9. Commercial Bank of Ethiopia, *The Ethiopian Economy*, Addis Ababa, 1970.
10. Information from Charles Rosen of the University of Chicago.
11. Quoted in Ambaw Ayele, "The Dynamics of Challenge—a case study: the Ethiopian Student Movement. Part I", 1973.
12. Legal Notice No. 10, 1950.
13. Investment Decree No. 51 of 1963.

14. Investment Proclamation No. 240 of 1966.
15. For a consideration of this see Timothy P. Bodman, "Income Tax exemption as an Incentive to Investment in Ethiopia", *Journal of Ethiopian Law*, Vol. VI, No. 1, 1969, pp. 215–25.
16. K. Ahooja, "Development and Legislation in Ethiopia", *Ethiopian Observer*, Vol. X, No. 4, 1966, pp. 277–78.
17. Among the shareholders in 1971 were: *Ato* Mammo Tadesse, Minister of Finance (in his wife's name), *Dejazmatch* Fessehazion Haile (Senator), *Ato* Getachew Mekasha (Minister of Information), *Ato* Tesfaye Teklewold, as well as the Prince Makonnen Hospital. The Directors included *Ato* Wondwossen Mengesha (Vice-governor of the National Bank), *Ato* Moulatou Kassaye (Director-General, Ministry of Finance) and *Ato* Asfa Demissie (Managing-Director Agricultural and Industrial Development Bank).
18. Figures from Duri Mohammed, "Private Foreign Investment in Ethiopia", *Journal of Ethiopian Studies*, 1969. However figures given in the *Ethiopian Herald* 21/10/73 suggested that the personnel of 4,500 permanent and 3,600 seasonal labourers were earning $13 million per annum then. The crisis in 1974 also set off a round of wage increases and wages are now higher.
19. This table is adapted from Duri Mohammed, *op. cit.*, p. 78.
20. F.O. 46049/J807/6/1. Howe to F.O. 12/2/45. Enclosing letter of resignation from A. D. Bethall to Haile Selassie.
21. A. D. Bethall, *op. cit.*
22. *Ibid.*
23. Profit estimates by Hickman Price: Report 21/11/44. Contained in Howe to F.O. 6/12/44. F.O. 371/41464/J4620/2/1. See also Howe to F.O. 8/1/45. F.O. 371/46073/J293/293/1.
24. In 1971 Directors of Indo-Ethiopian included: *Ato* Tadesse Mogesse, Vice-Minister, Communications and Industry (Vice-Chairman); *Ato* Wondwossen Mengasha, Vice-governor National Bank of Ethiopia (Chairman) and *Bajirond* Gezahegn Gebre Mariam, Assistant Minister of Finance.
25. Directors of Sabean Utility Corporation in 1971 included: *Ato* Akalework Habtewold (Minister of Justice); *Ato* Wondwossen Mengesha (Vice-governor of the National Bank of Ethiopia); Dr. Haile Giorghis Workineh (Lord Mayor of Addis Ababa); *Tsahfe Taezaz* Tefarra Work Kidane Wold (Minister of the Imperial Palace). Directors of the Cotton Company in 1971 included: *Ato* Menassie Lemma (Governor of the National Bank of Ethiopia and Minister of State, Finance); *Ato* Aklilu Habtewold (Prime Minister); *Ato* Yilma Deressa (Crown Councillor); *Ato* Abeba Retta (Minister of Agriculture). Fibre Company Directors in 1968 included: *Ato* Menassie Lemma; *Ato* Aklilu Habtewold; *Ato* Tefari Lemma (Vice-Minister of Finance) and His Imperial Highness the Crown Prince (Chairman). Among the shareholders a year earlier were: *Ato* Menassie Lemma, H.I.H. Princess Tegnagnawork, *Afa Negus* Zewde Ayele, *Ras* Mesfin Sileshi, *Dejazmach* Makonnen Desta, Debra Libanos monastery, Ethiopian Orthodox Church.

26. *Ethiopian Herald*, 28/2/73.
27. Besides the Tenneco concession two others were granted in March 1973. One to a consortium of four U.S. companies led by Voyager Petroleum Ltd. was for 34,400 square kilometres in Sidamo and Bale. The second to two other U.S. firms—Whitestone Ethiopia Petroleum Co. and Louisiana Land and Exploration Co.—is for 81,500 square kilometres in Hararge and Bale. Both groups expect to start test drilling in 1976.
28. K. Ahooja, *op. cit.*, p. 273.
29. By Ato Hailu Guade, Assistant Minister of Public Health in the *Ethiopian Herald*, 2/6/74. The two main Israeli investments are Incode —the meat packing firm in Asmara—and Epharm. Israeli firms have been involved in other areas however—Solel Boneh Overseas and Harbour Works Co. were both involved in laying water pipes in Harar and the former have also handled road construction projects and the Bole airport extensions.
30. It may be noted that the cut-back in U.S. presence involving the phasing down of the Kagnew base, the ending of the Mapping Mission, etc. has not affected private U.S. finance. In January 1974 for example the Mille Farms Co. was set up with 50 per cent U.S. private capital. (*Ethiopian Herald*, 26/1/74.)
31. Commercial Bank of Ethiopia. *Monthly Report*, January/February 1973, Addis Ababa.
32. Agricultural and Industrial Development Bank, *Report*, Addis Ababa, 1972. Government policy has in fact been retrogressive. The Development Bank (forerunner of the Agricultural and Industrial Development Bank) made small agricultural loans from its foundation in 1951 for ten years—lending 1,285 people 1,474,085 Eth.$. In 1961 these were discontinued on the grounds of supervisory expense. The minimum amount for a loan was then raised to $10,000. It is not clear what the Agricultural and Industrial Development Bank's minimum is today but it seems to be comparable for individual loans.
33. S. Gryziewicz, Legesse Tickeher, Mammo Bahta, "An Outline of the Fiscal System in Ethiopia", *Ethiopia Observer*, Vol. VIII, No. 4, 1965, pp. 293–322.
34. It is possible to argue perhaps that the last remnants of the Italian settlers could be equated with a national bourgeoisie. They do operate substantial enterprises especially in Eritrea—for example Melotti brewery, Cottonificio Baratolo, Eleberet—which do not have outside capital. However, even if this is acceptable, their numbers are dwindling and the majority would repatriate their capital to Italy if they were allowed to do so.
35. See Eshetu Chole, "The mode of Production in Ethiopia", *op. cit.*: North California Chapter of E.S.U.N.A., "Class Analysis in the Ethiopian Society", *Challenge*, Vol. XII, No. 1, November 1971 and "Imperialism in Ethiopia", *Challenge*, Vol. XI, No. 1, January 1971.

ᅟ

Chapter Six

1. R. Greenfield, *op. cit.*, p. 236.
2. Greenfield claims that there was a Shoan element to this and that Belai's mother was Shoan. While the latter is true there is no evidence of Shoan complicity in the escape and it appears to have been purely Gojjami in idea. It can in any case hardly be called a plot, although it was related to the tax problems of 1942–44.
3. See also A. Hoben, *op. cit.*, p. 219 for a different view.
4. A. Hoben, *op. cit.*, p. 223.
5. From Asmara he was sent to the Seychelles where he remained until 1947, when the British sent him back to Ethiopia. The Emperor had complained very strongly about this and demanded Haile Selassie Gugsa on many occasions. The British apparently however promised him political asylum in 1941 and refused to back down, on the grounds of morality.
6. See Haile Selassie Gugsa's conversation with the Governor of Eritrea quoted on pp. 29, 30 and Note 2 on p. 276.
7. These *awrajas* were the centre of the revolt—Blatta Haile Mariam himself came from Tembien and had lands in Enderta. The revolt also spread to Maichew, Agame and Adwa *awrajas*; indeed there is no doubt that he enjoyed very considerable support all over the province.
8. The following account of the revolt is taken from the reports drawn up by the British advisers attached to the Ethiopian Government forces and are to be found in F.O. 371/35607/35608. It is supplemented by conversations with survivors from *Blatta* Haile Mariam's forces; and others involved in the revolt.
9. This licence has been limited by the appointment of Shoan directors to the province, and by the fact that *Ras* Mangasha is married to a granddaughter of the Emperor, Princess Aida. There are signs that this may not still be sufficient. In the early 1970s there were a number of incidents in Tigre and some gun-running from Eritrea into Shire *awraja* in north-west Tigre. Eritrean Liberation Front propaganda has however not yet been aimed at the Christian Tigrinya speakers to any great extent.
10. Information given in conversation by the Administrator of the monastery in 1969.
11. For details see S. A. Longrigg, *A Short History of Eritrea*, Oxford, 1945, and G. K. N. Trevaskis, *Eritrea, a Colony in Transition 1941–52*, London, 1960. Eritrean Liberation Front booklets; *United Nations Documents on Eritrea*; *Eritrea, a Victim of U.N. Decision and Ethiopian Aggression*, New York, 1971.
12. G. K. N. Trevaskis, *op. cit.*
13. Accounts of the E.L.F. are sketchy. Details of some aspects of the struggle particular to its wider aspects may be found in C. Clapham, "Ethiopia and Somali" in *Conflicts in Africa*, Adelphi Papers No. 93, International Institute for Strategic Studies, 1962; J. F. Campbell, "Rumblings along the Red Sea: The Eritrea Question", *Foreign Affairs*, April, 1970; Godfrey Morrison: *The Southern Sudan and*

Eritrea: Aspects of wider African Problems, Minority Group Report No. 5, Revised edition, 1973; R. L. Hess, *Ethiopia: The Modernisation of Autocracy*, Ithaca, 1970.

14. Quoted in Taye Geremaw, "Rebellion in Eritrea: Who is behind it; What are its aims." *New Middle East*, April, 1971.

15. Personal information.

16. This is not apparent from the Front's communiqués. A communiqué of November 1968 said "An Eritrean Liberation Army force in the first region has ambushed . . . a convoy of vehicles on its way to rescue Halhal centre. The convoy consisted of six cars, four of which were destroyed and two took to flight. The battle resulted in the death and injury of a great number of enemy soldiers. Our forces returned safely to base".

17. Osman Saleh Sabbe, the Secretary-General of the E.L.F. apparently allowed El Fatah to use the E.L.F. duplicating facilities for their first communiqué. Personal communication from Peter Hellyer, Editor, Third World Reports.

18. E.L.F. claims have to be treated with even more circumspection, 1970–72, because of the splits within the movement. Some of the actions mentioned especially in 1972 refer to the "civil war" and not to operations against the Ethiopian army.

19. *Africa Confidential*, 27 April 1973.

20. For an account of this Congress see R. Lobban, "Eritrean Liberation Front; a close-up view", *Munger Africana Library Notes 13*, September 1972.

21. *Third World Reports*, Vol. 4, No. 7, September 1973.

Chapter Seven

1. The Oromo in Wollo have remained more committed to Islam; those who settled nearer to Gondar and in Begemeder were by and large converted.

2. Imperial government policy has been to allow foreign missionaries to operate in non-Christian areas. Considerable pressure has however been used to limit conversion and the government prefers the missionaries to carry out medical and educational activities.

3. The major sources for this revolt are the Italian consular reports from Dessie and Adwa which are extremely detailed. They belong to the series ASMAI 54/1–11 but have not been individually identified here.

4. No evidence is adduced for this but it is possible that the French were looking for a way to counteract Italian influence in Ethiopia. It gains some credence from the fact that one of *Lij* Iyasu's son's was under French protection at Tadjura from 1935 into the early 1940s.

5. The old Sultan actually died in 1932 and it was his son and successor who contacted the Italians.

6. F.O. 371/20206/J6142/4044/1. Enclosed in Erskine to F.O. 24/6/36.

7. The main source for this episode is Captain Erskine. His own involvement is not above suspicion and it is more than likely that he helped to draw up some of the documents sent to London. This does not of

course invalidate the sentiments expressed in them. His dispatches are to be found in F.O. 371/20206/20207/20208; as are the various documents sent by the government of the Western Galla.

8. The delegation which went to Gambella, the British held enclave on the Baro river, had "full power to conduct negotiations and to sign treaties with the British Government". This was conferred on them by *Dejazmatch* Hable Mariam.

   Other memoranda had also been sent through Gambella. In no case were answers apparently received direct from the Foreign Office, which at the time was not prepared to further compromise Anglo-Italian relations by interference in what was, by then, regarded as an Italian sphere influence.

9. There was an outbreak of trouble when the government attempted to measure land in the later 1960s (after the passing of the Agricultural Income Tax Law). Before it had a chance to reach any sizeable scale the government backed down.

10. I am much indebted to Aberra Ketsela for a detailed account of the revolt, "The Rebellion in Bale, 1963–1970", Haile Selassie I University, B.A. Thesis, 1971. This has been supplemented by information from individuals involved on both sides.

11. *Analysis of Revolution in Ethiopia* put out by the Ethiopian National Liberation Front, 1973.

12. The Front also operated in Sidamo; especially in Borana. An attack was made on Neghelli airfield in 1966/7—only a few kilometres from Neghelli town where a brigade of the 4th Division was stationed. In 1966–67 it was necessary to station Territorials along the Kebra Mengest to Neghelli road; and the road from Neghelli south to Kenya was usable only under military conveyance.

13. As always calculation of the numbers involved is difficult. In 1966–67 one army estimate put the guerillas at 5,000. This is probably exaggerated; more reasonable would be around 2,000. Towards the end of 1969 some 500 were still under arms in the Dolo forest area.

14. "Communiqué for the Establishment of the Ethiopian National Liberation Front", 1/8/71.

15. See *Third World Reports*, Vol. 4, No. 4, June 1973.

16. See C. Clapham, "Ethiopia and Somalia", *op. cit.* and C. J. Jaenan: "The Somali Problem", *African Affairs*, Vol. 56, April 1957, pp. 147–57.

17. "Somaliland Claim", *African Affairs*, Vol. 55, January 1956, pp. 15–16.

18. Ministry of the Interior Annual Report, 10/9/42. Copy in F.O. 371/35626/J75/78/1. Howe to F.O. 1/12/42.

19. It is relevant that the first two Prime Ministers of Somalia (1960–67) both came from the Darod clan, which is one of the main inland groups. Most of the Somalis in southern Ethiopia and northern Kenya come from this clan. For details of this and for further information see I. M. Lewis, *Peoples of the Horn of Africa*, London, 1955.

20. There were some violent clashes on the border around Dolo, and Ethiopia reinforced the brigade at Jigjiga in Hararge. The Emperor's

grandson-in-law was also appointed to the command of the 3rd Division which is stationed in Hararge.

21. This is equivalent to £16·50 and £3,000 or $U.S.40 and U.S.$7,200.
22. For full details of this see Aberra Ketsela, *op. cit.*
23. In 1970 there were 45 elementary schools but only 14 of these went through grades 1 to 6. There were 5 Junior Secondary (grades 7 and 8) and 1 secondary school. In the three years 1967–70 the enrolment doubled in the primary and junior secondary schools and tripled in the secondary school. For 1970 the percentage of the school age population enrolled was: 8·8 per cent—Fassil Awraja; 5·7 per cent —Genale; 5·7 per cent—Wabe; 2·7 per cent—Delo; 0·5 per cent— El Kere. In the primary sector a total of 12,036 out of a primary age population of 212,400 are enrolled. (Ministry of Education figures.)
24. See A. Orent, *op. cit.*
25. The 1967–68 Statistical Abstract gives 7,673,100 as the population for Arussi, Bale, Gomu-Goffa, Kafa, Sidamo, and Harage. However this is underestimated by at least a million. The population of Bale is given as 159,800 instead 1,300,000. The other figures may also be underestimated.

	Rural	Urban
Arussi	1,069,400	41,400
Bale	139,800	20,000
Gemu Gofa	818,500	22,000
Kafa	635,100	53,300
Sidamo	1,430,900	91,000
Hararge	3,189,200	152,500

26. The Mecha group of Oromo are found mainly in Southern Shoa.

Chapter Eight

1. R. Greenfield, *op. cit.*, pp. 224–48, which gives an account of patriot activities. See also Wo. Salome Gabre Egziabher, "The Ethiopian Patriots: 1936–41", *Ethiopian Observer*, Vol. XII, No. 2, and "The Patriotic Works of *Dejazmatch* Aberra Kassa and *Ras* Abebe Aragaye". Paper presented to Third International Conference of Ethiopian Studies, Addis 1968. A. Mockler, *Haile Selassie's War.*
2. A. Mockler, *op. cit.*
3. F.O. 371/31602/J1152/973/1. Howe to F.O. 9/3/42.
4. Student pamphlet 29/11/69.
5. The most detailed account of the coup is to be found in R. Greenfield, *op. cit.*, pp. 375–452, to which I am indebted. See also C. Clapham, "The Ethiopian Coup d'Etat of December 1960", *Journal of Modern African Studies*, Vol. 6, No. 4, 1968, pp. 495–507. D. C. Watt, The Decembrists: Russia 1825. Ethiopia 1960, *International Relations:* April 1963. D. N. Levine, "The Military in Ethiopian Politics", *op. cit.*
6. By R. Greenfield, *op. cit.*, and R. L. Hess, "Ethiopia", in *National Unity and Regionalism in Eight African States*", ed. G. M. Carter, Ithaca, 1966, and *Ethiopia: the Modernisation of an Autocracy, op. cit.*

7. Quoted from D. C. Watt, *op. cit.* This transcription comes from the B.B.C. and differs a little from that recorded by Greenfield. The only difference of importance is item 9. "Members of the Armed Forces will have more clearly defined privileges and personal freedom . . ." Greenfield, *op. cit.*, p. 403.
8. C. Clapham, "The Ethiopian Coup", *op. cit.*, p. 502.
9. R. Greenfield, *op. cit.*, p. 417.
10. Haile Selassie himself apparently viewed it as a Moja family matter.
11. The only discussions of the Ethiopian army are to be found in Ross K. Baker, "The Ethiopian Army and Political Stability: Prospects and Potentials", *Middle Eastern Studies*, Vol. 6, No. 3, October 1970, and D. N. Levine: "The Military in Ethiopian Politics", *op. cit.*
12. 1973 :   1 bomber squadron—4 Canberra B-2
              1 fighter-bomber squadron—12 F-86 F
              1 counter-insurgency squadron—6 T-28 A
              1 fighter squadron—15 F-5A
              16 transport aircraft
              46 training aircraft (in three squadrons)
              14 helicopters.
    In 1971 there were 48 combat aircraft, including T-28 As, but only six helicopters.
    The Military Balance 1973–74 and 1971–72, International Institute of Strategic Studies, 1972 and 1973.
13. B.B.C. Monitoring Service Report, 28/4/74. This account of the crisis draws on news and media reports, Addis Ababa Radio broadcasts, pamphlets, the *Ethiopian Herald* and personal information.
14. These estimates are based on C. Clapham, *Registrar of Appointments from the Negarit Gazeta*, *op. cit.*
15. The 1972 figures come from a source in the Ministry of Defence; both were supplied by Army officers.
16. One figure for other ranks supplied by a middle ranking officer was 22 per cent Amhara, 45 per cent Oromo, 12 per cent Tigre, 22 per cent others. These however are extremely surprising (particularly the "others") and do not reflect other estimates.
17. For a detailed account of the Ethiopian Student Movement up to 1967 see Ambaw Ayele, "The Dynamics of Challenge, a Case Study: The Ethiopian Student Movement", Pt. I, 1973(?) to which I am indebted. The student movement is also discussed in R. L. Hess, "Ethiopia", *op. cit.*
18. In *Challenge*, Vol. XIII, No. 1, August 1973, the figure is given as "more than 30 students were massacred". As a lecturer at the University at the time, I think this figure is too high even allowing for deaths from wounds. The difficulty in getting an accurate count was due to the immediate scattering of the students and not all returned when the University re-opened—at least a dozen fled to Somalia and the Sudan; others abandoned any further hope of education.

Chapter Nine

1. As itemized by M. Bloch, *Feudal Europe*, London 1961. See also M. Dobb, *Studies in the Development of Capitalism*, International Publishers, New York, 1963.
2. An instructive parallel to this may be seen in late sixteenth century Japan with the establishment of a central authority by the Tokugawa Shoganate. See Toshio G. Tsukahira, *Feudal Control in Tokugawa, Japan, the Sankin Kotae System*, Harvard, 1966; James Murdoch, *History of Japan*, London, 1925/6.
3. Zenon Merida, "Ethiopia", *New Left Review*, No. 30, March/April 1965.
4. D. L. Levine, *Wax and Gold. Tradition and Innovation in Amhara Culture*, Chicago, 1965.
5. See D. L. Levine, *Wax and Gold, op. cit.* and Haile Wolde Mikael: "The lack of precision in the Ethiopian Social and Economic life and its implications for modernising Ethiopia". Arts Seminar paper, Haile Selassie I University, 1969.
6. Gedamu Abraha, "Wax and Gold", *Ethiopian Observer*, XI, No. 3, September 1968, pp. 226–43.
7. Commercial Bank of Ethiopia, *The Ethiopian Economy*, Addis Ababa, 1970, pp. 93–100.

Select Bibliography

Books

Abir, M., *Ethiopia—the Era of the Princes*, London, 1968.

Assefa Bequele and Eshetu Chole, *A Profile of the Ethiopian Economy*, Nairobi, 1969.

Berhanou Abbebe, *Evolution de la Propriété Foncière au Chao (Ethiopie) au règne de Menelik a la Constitution de 1931*, Paris, 1971.

Bloch, M., *Feudal Europe*, tr. L. A. Manyon, London, 1961.

Bruce, J., *Travels to discover the source of the Nile 1768–73*, Edinburgh, 1790.

Clapham, C., *Haile Selassie's Government*, London, 1969.

Crummey, D., *Priests and Politicians*, Oxford, 1972.

Dobb, M., *Studies in the Development of Capitalism*, New York, 1963.

Ginzberg, E. and Smith, H. A., *Manpower Strategy for Developing Countries*, New York, 1967.

Greenfield, R., *Ethiopia, a New Political History*, London, 1965.

Hess, R., *Ethiopia: Modernisation of an Autocracy*, Ithaca, 1970.

Hoben, A., *Land Tenure among the Amhara of Ethiopia: the Dynamics of Cognatic Descent*, Chicago, 1973.

Huntingford, G. W. B., *The Land Charters of Northern Ethiopia*, Addis Ababa, 1965.

Kaplan, I., et al. *Area Handbook for Ethiopia*, Washington, 1971.

Levine, D., *Wax and Gold*, Chicago, 1966.

Lewis, H. S., *A Galla Monarchy*, Madison, 1965.

Lewis, I. M., *Peoples of the Horn of Africa*, London, 1955.

Lipsky, G. A., *Ethiopia, its people, its society, its culture*, New Haven, 1962.

Longrigg, S. A., *A Short History of Eritrea*, Oxford, 1945.

Mann, H. S., *Land Tenure in Chore (Shoa)*, Addis Ababa, 1963.

Mathew, D., *Ethiopia, the Study of a Polity 1540–1935*, London, 1947.

Messing, S. D., *The Target of Health in Ethiopia*, New York, 1972.

Mockler, A., *Haile Selassie's War*, forthcoming.

Murdoch, J., *History of Japan*, London, 1925–26.

Neckby, B., *CADU, an Ethiopian Experiment in Developing Peasant Farming*, Stockholm, 1971.

Pankhurst, R., *State and Land in Ethiopian History*, Addis Ababa, 1966.

Pankhurst, R., *Economic History of Ethiopia*, Addis Ababa, 1968.

Perham, M., *The Government of Ethiopia*, London, 1969 (2nd Edition).

Rubenson, S., *King of Kings, Tewodros of Ethiopia*, Addis Ababa, 1966.

Schwab, P., *Decision-making in Ethiopia*, London, 1972.

Shack, W. A., *The Gurage, a people of the Ensete Culture*, Oxford, 1966.

Simoons, F. J., *Northwest Ethiopia, Peoples and Economy*, Madison, 1960.

Stauder, J., *The Majangir: Ecology and Society of a Southwestern Ethiopian People*, Cambridge, 1971.

Tadesse Tamrat, *Church and State in Ethiopia 1270–1527*, Oxford, 1972.

Trimingham, J. S., *Islam in Ethiopia*, Oxford, 1952.

Toshio G. Tsukahira, *Feudal Control in Tokugawa, Japan: the Sankin Kotae System*, Harvard, 1966.

Trevaskis, G. K. N., *Eritrea, a Colony in Transition*, London, 1960.

Wallis Budge, Sir E. A., *The Queen of Sheba and Her Only Son Menelek I*, London, 1932.

Articles, Pamphlets and Monographs

Abir, M., "Red Sea Politics", in *Conflicts in Africa*, Adelphi Papers, No. 93, International Institute for Strategic Studies, 1972.

"Agriculture Sector Survey—Ethiopia, Vols. I–III", International Bank for Reconstruction and Development, 15 January 1973.

Ahooja, K., "Development and Legislation in Ethiopia", *Ethiopian Observer*, Vol. X, No. 4, 1966.

Alemayehu Seifu, "Eder in Addis Ababa: a Sociological Study", *Ethiopian Observer*, Vol. XII, No. 1, 1969.

Assefa Bequele, "The Educational Framework of Economic Development in Ethiopia", *Ethiopian Observer*, Vol. XI, No. 1, 1967.

Assefe Dula, "Land Tenure in Chercher Province", *Ethiopian Observer*, Vol. IV, No. 2, 1961.

Billign Mandafro, "Agricultural Communities and the Civil Code", *Journal of Ethiopian Law*, Vol. 6, No. 1, 1969.

Bodman, T. P., "Income Tax Exemption as an Incentive to Investment in Ethiopia", *Journal of Ethiopian Law*, Vol. 6, No. 1, 1969.

"Budget for the year 1958", *Ethiopian Observer*, Vol. III, No. 2, 1959.

"Budget for the year 1965/6", *Ethiopian Observer*, Vol. X, No. 3, 1966.

Campbell, J. F., "Rumblings along the Red Sea, the Eritrean Question", *Foreign Affairs*, April 1970.

Clapham, C., "The Ethiopian Coup d'Etat of December 1960", *Journal of Modern African Studies*, Vol. VI, No. 4, 1968.

Clapham, C., "Imperial Leadership in Ethiopia", *African Affairs*, LXVIII, April 1969.

Clapham, C., "Ethiopia and Somalia", in *Conflicts in Africa*, Adelphi Papers No. 93, International Institute for Strategic Studies, 1972.

Cohen, J. M., "Ethiopia after Haile Selassie", *African Affairs*, October 1973.

Crummey, D., "Tewodros as Reformer and Moderniser", *Journal of Modern African History*, Vol. X, No. 3, 1969.

de Young, M., "The Internal Marketing of Agricultural Products and its Influence on Agricultural Productivity", *Ethiopian Observer*, Vol. XI, No. 1, 1967.

Duri Mohammed, "Private Foreign Investment in Ethiopia", *Journal of Ethiopian Studies*, Vol. VII, No. 2, 1969.

"Economic Survey of Ethiopia", *African Development*, November 1971, May 1973, May 1974.

"The Economy of Ethiopia, 5 Vols.", International Development Association, 1967.

Ephraim Isaac, "Social Structure of the Ethiopian Church", *Ethiopian Observer*, Vol. XIV, No. 4, 1971.

"Eritrean Liberation Front Statement", *Third World Reports*, Vol. 4, No. 7, 1973.

"Eritrea, a Victim of U.N. Decision and Ethiopian Aggression", New York, 1971.

Eshetu Chole, "Taxation and Economic Development in Ethiopia", *Ethiopian Observer*, Vol. XI, No. 1, 1967.

Eshetu Chole, "The mode of Production in Ethiopia and the realities thereof", *Challenge*, Vol. XII, No. 1, November 1971.

"The Ethiopian Economy", Commercial Bank of Ethiopia, Addis Ababa, 1970.

"The Ethiopian National Liberation Front: Analysis of Revolution in Ethiopia", 1973.

"Ethiopian National Liberation Front: Communiqué for the Establishment of the Front", 1973.

"Famine in Ethiopia—the Starving Granary of the Middle East", *African Red Family*, Vol. I, Nos. 5–6, 1973.

Gamst, F., "Peasantries and Elites without Urbanism: the Civilisation of Ethiopia", *Comparative Studies in Society and History*, Vol. 12, No. 4, 1970.

Gebre-Wold Ingida Work, "Ethiopia's Traditional System of Land Tenure and Taxation", *Ethiopian Observer*, Vol. V, No. 4, 1962.

Gedamu Abraha, "Wax and Gold", *Ethiopian Observer*, Vol. XI, No. 3, 1968.

Geraghty, T., "People, Practice, Attitudes and Problems in the Lower Courts of Ethiopia", *Journal of Ethiopian Law*, Vol. VI, No. 2, 1969.

Gryziewiez, S., Legesse Tickeher, Mammo Bahta, "An Outline of the Fiscal System in Ethiopia", *Ethiopian Observer*, Vol. VIII, No. 4, 1965.

Haile Menkerios, "Notes on Land Tenure in Ethiopia", *Challenge*, Vol. IX, No. 2, 1969.

"Hearings before the sub-committee on the United States security agreements and commitments abroad of the Committee on Foreign Relations", U.S. Senate, 2nd Session, Part 8, June 1970, Washington.

Henock Kifle, "An Analysis of the CADU Credit Development Programme 1968–69 to 1970–71", CADU Publications, No. 66, 1971.

Hoben, A., "Social Anthropology and Development Planning in Ethiopia", *Journal of Modern African Studies*, Vol. X, No. 4, 1972.

Hovarth, R. J., "The Wandering Capitals of Ethiopia", *Journal of African History*, Vol. X, No. 2, 1969.

Jaenan, C. J., "The Somali Problem", *African Affairs*, Vol. 56, April 1957.

Lawrence, J. C. D. and Mann, H. S., "F.A.O. Land Policy Project", *Ethiopian Observer*, Vol. IX, No. 4, 1966.

Levine, D. N., "Haile Selassie's Ethiopia—Myth or Reality", *Africa Today*, May 1961.

Lewis, H. S., "Origins of the Galla and Somali", *Journal of African History*, Vol. VII, No. 1, 1966.

Lobban, R., "Eritrean Liberation Front: a Close-up View", *Munger Africana Library Notes*, 13 September 1972.

Mahteme Selassie Wolde Maskal, Balambaras, "The Land System of Ethiopia", *Ethiopian Observer*, Vol. I, No. 9, 1957.

Marcus, H., "The Organisation of Menilek's Palace and Imperial Hospitality", *Rural Africana*, Spring, 1970.

Markakis, J. and Beyene Asmalash, "Representative Institutions in Ethiopia", *Journal of Modern African Studies*, Vol. V, No. 2, 1967.

Market Reports 1972–73, Commercial Bank of Ethiopia, Addis Ababa.

Messing, S. D., "Group Therapy and Social Status in the Zar Cult of Ethiopia", in *Culture and Mental Health* (Ed. Opler, M. K.), New York, 1959.

The Military Balance 1973–74, International Institute for Strategic Studies, London, 1973.

Monthly Bulletins 1972–73, Commercial Bank of Ethiopia, Addis Ababa.

Morgan, M., "Continuities and Traditions in Ethiopian History: an Investigation of the reign of Tewodros", *Ethiopian Observer*, Vol. XII, No. 4, 1969.

Morrison, G., "The South Sudan and Eritrea. Aspects of Wider African Problems", *Minority Group Report*, No. 5, Revised Ed. 1973.

Nadel, S. F., "Land Tenure on the Eritrean Plateau", *Africa*, Vol. XVI, 1946.

North Californian Chapter of the Ethiopian Student Union of North America, "Class Analysis in Ethiopian Society", *Challenge*, Vol. XII, No. 1, 1971. "Imperialism in Ethiopia", *Challenge*, Vol. XI, No. 1, January 1971.

Pankhurst, R., "Misoneism and Innovation in Ethiopian History", *Ethiopian Observer*, Vol. VII, 1964.

Quarterly Bulletins, National Bank of Ethiopia, Addis Ababa, 1968–73.

Ramahto, D., "Conditions of the Ethiopian Peasantry, *Challenge*, Vol. X, No. 2, 1970.

"Rebels Preparing Offensive", *Third World Reports*, Vol. 4, No. 4, 1973.

Schwab, P., "Rebellion in Ethiopia", *East African Journal*, Vol. VI, No. 11, 1969.

Sileshi Wolde-Tsadik, "Land Taxation in Hararge Province", *Agricultural College Bulletin*, No. 47, June 1966.

Sileshi Wolde-Tsadik, "Land Ownership in Hararge Province", *Agricultural College Bulletin*, No. 48, June 1966.

Sjöstrom, R. and M., *Y.D.L.C.—a Literacy Campaign in Ethiopia*, Scandinavian Institute of African Studies, Research Report, No. 20, Uppsala, 1973.

Stähl, M., *Contradictions in Agricultural Development*, Scandinavian Institute of African Studies, Research Report, No. 14, Uppsala, 1973.

Summary of Economic Data, Ethiopia 1971, Economic Commission for Africa, Addis Ababa, 1973.

Tadesse Tereffe, "Progress, Problems and Prospects in Ethiopian Education", *Ethiopian Observer*, Vol. VIII, No. 1, 1964.

Tayar, G., "Ethiopia's Rebellion", *Africa Report*, Vol. XIV, No. 8, 1969.
Taye Geremaw, "Rebellion in Eritrea: Who is Behind it; What are its aims", *New Middle East*, April 1971.
Watt, D. C., "The Decembrists: Russia 1825. Ethiopia 1960", *International Relations*, April 1963.

Official Publications (Ethiopian)

Administrative Directory of the Imperial Ethiopian Government, 7th edition, 1967, 9th edition, 1969, Addis Ababa, 1967–69.
Agricultural and Industrial Development Bank Report, Addis Ababa, 1972.
Budget for the Fiscal Year, 1970–71, Addis Ababa, 1970.
Budget for the Fiscal Year, Draft, 1971–72, Addis Ababa, 1971.
Field Study in the Systems of Land Tenure and Landlord Tenant Relationships Tabor Woreda (*Sidamo*), Ministry of Land Reform and Administration, Addis Ababa, 1966.
Land Tenure Surveys of the Provinces, Ministry of Land Reform and Administration, Addis Ababa, 1967–70.
Negarit Gazeta, Decrees, Proclamations, Legal Notices and Orders are published in this. Addis Ababa, 1941–onwards.
Report on the Organization of Education in Ethiopia 1971–73 and Report on Major Trends in Educational Development, Ministry of Education and Fine Arts, Addis Ababa, 1973.
School Census for Ethiopia 1966–68, Ministry of Education and Fine Arts, Addis Ababa, 1968.
Second Five Year Development Plan 1963–67, Addis Ababa, 1962.
Selected Speeches of H.I.M. Haile Selassie 1st, Addis Ababa, 1967.
Statistical Abstracts, 1965, 1966, 1967 and 1968, 1969 and 1970, Central Statistical Office, Addis Ababa.
Sample Surveys of the Provinces and of Towns, Central Statistical Office, Addis Ababa.
Third Five Year Development Plan 1968–73, Ministry of Planning and Development, Addis Ababa, 1968.

Official Publications (British and Italian)

Italian Foreign and Colonial Office Archives, Ethiopia: ASMAI series 54/1–38 (1896–1936).
British Foreign Office Archives. Public Records Office Series F.O. 371/F.O. 401.

Unpublished Sources

Aberra Ketsela, "The Rebellion in Bale 1963–70", B.A. Thesis, Haile Selassie 1st University, 1971.
Ambaw Ayele, "The Dynamics of Challenge—a case study, the Ethiopian Student Movement", Pt. I, 1973.

Bauer, D., "Land, Leadership and Legitimacy among the Inderta", Ph.D. Thesis, Rochester, 1972.

Clapham, C., "Index of Appointments in the Negarit Gazeta 1942–63".

Hoben, A., "The Role of Ambilineal Descent Groups in Gojjam: Amhara Social Organisation", Ph.D. Thesis, Berkeley, 1963.

Hoben, S., "Situational Constraints on Semantic Analysis, an Amharic case", Ph.D. Thesis, Rochester, 1972.

MacArthur, J. D., "Some aspects of Land Policies in Ethiopia", November 1971.

Morton, A. L., "Some aspects of Spirit Possession in Ethiopia", Ph.D. Thesis, London School of Economics, 1973.

Orent, A., "Lineage Structure and the Supernatural; the Kafa of South West Ethiopia", Ph.D. Thesis, Boston, 1969.

Sandford, D., "Memorandum on Land Tenure, Registration and Measurement in Ethiopia", Addis Ababa, 1944.

Index

(This index does not include Notes or Bibliography)
(Text references precede Preface references)

NAME INDEX

SUBJECT INDEX

finance—*contd.*
  investment provision, 164
  lending of imperial money, 76
  loan repayments, 160
  planned investment, 158
  sectional disbursement of credits, 159
  tourism, 139–40
  see also Five Year Plans, Taxation, Trade
Finance, Ministry of, 45, 47, 55, 56, 66, 67, 68, 69, 75, 76, 77, 78, 81, 82, 83, 85, 125, 136, 147, 159, 184, 222, xiii
Five Year Plans, 153, 158, 159, 164
  Second Five Year Plan, 137
  Third Five Year Plan, 101, 121, 137, 145, 147, 156, 158, 162
  Fourth Five Year Plan, 139, 140
France, 85

gebbar, (land), 111, 112, 113, 130, 182, 257
gebbars, 13, 14
Ge'ez, 5, 60, 61
Gibe areas, 8
godfathers, 45
Gojjam, province of, 4, 9, 10, 26, 29, 31, 32, 33, 34, 39, 43, 48, 49, 56, 57, 68, 79, 88, 92, 96, 102, 103–4, 105, 107, 116, 117, 121, 122, 146, 175, 177, 178, 179, 181, 182, 183–6, 191, 245, 257, 259, 262, 263
  royal house of, 32, 189
Gomu-Goffa, province of, 43, 48, 55, 56, 74, 80, 92, 116, 117, 118, 119, 120, 121, 122, 126, 146, 162
Gondar, 1, 2, 3, 4, 5, 6, 7, 8, 9, 10, 204
Gore, 29
governors, 4, 27, 28, 31, 33, 34, 39, 83, 84
  see also awraja, meslenie, woreda
guebbars (feasts), 18
gult, 5, 14, 17, 19, 27, 48, 55, 76, 107–8, 109, 117, 256, 257
  definition, 4
gult-gej
  definition, 4
  services owed to, 13

Haile Selassie Foundation, xiii
Haile Selassie I University, 91, 248–9
  see also students
Haimanote Abew, 61
Harar, province of, 12, 31
  town of, 76, 80, 85, 89
Harar Military Academy, 243, 246, 247
  class structure, 86
Hararge, province of, 26, 31, 48, 49, 51, 56, 80, 92, 116, 117, 118, 119, 120, 121, 122, 141, 146, 147, 162, 216, 220, 221
Holeta Military Academy, 85, 86, 235, 243
House of Solomon (myth of), 3, 6, 9, 10, 16, 20, 21, 26, 53

I.D.A., 139, 159
Ichenge, 2, 53, 58, 190
Illubabor, province of, 48, 49, 51, 56, 80, 92, 116, 117, 118, 119, 120, 121, 122, 141, 146, 257
imperial estates, 110–11, 126
  balderas, 110
  bet iqa, 110
  gann gebb, 110
  hudad, 110
  woregenu, 110
imperial system, Ch. II–III, xiii, xviii
  and church, 52–62
  controls, 63, 66, 72, 75, 82, 97, 175–6, 187, 227, 255, 265–6
  of army, 87
  of education, 88–9
  historical, 2, 3, 6, 17–18
  use of governors, 34
  use of judges, 47–8
  use of land grants, 112–13
  exploitation, 204
  myths, 5, 6, 10, 16, 21, *see also* House of Solomon
  opposition to, Ch. VI, Ch. VII, Ch. VIII
  patronage, 86, 110
  Pen, Ministry of, 73, 74, 75, 82
  powers, 6, 10, 11, 71, 175, 176
  relationship with nobility, 5–6, 11, 31, 32, 33, 34, 35, 227–51
  see also feudalism, Haile Selassie I
Income Tax Authorities, 67
Income Tax Decree (1956), 149
Income Tax Proclamation (1961), 149, 184
India, 85, 94, 147, 154
industry, Ch. V, 237
  GDP, 139
  industrial growth, 145
  industrial sectors, 146
  regional distribution, 146
  see also coffee, cotton, mining, sugar, textiles
Information, Ministry of, xiv
Interior, Ministry of, 39, 45, 73, 83, 85, 107, 111, 222, 245
  see also Local Self Government Order
Investment Committee, 150
Islam, 5, 6, 7, 9, 11, 12, 17, 52, 57, 191, 193, 194, 196, 197, 223, 224, 225
  Islamic Courts, 52, 223
  Moslem League, 194, 195

ETHIOPIAN PROVINCES & TOWNS

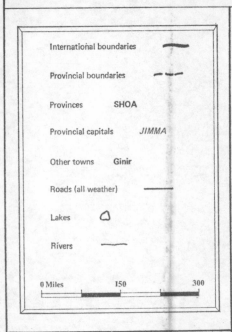

International boundaries	
Provincial boundaries	
Provinces	SHOA
Provincial capitals	*JIMMA*
Other towns	Ginir
Roads (all weather)	
Lakes	
Rivers	

0 Miles   150   300

Ethiopia in the African Continent

Sudan

Tesser

BEGEMED

GOJJAM

Blue Nile

WOLLEGA

NEKEMT

Dembidollo

Gambella

R.Baro   *GORE*

ILLUBABOR   *JIMMA*

Bonga

KAFFA

ARBAMIN

Maji

R.Omo

GOM
GOF

L. Rudolph